First World War
and Army of Occupation
War Diary
France, Belgium and Germany

19 DIVISION
57 Infantry Brigade
Gloucestershire Regiment
8th Service Battalion
17 July 1915 - 31 March 1919

WO95/2085/1

The Naval & Military Press Ltd
www.nmarchive.com
Published in association with The National Archives

Published by

The Naval & Military Press Ltd

Unit 10 Ridgewood Industrial Park,

Uckfield, East Sussex,

TN22 5QE England

Tel: +44 (0) 1825 749494

www.naval-military-press.com

www.nmarchive.com

This diary has been reprinted in facsimile from the original. Any imperfections are inevitably reproduced and the quality may fall short of modern type and cartographic standards.

© **Crown Copyright**
Images reproduced by permission of The National Archives, London, England, 2015.

Contents

Document type	Place/Title	Date From	Date To
Heading	WO95/2085/1		
Heading	10th Bn Roy. Warwickshire Regt Jly 1915-Mar 1919		
Heading	8th Bn Gloucestershire Regt Jly 1915-Mar 1918		
Heading	8th Battn. The Gloucestershire Regiment. December 1915		
War Diary	Robecq	01/12/1915	03/12/1915
War Diary	Le Touret	04/12/1915	10/12/1915
War Diary	Near Riche Bourg L'Avoue	11/12/1915	12/12/1915
War Diary	Reserve Billets In Kings Road	16/12/1915	21/12/1915
War Diary	Trenches Quinque Rue to Farm Corner	21/12/1915	23/12/1915
War Diary	Brigade Reserve Kings Road Billets	24/12/1915	27/12/1915
War Diary	Billet between Locon and Les Lobes	28/12/1915	30/12/1915
War Diary	Divisional Reserve	31/12/1915	31/12/1915
Heading	8th Battn. The Gloucestershire Regiment. November 1915		
War Diary	Trenches Ind I A Just North of Givenchy	01/11/1915	05/11/1915
War Diary	Old British Line Trenches Festubert Ind I b.	05/11/1915	05/11/1915
War Diary	Old British Line Reserve Trenches Ind I b Festubert	06/11/1915	09/11/1915
War Diary	La Tombe Willot Billets	10/11/1915	11/11/1915
War Diary	Billet La Tombe Willot near Locon	11/11/1915	13/11/1915
War Diary	La Tombe Willot Billets	14/11/1915	16/11/1915
War Diary	Ind II b Trenches tube station	17/11/1915	20/11/1915
War Diary	Ind II Trenches near Tube Station Epinette	21/11/1915	21/11/1915
War Diary	Epinette Posts	22/11/1915	23/11/1915
War Diary	Les Lobes	24/11/1915	25/11/1915
War Diary	Robecq	26/11/1915	30/11/1915
Heading	8th Battn. The Gloucestershire Regiment. September & October 1915		
War Diary	Trenches Sub Sec Ind. 2.c. Near Richebourg L'Avoue	01/09/1915	13/09/1915
War Diary	Locon X, 1	14/09/1915	16/09/1915
War Diary	near Locon W.1.a.	17/09/1915	24/09/1915
War Diary	Le Hamel Marais	25/09/1915	25/09/1915
War Diary	Le Touret	26/09/1915	28/09/1915
War Diary	Trenches Ind IIb near Festubert	29/09/1915	02/10/1915
War Diary	Le Hamel	03/10/1915	03/10/1915
War Diary	Lacouture	04/10/1915	07/10/1915
War Diary	Vielle Chapelle	08/10/1915	11/10/1915
War Diary	Ind IV b. Trenches Farm Corner To Vine Street	12/10/1915	12/10/1915
War Diary	Trenches Ind IV b. Farm Corner to Vine Street	13/10/1915	20/10/1915
War Diary	Le Hamel	20/10/1915	28/10/1915
War Diary	Ind I.A. Trenches Just North Of Givenchy	29/10/1915	31/10/1915
Heading	8th Battn. The Gloucestershire Regiment. August 1915		
War Diary	Caudescure	01/08/1915	03/08/1915
War Diary	Estaires	04/08/1915	10/08/1915
War Diary	Laventie	10/08/1915	14/08/1915
War Diary	Estaires	16/08/1915	16/08/1915
War Diary	Caudescure	17/08/1915	27/08/1915
War Diary	Marmuse	28/08/1915	28/08/1915
War Diary	Trenches	29/08/1915	31/08/1915
Heading	8th Battn. The Gloucestershire Regiment. July 1915		

Heading	War Diary 8th (Ser) Bn Gloucestershire Reg. from 17th July to 31st July (inclusive) 1915 Volume I		
War Diary	Tidworth	17/07/1915	17/07/1915
War Diary	House	18/07/1915	18/07/1915
War Diary	Tidworth	18/07/1915	18/07/1915
War Diary	Boulogne	19/07/1915	19/07/1915
War Diary	Ponta Briques	19/07/1915	19/07/1915
War Diary	Watten	20/07/1915	20/07/1915
War Diary	North Leulinehem	20/07/1915	23/07/1915
War Diary	Renescure	24/07/1915	24/07/1915
War Diary	Isbergues	25/07/1915	30/07/1915
War Diary	Haverskerque	31/07/1915	31/07/1915
Heading	8th Geistingen Vol 6		
War Diary	Les Lobes	01/01/1916	01/01/1916
War Diary	Billets	02/01/1916	04/01/1916
War Diary	Trenches Copse Street to Oxford Street	05/01/1916	06/01/1916
War Diary	Trenches Copse Street to Oxford Street just South of Neuve Chapelle	07/01/1916	08/01/1916
War Diary	Billets Croix Barbee	09/01/1916	10/01/1916
War Diary	Croix Barbee Billets	11/01/1916	12/01/1916
War Diary	Trenches from Copse Street to Oxford Street just South of Neuve Chapelle	13/01/1916	15/01/1916
War Diary	Trenches from Copse Street to Oxford Street	16/01/1916	16/01/1916
War Diary	Trenches between Copse Street and Oxford Road just South of Neuve Chapelle	17/01/1916	17/01/1916
War Diary	Billets near Croix Barbee	18/01/1916	20/01/1916
War Diary	Croix Barbee	21/01/1916	21/01/1916
War Diary	Billets at Hamet Billet	22/01/1916	31/01/1916
Operation(al) Order(s)	8th Gloucestershire Regt Order No 1	20/01/1915	20/01/1915
Operation(al) Order(s)	8th Gloucestershire Regt Order No 8	20/01/1915	20/01/1915
Heading	8th Gloucestershire Vol 8		
War Diary	Billets in Hamet Billet	01/02/1916	19/02/1916
War Diary	Lagorgue	20/02/1916	24/02/1916
War Diary	Trenches Sign Post Lane to Moated Grange Street	24/02/1916	26/02/1916
War Diary	Riez Bailleul Billets	27/02/1916	28/02/1916
War Diary	Trenches Sign Post Lane To Moated Grange Street	28/02/1916	29/02/1916
Operation(al) Order(s)	8th Gloucestershire Regt Order No. 24	23/02/1916	23/02/1916
Miscellaneous	Operation Order By Lieut Col G.D.M. Moore	28/02/1916	28/02/1916
War Diary	Trenches Sign Post Lane-Moated Grange Street	01/03/1916	03/03/1916
War Diary	Billets Riez Bailleul	04/03/1916	07/03/1916
War Diary	Regnier Le Clerc	09/03/1916	13/03/1916
War Diary	Riez Bailleul	14/03/1916	14/03/1916
War Diary	Trenches Sign Post Lane To Moated Grange Street.	15/03/1916	21/03/1916
War Diary	Riez Bailleul	23/03/1916	24/03/1916
War Diary	Trenches Sign Post Lane To Moated Grange Street	27/03/1916	28/03/1916
War Diary	Riez Bailleul	29/03/1916	31/03/1916
Operation(al) Order(s)	Operation Order by Lieut Col G.D Moore Comding 8th battn Gloucestershire Regt	06/03/1916	06/03/1916
Miscellaneous	Operation Order by Lieut Col.G.D Moore Comding 8th Bn Gloucestershire Regt.	13/03/1916	13/03/1916
Miscellaneous	Operation Order by Lieut Col.G.D Moore Comdg 8th Bn Gloucestershire Regt.	14/03/1916	14/03/1916
Miscellaneous	Operation Order by Major C.N. Harding Comdg 8th Bn Gloucestershire Regt	26/03/1916	26/03/1916
Miscellaneous	Lieut Priestley		
War Diary	Regnier Le Clerc	01/04/1916	05/04/1916

Type	Location	Start	End
War Diary	Riez Bailleul	06/04/1916	15/04/1916
War Diary	Trenches Sign Post Lane To Moated Grange Street	16/04/1916	16/04/1916
War Diary	Lagorgue	17/04/1916	17/04/1916
War Diary	Hamet Billet	18/04/1916	20/04/1916
War Diary	Cresques	21/04/1916	30/04/1916
War Diary	Cresques 1st Army Training Area	01/05/1916	07/05/1916
War Diary	Vignacourt	08/05/1916	28/05/1916
War Diary	St Riquier	30/05/1916	31/05/1916
Operation(al) Order(s)	Operation Order by Lieut Col G.D.N Moore Comdg 8th Bn Gloucestershire Regt.	07/05/1916	07/05/1916
Operation(al) Order(s)	8th Gloucestershire Regt. Order No. 1	29/05/1916	29/05/1916
War Diary	St Riquier	01/06/1916	09/06/1916
War Diary	Vignacourt	10/06/1916	14/06/1916
War Diary	Rainneville	16/06/1916	27/06/1916
War Diary	Franvillers Wood	27/06/1916	30/06/1916
Operation(al) Order(s)	8th Bn Gloucestershire Regt. Order No. 3	03/06/1916	03/06/1916
Miscellaneous	Reference Training Area Map 1/20,000		
Operation(al) Order(s)	8th Gloucestershire Regt. Order No. 8	15/06/1916	15/06/1916
Operation(al) Order(s)	8th Bn Gloucestershire Regt. Order No. 9	26/06/1916	26/06/1916
Heading	8th G'cesters Vol 7		
Heading	8th Battn. The Gloucestershire Regiment. July 1916		
War Diary	Millencourt	01/07/1916	01/07/1916
War Diary	Tara-Usna Line	02/07/1916	03/07/1916
War Diary	La Boisselle	04/07/1916	05/07/1916
War Diary	Albert	06/07/1916	09/07/1916
War Diary	Millencourt	10/07/1916	19/07/1916
War Diary	Fricourt	20/07/1916	20/07/1916
War Diary	Bazentin Le-Petit	21/07/1916	23/07/1916
War Diary	Becourt	24/07/1916	29/07/1916
War Diary	Bazentin Le-Petit	30/07/1916	31/07/1916
Heading	1/8th Battalion Gloucestershire Regiment August 1916		
War Diary	Becourt Wood	01/08/1916	01/08/1916
War Diary	Bresle	02/08/1916	03/08/1916
War Diary	Bouchon	04/08/1916	06/08/1916
War Diary	Bailleul	07/08/1916	07/08/1916
War Diary	Dranoutre	08/08/1916	22/08/1916
War Diary	Aircraft Farm	23/08/1916	31/08/1916
War Diary	Dranoutre	01/09/1916	18/09/1916
War Diary	Neuve Eglise	19/09/1916	20/09/1916
War Diary	Grand Sec Bois	21/09/1916	06/10/1916
War Diary	Amplier	06/10/1916	06/10/1916
War Diary	Bois de Warnimont	08/10/1916	16/10/1916
War Diary	Warloy	17/10/1916	22/10/1916
War Diary	Ovillers	23/10/1916	26/10/1916
War Diary	Ovillers Post	27/10/1916	20/11/1916
War Diary	Warloy	21/11/1916	22/11/1916
War Diary	Herissart	23/11/1916	23/11/1916
War Diary	Canaples	24/11/1916	24/11/1916
War Diary	Saouen	25/11/1916	25/11/1916
War Diary	St Ouen	26/11/1916	26/11/1916
War Diary	Gezaincourt	27/11/1916	10/12/1916
War Diary	Beauval	11/12/1916	13/12/1916
War Diary	La Vicogne	14/12/1916	14/12/1916
War Diary	Beauval	15/12/1916	09/01/1917
War Diary	Amplier	10/01/1917	10/01/1917
War Diary	Bayencourt	11/01/1917	15/01/1917

War Diary	Trenches Hebuterne	16/01/1917	21/01/1917
War Diary	Courcelles	23/01/1917	21/02/1917
War Diary	Trenches	22/02/1917	25/02/1917
War Diary	Bertrancourt	26/02/1917	26/02/1917
War Diary	Bus	27/02/1917	01/03/1917
War Diary	Louvencourt	02/03/1917	08/03/1917
War Diary	Gezaincourt	09/03/1917	09/03/1917
War Diary	Fortel	10/03/1917	11/03/1917
War Diary	Croisette	12/03/1917	12/03/1917
War Diary	Floringhem	13/03/1917	14/03/1917
War Diary	St Hilaire	15/03/1917	16/03/1917
War Diary	Steenbecque	17/03/1917	17/03/1917
War Diary	Merris	18/03/1917	20/03/1917
War Diary	Murrumbidgee Camp	21/03/1917	21/03/1917
War Diary	Diependaal Sector	22/03/1917	27/03/1917
War Diary	Murrumbidgee Camp	28/03/1917	29/03/1917
War Diary	Moolenacker	30/03/1917	02/04/1917
War Diary	Hazebrouck	03/04/1917	03/04/1917
War Diary	Longueness	04/04/1917	05/04/1917
War Diary	Zudausques	06/04/1917	17/04/1917
War Diary	Arques	18/04/1917	18/04/1917
War Diary	Haze Brouck	19/04/1917	19/04/1917
War Diary	Scherpenberg Carnarvon Camp	20/04/1917	29/04/1917
War Diary	Carnarvon Camp	30/04/1917	30/04/1917
War Diary	Toronto Camp (G18a Sheet 208 1/40,000)	01/05/1917	01/05/1917
War Diary	Railway Dugouts	02/05/1917	05/05/1917
War Diary	Centre Sector (Hill Sixty Sector)	06/05/1917	11/05/1917
War Diary	Toronto Camp	12/05/1917	12/05/1917
War Diary	Zon Camp	13/05/1917	19/05/1917
War Diary	Ridge Wood De Zon Camp	20/05/1917	20/05/1917
War Diary	Ridgewood & Murrumbidgee Camp	22/05/1917	25/05/1917
War Diary	Murrumbidgee Camp	26/05/1917	26/05/1917
War Diary	Carnarvon Camp	27/05/1917	29/05/1917
War Diary	Ascot Camp	30/05/1917	06/06/1917
War Diary	La Clytte	06/06/1917	06/06/1917
War Diary	Wytschaete Beek	07/06/1917	07/06/1917
War Diary	Onraet Wood	07/06/1917	07/06/1917
War Diary	Oosttaverne	08/06/1917	09/06/1917
War Diary	Grand Bois	10/06/1917	10/06/1917
War Diary	Dezon Camp	14/06/1917	14/06/1917
War Diary	Grand Bois	15/06/1917	19/06/1917
War Diary	Dezon Camp	20/06/1917	20/06/1917
War Diary	M. 20a.1.8 (Sheet 28 1/40,000)	21/06/1917	01/07/1917
War Diary	N 16 C 9.3	02/07/1917	02/07/1917
War Diary	Ridge Defences	03/07/1917	07/07/1917
War Diary	Right Sub Sector Oosttaverne	08/07/1917	10/07/1917
War Diary	Ridge Defence	11/07/1917	11/07/1917
War Diary	Rossignol Wood	12/07/1917	22/07/1917
War Diary	Oosttaverne	23/07/1917	28/07/1917
War Diary	Ridge Defences Oosttaverne	29/07/1917	29/07/1917
War Diary	Locre	30/07/1917	31/07/1917
War Diary	Rossignol Wood	01/08/1917	02/08/1917
War Diary	Doncaster Huts	03/08/1917	03/08/1917
War Diary	Kemmel	04/08/1917	05/08/1917
War Diary	Denys Wood	06/08/1917	07/08/1917
War Diary	St Jan Cappel	08/08/1917	08/08/1917

War Diary	Jan Cappel	09/08/1917	10/08/1917
War Diary	Fromentel	11/08/1917	22/08/1917
War Diary	Le Waast	23/08/1917	28/08/1917
War Diary	Le-Nieppe	29/08/1917	29/08/1917
War Diary	Strazeele	30/08/1917	06/09/1917
War Diary	Mont Noir	07/09/1917	11/09/1917
War Diary	Bois Confluent	12/09/1917	13/09/1917
War Diary	Klein Zillebeke	14/09/1917	14/09/1917
War Diary	Beaver Camp	15/09/1917	18/09/1917
War Diary	Klein Zillebeke	19/09/1917	21/09/1917
War Diary	Beaver Camp	22/09/1917	27/09/1917
War Diary	Line	28/09/1917	30/09/1917
War Diary	Shrewsbury Forest	01/08/1917	01/08/1917
War Diary	Hill 60	02/10/1917	05/10/1917
War Diary	Bois Carre	06/10/1917	11/10/1917
War Diary	Line	12/10/1917	14/10/1917
War Diary	Spoil Bank	15/10/1917	17/10/1917
War Diary	Hessian Wood	18/10/1917	19/10/1917
War Diary	Bois Carre	20/10/1917	27/10/1917
War Diary	Rossignol	28/10/1917	28/10/1917
War Diary	Rossignol Camp	29/10/1917	04/11/1917
War Diary	Spoil Bank	05/11/1917	07/11/1917
War Diary	Hessian Wood	08/11/1917	09/11/1917
War Diary	Bois Carre	10/11/1917	10/11/1917
War Diary	Merris	11/11/1917	12/11/1917
War Diary	Blaringhem	13/11/1917	29/11/1917
War Diary	Wardrecques	30/11/1917	05/12/1917
War Diary	Bienvillers	06/12/1917	07/12/1917
War Diary	Etricourt	08/12/1917	08/12/1917
War Diary	Ribecourt	09/12/1917	12/12/1917
War Diary	Wardrecques	01/12/1917	05/12/1917
War Diary	Bienvillers	06/12/1917	07/12/1917
War Diary	Etricourt	08/12/1917	08/12/1917
War Diary	Ribecourt	09/12/1917	17/12/1917
War Diary	Havrincourt	18/12/1917	20/12/1917
War Diary	Line	21/12/1917	24/12/1917
War Diary	Ribecourt	13/12/1917	17/12/1917
War Diary	Havrincourt	18/12/1917	20/12/1917
War Diary	Line	21/12/1917	24/12/1917
War Diary	Kaiser Trench	25/12/1917	25/12/1917
War Diary	Fork Avenue	26/12/1917	27/12/1917
War Diary	Line	28/12/1917	31/12/1917
War Diary	Kaiser Trench	25/12/1917	25/12/1917
War Diary	Fork Avenue	26/12/1917	27/12/1917
War Diary	Line	28/12/1917	05/01/1918
War Diary	Havrincourt Wood	06/01/1918	08/01/1918
War Diary	Line	09/01/1918	15/01/1918
Miscellaneous			
War Diary	Line	01/02/1918	06/02/1918
War Diary	Havrincourt Wood	07/02/1918	09/02/1918
War Diary	Line	10/02/1918	14/02/1918
War Diary	Beaulencourt Alma Camp	15/02/1918	16/02/1918
War Diary	Jericho Camp	17/02/1918	28/02/1918
Heading	1/8th Battalion Gloucestershire Regiment April 1918		
War Diary		01/04/1918	30/04/1918

Heading	8th Battalion The Gloucestershire Regiment March 1918		
War Diary	Jericho Camp	01/03/1918	07/03/1918
War Diary	Salamanca Camp	08/03/1918	21/03/1918
War Diary	In The Line	22/03/1918	30/03/1918
War Diary	Rossignol Camp	31/03/1918	31/03/1918
Miscellaneous		24/03/1918	24/03/1918
War Diary		01/05/1918	11/05/1918
War Diary	Tunnellers Camp	12/05/1918	18/05/1918
War Diary	Sarry	19/05/1918	28/05/1918
War Diary	Chambrecy	29/05/1918	18/06/1918
War Diary	Haunt Villers	19/06/1918	20/06/1918
War Diary	Suroger	21/06/1918	21/06/1918
War Diary	Broussy Le Petit	22/06/1918	30/06/1918
War Diary	Semoine	01/07/1918	03/07/1918
War Diary	Remilly	04/07/1918	11/07/1918
War Diary	Lozinghem	12/07/1918	20/07/1918
War Diary	St Hilaire	21/07/1918	30/07/1918
War Diary	Lozinghem	31/07/1918	05/08/1918
War Diary	Gosnay	06/08/1918	06/08/1918
War Diary	Line	07/08/1918	10/08/1918
War Diary	Chocques	11/08/1918	15/08/1918
War Diary	Line	16/08/1918	21/08/1918
War Diary	Vendin	22/08/1918	22/08/1918
War Diary	Annezin	23/08/1918	28/08/1918
War Diary	Line	29/08/1918	11/09/1918
War Diary	Nr Locon	12/09/1918	29/09/1918
War Diary	Essars	30/09/1918	01/10/1918
War Diary	Cauchy-A-La Tour	02/10/1918	02/10/1918
War Diary	Bours	03/10/1918	04/10/1918
War Diary	St Amand	05/10/1918	07/10/1918
War Diary	Graincourt	08/10/1918	09/10/1918
War Diary	Anneux	10/10/1918	10/10/1918
War Diary	Cambrai	11/10/1918	16/10/1918
War Diary	Cauroir	17/10/1918	17/10/1918
War Diary	St Albert	18/10/1918	19/10/1918
War Diary	Line	20/10/1918	24/10/1918
War Diary	Avesnes	25/10/1918	26/10/1918
War Diary	Caurior	27/10/1918	02/11/1918
War Diary	St Aubert	03/11/1918	03/11/1918
War Diary	Sepmeries	04/11/1918	04/11/1918
War Diary	Maresches	05/11/1918	05/11/1918
War Diary	Jenlain	06/11/1918	06/11/1918
War Diary	La Flamengrie	07/11/1918	08/11/1918
War Diary	Taisnieres	09/11/1918	10/11/1918
War Diary	Bettrechies	11/11/1918	14/11/1918
War Diary	Sepmeries	15/11/1918	15/11/1918
War Diary	St Aubert	16/11/1918	16/11/1918
War Diary	Caurior	17/11/1918	28/11/1918
War Diary	Autheux Boisbergues	29/11/1918	30/11/1918
War Diary	Candas	01/12/1918	31/03/1919

WO95/20885/1

19TH DIVISION
57TH INFY BDE

10TH BN ROY. WARWICKSHIRE REGT

JLY 1915 - MAR 1919

Box 2085

19TH DIVISION
57TH INFY BDE

8TH BN GLOUCESTERSHIRE REGT
JLY 1915 - MAR 1919

57th Inf.Bde.
19th Div.

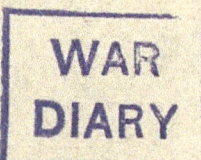

8th BATTN. THE GLOUCESTERSHIRE REGIMENT.

D E C E M B E R

1 9 1 5

Army Form C. 2118.

WAR DIARY
or
INTELLIGENCE SUMMARY.

8th Gloucestershire Regt

(Erase heading not required.)

Place	Date	Hour	Summary of Events and Information	Remarks and references to Appendices
ROBECQ	1915 1st Dec.		Company Training. One of	
	2nd		Company Training. One officer and one N.C.O. went on leave today. G.O.C. 57th Brigade held an inspection of companies in marching order at 2:30pm	
	3rd		Two men went on leave today. All companies bathed at the Brewery Baths, ROBECQ. Throughout the day. Very wet day today.	
LE TOURET	4th		Battalion moved from ROBECQ to LE TOURET and took over billets formerly occupied by 4th Batt Leicester Regt. and 9th Cheshire Regt. Going to the withdrawal of the 46th Division from the XIth Corps, 19th Division hand into the front line the 57th Brigade being in Divisional Reserve. Rained continuously today. The Adjutant went on leave today	MP
	5th		Very wet. Brigade General visited billets today.	MP
	6th		Wet again. Companies physical training & route marches.	MP
	7th		C.O. went to Conference at Brigade at 10 a.m. Companies Route marches & physical training Battalion near us very active.	MP
	8th		Two officers made a reconnaissance & sketch of ground over which the Battn would make counter attack. Enemy sent over about 20 H.E. Shells trying to locate Battery. No appreciable damage	MP
	9th		Very wet. Companies kit inspection	MP

Army Form C. 2118.

WAR DIARY
or
INTELLIGENCE SUMMARY.   8th Gloucester Regt

(Erase heading not required.)

Place	Date	Hour	Summary of Events and Information	Remarks and references to Appendices
LE TOURET	10 Dec		C.O. visited H.Q. of the 6th Wiltshire Regt preparatory to taking over their line of trenches tomorrow. Remaining Companies training took an interception from front line.	
New RICHEBOURG L'AVOUÉ	11 Dec		Battalion moved into trenches extending from QUINQUE RUE crossing to FARM CORNER. "B" and "D" Coy in firing line, "A" Coy in reserve line, and "C" Coy in billets on RUE DU BOIS and RUE EPINETTE, as there were only room for one Company in the reserve line. Battalion H.Q. on RUE DU BOIS. Battalion on our right 11th Battn. Middlesex Regt, on our left 10th Worcestershire Regt. Condition of trenches deplorable. Only halfway island positions. Companies in firing line for 48 hours & relieved for two days taken up with men. No sleeping accommodation in trenches.	
	12th		Visited by Acting Brigadier and Acting G.O.C. Division. In Evening C.O. and Brigadier visited front line. 15th Battn Welsh Regt, 28th Division arrived in day to be attached to the Battn for 3 days instruction. One platoon was attached to each company. Our Artillery very active especially in Evening. 2 platoons of D Coy were withdrawn from firing line owing to overcrowding and were accommodated in billets in RUE DU BERCEAU.	
	13th		Our Artillery fired salvoes during last night. O.C. made promises visited "D" Company and find there were no arrangements for relief on Wednesday night. The Companies under front line were relieved this evening. "A" Coy & 2 platoons relieved 1st "D" Coy, "C" Coy relieved "B" Coy.	
	14th		C.O. & Adjutant of 8th North Staffordshire Regt, visited H.Q. to make prior arrangements for relief on Wednesday night.	

Army Form C. 2118.

WAR DIARY
or
INTELLIGENCE SUMMARY.
(Erase heading not required)

8th Gloucester Regt

Place	Date	Hour	Summary of Events and Information	Remarks and references to Appendices
NEAR RICHEBOURG L'AVOUÉ	Dec 14th		CO visited front line trenches this evening.	
"	15/12		Our artillery was very active all day, and there was some retaliation from the enemy. About 2.30 p.m. a shell fell into CHOCOLATE POST killing one man & wounding 4 others. The 8th North Staffords relieved the Battalion in the Trenches. Relief completed by 7.30 p.m. and companies marched to billets in KING GEORGES ROAD, KINGS ROAD and RUE DES BERCEAUX. The C.O. Lt Col J.S. Hobbs gave over command of the regiment to Major G.D.M. Moore today and departed to England. Major P.W. Parkinson left the battalion to take over command of the 10th Royal Warwickshire Regt handing over command of "B" to Capt Brooke.	
Reserve Billets in KINGS ROAD	16/12/15		The Battalion is in Brigade Reserve. Companies had thorough kit inspection & feet inspection today & working parties were supplied for night work in the trenches under R.E. Supervision.	
"	17/12/15		Cleaning up. Working parties for R.E. again supplied tonight.	
"	18/12/15		Same as 17th.	
"	19/12/15		The B Coy 15th Welch Regt ceased to be attached to the Battalion today	

Army Form C. 2118.

8th Gloucester Regt

WAR DIARY
or
INTELLIGENCE SUMMARY.
(Erase heading not required.)

Place	Date	Hour	Summary of Events and Information	Remarks and references to Appendices
	Dec 19th		The Battalion went into trenches today and relieved the 8th North Staffordshire Regt who took over our billets. Companies marched independently B. & D. into front line trenches, C. Coy into Reserve Trenches and A. & 40 men of B. into Reserve billets. Batt HQ. on Rue du Bois near HAYSTACK POST. Relief completed by 9.30 p.m. Fine moonlight night. Patrols were sent out from front line towards german lines during the night and one patrol reported enemy working on MOUND, FME COUR D'AVOUE and trenches. Artillery were informed and fired on the objects. The germans also had patrols out and about 12 men strong.	
	20th		Enemy shelled out right section trenches near ROPE KEEP at 11 am and 3 p.m. but no damage was done. Our guns retaliated heavily. A patrol from D. Coy on right went out at night and reported ground towards german trench very swampy.	
	21st	2 a.m	The 58th Brigade on our left, having arranged to loose gas onto the german trenches, & then send six small columns of 2 officers & 20 men	

Army Form C. 2118.

WAR DIARY
or
INTELLIGENCE SUMMARY.
(Erase heading not required.)

8th Gloucester Regt

Place	Date	Hour	Summary of Events and Information	Remarks and references to Appendices
Trenches QUINQUE RUE to FARM CORNER	21st		each to occupy the German Trenches. The Battalion was ordered to wear smokehelmets in the front line and A Coy was moved from shelters in RUE DU BOIS to join C Coy in Reserve Trench at 12.45.a.m.	
		1.30 a.m.	Orders were received cancelling the action owing to unfavourable wind. A Coy was therefore withdrawn yesterday. No. 20 (?) of B Coy. 14th Welch Regt arrived to be attached to Battalion for instruction in trench warfare, one platoon was therefore sent to each company.	
		3.15 a.m.	Enemy fired 15 shrapnel shells on the Company H.Q. on our left section of front-line trenches, wounded one man.	
		11 a.m.	Our artillery bombarded MOULIN D'EAU works & parapets. Little effect.	
			A german machine gun played at intervals on PRINCE'S ROAD, the road from Batn. H.Q. to the trenches. Our artillery fired three bursts of fire during the night.	
do.	22nd	6 p.m.	A Coy from RUE DU BOIS relieved D Coy in right section front-line Trenches. D Coy took up Reserve trenches Tube Station from C Coy who moved up	

Army Form C. 2118.

8th Gloucester Regt

WAR DIARY
or
INTELLIGENCE SUMMARY.
(Erase heading not required.)

Place	Date	Hour	Summary of Events and Information	Remarks and references to Appendices
Trenches QUINQUE RUE to 22nd FARM CORNER.			and relieved B. Coy in left section front line trenches, the latter Company moving back into shelters in RUE DU BOIS. Our artillery fired steadily throughout the day. Enemy retaliated weakly causing no casualty.	
		9 p.m.	Battalion Division on our right made gas attack on enemy trenches and there was much artillery bombardment on both sides. Attack subsided at 11 p.m.	
do	23/12/15	12 noon	Enemy shelled Orchard S.21.a.4.7. in reserve line trenches, demolishing one dug out, killing two men and wounding a third.	
		2 p.m.	Right section of front line (A Coy) was shelled for half an hour by shrapnel and blew a hole in the parapet and wrecked one sheller but caused no casualties.	
		6 p.m.	Relief by North Stafford commenced and finished about 9 p.m. Very wet night and the handing over gum boots caused much delay. The Battalion moved into billets in KINGS, KING GEORGE'S, ROAD, and GRUB STREET and occupied three posts.	

Army Form C. 2118.

8th Gloucester Reg

WAR DIARY
INTELLIGENCE SUMMARY.
(Erase heading not required.)

Place	Date	Hour	Summary of Events and Information	Remarks and references to Appendices
	December			
Brigade Reserve	24th		Whilst the Battalion was in the trenches, we formed the right of the 11th Corps line upto QUINQUE RUE Crossing, the Battalion on our right forming part of the 12th Division. On our left was a battalion of our own brigade, the 57th Brigade.	
KINGS ROAD Billets	25th		Companies carried out kit inspection, and 200 men were found for trench working parties under R.E. supervision. Holy communion 9.15 a.m. Divine service in Company billets. Otherwise Christmas Day was not otherwise recognised, except for an easy day.	
"	26th		Companies went on with their kit inspection, and 200 men were found for trench work under R.E. in the evening.	
"	27th		The 7th South Lancashire Regt arrived in the morning and took over our billets. Companies marched independently, to billets between LOCON and LES LOBES, the battalion thus moving with the rest of the Brigade into Divisional Reserve. Mr Ben Tillett addressed A Coy this afternoon.	
Billets between LOCON and LES LOBES	28th		Kit inspection by companies, 'cleaning up billets.	
	29th		— do. —	

Army Form C. 2118.

8th Gloucester Regt

WAR DIARY
or
INTELLIGENCE SUMMARY.

(Erase heading not required.)

Instructions regarding War Diaries and Intelligence Summaries are contained in F. S. Regs., Part II. and the Staff Manual respectively. Title pages will be prepared in manuscript.

Place	Date	Hour	Summary of Events and Information	Remarks and references to Appendices
BILLETS Between LOCON and LES LOBES	December 30th	10.30 a.m.	C.O. inspected "D" Coy at 10.30 a.m. and "B" Coy at 11.30 a.m. "A" & "C" practised route marching in "Drill Tube helmets". "B" & "D" route marched in the afternoon.	
Divisional Reserve	31st	10.30 a.m.	C.O. inspected "A" Coy at 10.30 a.m. and "C" Coy + Transport at 11.30 a.m. and H.Q. at 12.15 p.m.	

G.M. Moore. Major
com dg 8th Gloucester Regt.

57th Inf.Bde.
19th Div.

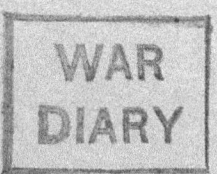

8th BATTN. THE GLOUCESTERSHIRE REGIMENT.

N O V E M B E R

1 9 1 5

INTELLIGENCE SUMMARY.

(Erase heading not required.)

Place	Date	Hour	Summary of Events and Information	Remarks and references to Appendices
TRENCHES in front 2nd I.B. North of GIVENCHY	1/15	8.30am	A smoke bomb was thrown in front of the LOOP. Our heavy guns fired several HE shells on ridge behind CRATER. Enemy retaliated with 3 HE shells on GRENADIER Trench near fire trench, which blocked up the trench for 4 yards, though one shell failed to explode.	
		8.30pm	A smoke bomb again fell near our wire in front of LOOP. Fired [?]	
		9 pm	7 rifle grenades fell short of our wire entanglement near LOOP, & did nothing. Enemy otherwise very quiet during the night. It rained heavily all day & night and the trenches consequently got into a shocking condition. In the front trenches the supervision trench, parados, & traverses fell down in several places, likewise several dugouts, & LOOP & GRENADIER communication trenches. Men wet through with no means of drying. Every dugout badly leaks, and the trenches will be untenable if rain continues.	⊕
—do—	2/15		Enemy very quiet today. Rained hard all day & last night. Communication trenches becoming impossible, and ration supply to front line is increasingly difficult. The front trenches are full of water, and there is no way of baling it out. Relief communication in front line is very difficult. The front companies are naturally having a very wretched time, but relief is impossible owing to the state	

INTELLIGENCE SUMMARY

(Erase heading not required.)

Instructions regarding War Diaries and Intelligence Summaries are contained in F. S. Regs., Part II and the Staff Manual respectively. Title pages will be prepared in manuscript.

Place	Date	Hour	Summary of Events and Information	Remarks and references to Appendices
Trenches SNDI a. Givenchy	2/11/15		of the communication trenches. The Colonel returned from several days leave today. Some enemy were seen walking in the open probably to avoid muddy communication trenches, to our snipers had some luck to fire at.	
North of Givenchy	3/11/15		Fine morning with some sunshine. No rain all day. Enemy very active probably a fresh regiment has arrived in front of us. Their Snipers were active from the CRATER and were shooting down GRENADIER Trench. One man of "B" Coy killed by sniper whilst working near GRENADIER Junction. Was buried at night near the front line, as it was impossible to carry his body down.	
		10 a.m.	Enemy also fired H.E Shells at our Reserve trenches and behind but only damaged a bit of the parapet.	
		11:30 a.m.	Our Snipers activity silenced the enemy's sniper by this time.	
		12:35 p.m.	Enemy fired some 12 Shrapnel shells over our trenches but did no harm, and our guns quickly retaliated + silenced them. The enemy during the day were engaged in baling out their trenches and several were seen walking about in the open & proved good targets for our snipers. Fine day & night.	

INTELLIGENCE SUMMARY.

(Erase heading not required.)

Place	Date	Hour	Summary of Events and Information	Remarks and references to Appendices
TRENCHES INDIA just north of GIVENCHY.	4/15	4.15am.	An engine, probably water pump, was heard working in enemy's line about house 34. Enemy during night used very few flares & none between 11pm & 5 a.m.	
		11 a.m.	Two snipers were shot by our snipers.	
		1 p.m.	A sentry spotted a party of germans collecting wood near house 34, & B Coy quickly manned the parapet & poured rapid fire on them. Three germans were seen to fall & others were later carried away.	
		2.45.	Our guns rapidly retaliated on enemy's guns which were annoying at the time. One man being wounded by shrapnel in B Coy. Communication trenches are now impassable owing to mud and falling in; & rations have to be carried up in the open. It was foggy up to 10. a.m. Today & fine all day & night.	Y.
	5/15.	5 am.	B Coy was relieved by a Coy R. Warwicks, and went into FESTUBERT POSTS. D Coy was relieved later in daylight & did not reach their posts at LE PLANTIN till late in the morning. A & C Coy moved into O.B. line trenches in 1nd I.B. and H.Q. during the morning, being relieved by the 10th Royal Warwicks. Fine day, but clear & not misty as we hoped for relief. Two men were wounded during relief, and as it was carried out in broad daylight, we were pretty fortunate.	

INTELLIGENCE SUMMARY.

(Erase heading not required.)

Place	Date	Hour	Summary of Events and Information	Remarks and references to Appendices
Old British Line Trenches FESTUBERT Ind I 8	5/11/15	8 p.m.	200 men from A & C Companies worked under R E & communication. Our position is now as 1st Reserve Battalion, with two companies in reserve trenches & two companies in posts in rear. The 10th Worcesters Regt hold Ind I b trenches in front of us, and the 10th Warwicks on our right hold Ind I a. trenches with 7th Division on their right at GIVENCHY and the 5-8th Brigade hold the trenches on the left of our Brigade	&
-do-	5/11/15	2.30 p.m.	The enemy sent over some twenty shells starting on FESTUBERT road then gradually decreasing range, all the time firing on BARNTON TRENCH till finally two incendiary shells actually burst on our reserve line parapet first by headquarters. One shell knocked some of the parapet down and set on fire the sandbags on the ammunition dugout. No damage was done however as the fire was quickly extinguished and the ammunition removed by the Sergeant Major & others. Another burst on parapet and sent up pieces of charcoal out of shell, and a third shell passed very close over the bomb-store. A man was wounded by indirect machine gun fire at 6 p.m. whilst getting water near BARNTON GATE.	&

INTELLIGENCE SUMMARY.

(Erase heading not required.)

Place	Date	Hour	Summary of Events and Information	Remarks and references to Appendices
Old British Line Reserve Trenches	6/11/15		Fine all day, white frost early morning.	
		4:30 a.m.	50 men from A + 50 from C with officers working under R.E. for 4 hours	
		5 p.m.	100 men from A + 100 from C Coy. working under R.E. for 4 hours.	
Ind 1st	7/15		Fine again today, work as on 6th.	
FESTUBERT	8/15		As on 7th.	
	9/15		Leave opened today. Major Moore & Capt Cox commenced their leave today also 5 N.C.O's and men. They are due to return on 16th Nov 1915. Fifty men from A Coy, 50 men from C Coy at work under R.E. on trenches for four hours from 9:30 a.m. It rained all afternoon and very hard at night.	
		6:45 p.m.	Companies of 8th South Lancs Regt commenced relieving our companies. Relief completed by 9:15 p.m. Companies marched to billets in vicinity of LA TOMBE WILLOT near LOCON, and settled down by 12 midnight.	
LA TOMBE WILLOT billets	10/15	10 a.m.	All companies had kit & foot inspection today. Major Harding, Capt Cooke, Lt/Major Vaughan and 1 N.C.O & 4 men went on leave today.	
	11/15	8:30 a.m.	40 men "A" Coy, 100 "B" Coy, 20 men "C" Coy & 140 "D" Coy were sent out in wagons for working in the trenches. They returned 6 p.m. "A" Coy & "C" Coy bathed at LOCON Baths in the morning	

INTELLIGENCE SUMMARY.

(Erase heading not required.)

Place	Date	Hour	Summary of Events and Information	Remarks and references to Appendices
Billets LA TOMBE WILLOT nr LEON.	11/11/15		From the 10th inst. the battalion ceased to belong to the INDIAN CORPS. From that date the 19th Division is incorporated in the 11th Corps 1st Army, together with the Guards Division and 46th Division. Capt Thomas, 1 N.C.O and two men went on leave today, the men to return on Nov 18th 1915. From today number of all ranks granted leave per diem has been reduced to four, and officers leave has been extended to 10 days.	
- do -	12/11/15	4.30am	2nd Lieut. Poole, one N.C.O. and two men went on leave today. Companies bathing at the LOCON Baths in the morning.	
		2.45 pm	G.O.C. Brigade (Gen. Twyford) inspected billets. Rain all day	
- do -	13/11/15		Rain all day. ~~Lieut Mason~~ No leave parties today owing to mines leave in the Channel.	
LA TOMBE WILLOT	14/11/15	8.30am	90 men of A Coy, 20 of B + 140 of C were sent out in wagons for work in the trenches and returned about 5 p.m.	
Billets.	15/11/15	11.30am	The B Battalion was inspected by Maj Gen Fasken, commanding 19th Division.	
	16/11/15	4.30am	Lieut Mason, 1 N.C.O. + 2 men left for leave. The C.O. went round the Ind II/r Trenches occupied by 6th Wilts whom we are relieving on 17th inst.	

INTELLIGENCE SUMMARY

or

(Erase heading not required.)

Place	Date	Hour	Summary of Events and Information	Remarks and references to Appendices
Ind III b Trenches Tube Station	17/11/15		Rained and sleet heavily during afternoon. Companies left billets at different times and relieved the 6th Wilts in Ind III b Trenches. Relief completed by 9 p.m. and was considerably assisted by the fine clear moon light night. Front line trenches are all mud & water, and parapet very low in several places. No dugouts, all having fallen in and only a few temporary shelters to which we added. Shelters made by placing corrugated iron sheets on parapet separator. A, D & C Companies are in front line & D in Reserve. A on the right resting on QUINQUE RUE with 2 platoons in fire trench & 2 in support. D in centre with 3 platoons in fire trench and one in support, and C with its left resting on RUE with 3 platoons in fire trench & one in support. The 10th Worcesters are on our right at the ORCHARD and the 46th Division on our left. Fine frosty night.	
	18/11/15		Enemy's snipers very active today and two of our men were killed and 5 wounded by bullets. The parapet having fallen down in several places in all the trenches, men have to be very careful how they pass up & down	

INTELLIGENCE SUMMARY.

(Erase heading not required.)

Place	Date	Hour	Summary of Events and Information	Remarks and references to Appendices
Ind II b. trenches.	18/7/15		Our snipers were very active during the day & claim several kills. Enemy quiet during the night, frosty night.	
TUBE STATION	19/7/15	11.30 a.m.	Enemy shelled our trenches but did no damage. Both our snipers and enemy's were active. Condition in the fire trench very bad. "B" Coy relieved "D" Coy in the fire trench during the evening, and "D" Coy came into Reserve Trench. One of our heavy guns sent several shells short of enemy's trenches during the afternoon, one shell striking our wire entanglement, another between the wire and parapet and a third exploded on the parapet and destroyed it. We had one man killed today.	
"	20/7/15		Enemy fired several shrapnel during the day on our trenches at various points, but did no damage.	
		7.30 p.m.	Officers patrol of B Coy reported enemy working party working at breach in their parapet near the CUPOLA, therefore at 9 p.m. in conjunction with our artillery, we fired rapid and machine gun on the breach, but the result was unknown. As our artillery had made several breaches in the enemy's parapet during the day, our front companies kept a continual fire onto the breaches to prevent enemy working at them. Sharp frost tonight.	

INTELLIGENCE SUMMARY.

(Erase heading not required)

Place	Date	Hour	Summary of Events and Information	Remarks and references to Appendices
In L II b Trenches near TUBE STATION EPINETTE	21/4/15		The Batteries supporting us in this section are Field. Q.86 & C.86 and Howitzer D.89. There was very little sniping today by the enemy, and our sniping during the last few days has made the enemy very careful in exposing himself now, so our snipers have little to shoot at.	
		3 p.m.	Enemy fired a few shrapnel on our left section, and were quickly silenced by our guns.	
		5 p.m.	Relief by 8th N. Staffs. commenced. Two platoons from each of the three Coys in front line came out in waders under cover of darkness, and changed into ordinary boots at TUBE STATION & handed over waders to the 6 platoons of North Staffs who went up & relieved the other platoons of the front line who returned and handed over their waders in the same way to the other platoons of 8 North Staffs. Thus all the relieving Coys coming went up to the front line in waders. The relief was completed by 9.30 p.m. goiudes conducting by a full moon. The Companies went back to brots and billets round EPINETTE, arriving in by 10 p.m., A & C Coys were in billets, B. Coy held CAILLOUX POST & D. Coy EPINETTE N-W. and DITCH and CHEVATTE POST.	

INTELLIGENCE SUMMARY.

(Erase heading not required.)

Place	Date	Hour	Summary of Events and Information	Remarks and references to Appendices
EPINETTE POSTS	22/7/15	6 pm	A Coy 40 men. B Coy. 40 men. C Coy 100 men & D Coy 40 men were out working under R.E. in 2nd & 6 Trenches during the night.	4
-do-	23/7/15	6 pm	Companies were relieved by Companies of 2nd Border Regt, 4th Lincolns, and 9th Devons, and marched to billets at LES LOBES.	4
LES LOBES	24/7/15		Remained.	
"	25/7/15	11 a.m	The Battalion left billets and marched to ROBECQ via LOCON, LES CHOQUAUX AVELETTE and South Bank of LA BASSÉE CANAL. The Battalion is now in Army Reserve. Leave was opened again and one officer, one N.C.O. & four men went on leave.	4
ROBECQ	26/7/15		Platoon Training. G.O.C 57th Brigade inspected billets this morning. A Snow storm at midday. One officer, one N.C.O, & 2 men left for leave today	4
"	27/7/15		Platoon Training. One officer and one N.C.O. & 2 men left on leave. Hard frost.	4
"	28/7/15		Sunday. One officer, 1 N.C.O. & 2 men left on leave today. Hard frost.	4
"	29/7/15		Company Training. One Officer, one N.C.O. & 2 men went on leave today. Rain today.	4
"	30/7/15		Company training. Fine & warm today. The Battalion Engineers are employed in improving billets, stopping leaks in roof, making tables & wash horses latrines etc. Much improvement is already visible.	

J. MOSS. Lt Col
Comd. 6th Yorkshire Regt.

57th Inf.Bde.
19th Div.

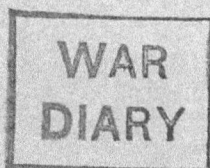

8th BATTN. THE GLOUCESTERSHIRE REGIMENT.

SEPTEMBER & OCTOBER

1 9 1 5

WAR DIARY
or
INTELLIGENCE SUMMARY
(Erase heading not required.)

Army Form C. 2118.

Instructions regarding War Diaries and Intelligence Summaries are contained in F.S. Regs., Part II. and the Staff Manual respectively. Title pages will be prepared in manuscript.

Place	Date	Hour	Summary of Events and Information	Remarks and references to Appendices
TRENCHES Sub-sec. 2nd 2.C. near RICHEBOURG L'AVOUÉ	Sept 1st		Our artillery during the day fired several shells on enemy's position, enemy's reply being feeble	
		5.30 pm.	Enemy's rifle grenades were fired at C Companies 1st line trench, but no damage was done.	
		10 pm.	C Company fired on party of Germans with machine gun, seen in old German trench in front of FERME COUR D'AVOUÉ. Result not known.	
		10.30 pm.	A & C Company working party again had to go back to their 1st line trenches, from working in front, owing to enemy's machine gun & artillery fire.	Ey.
		10.30 pm.	Enemy's machine gun fire swept along parapet of Reserve Trenches, and two men of B. Coy working in pond) were wounded.	
- do -	2/9/15	11 am.	Corporal Cox "C" Company shot three Germans who were crawling about near old German Trench, two rolled over, & the third crawled away wounded. The same N.C.O. fired at a German seen by listening post at 5.30 p.m. After the shot, the man ran away with his clothes in flames.	
		2.30 pm.	Our guns shelled FERME COUR D'AVOUÉ + at Midday the Germans shelled house along Rue du BOIS, just behind our Reserve Trenches	
		7 pm	B & D Companies relieved A & C Companies in 1st line & support Trenches and A & C took up positions in Reserve Trenches. B Coy who took over WATER KEEP and C Company FALLENTREE KEEP.	Ey

INTELLIGENCE SUMMARY.

(Erase heading not required.)

Place	Date	Hour	Summary of Events and Information	Remarks and references to Appendices
TRENCHES Sub-sec 2nd 2.C. near RICHEBOURG L'AVOUE	3/9/15	8.45am	One hostile shell pitched onto A Coy's entrenching tool store in Reserve Trench, but failed to explode.	
		11.am	2-3 hostile shells burst in vicinity of Reserve Trenches but did not damage.	
		12pm to 2.p.m.	hostile howitzers fired on our guns some way in our rear. Several failed to explode.	
		9 pm	A & B Coys in 1st line worked in front of parapet, & prevented enemy from snapping the presence of working parties, by posting men on the flanks to fire continuously.	
	4/9/15		Enemy shelled FALLEN TREE KEEP and houses behind Reserve Trenches, during morning, no damage done. Our guns pretty active by day, and by night fired salvoes on 7th COUR D'AVOUÉ. Companies in front line fired 5 rounds rate on machine gun position near F^{me} COUR D'AVOUÉ. Trenches very wet & muddy from rain.	
	5/9/15	11pm	FALLEN TREE KEEP shelled during morning, no damage. 1st line fired 5 minutes "hate" in conjunction with 89th Punjabis on our left, on F^{me} Du BOIS where working parties were at 11 p.m. At 11.30 am an enemy fired 16 shells and machine gun on "D" Coy Trenches no damage.	
	6/9/15	11.a.m.	Lieut Mason, 2nd Lt Fitzgerald & one man of D Coy, patrolled old german communication trench 100 yards in front of 1st line trenches, & found several dead germans. They brought back valuable information in the shape of articles of equipment and newspapers. At 8 p.m. a signaller read a german signalling lamp & made out the words "Kitchen, Transport, Halt, Officer."	

INTELLIGENCE SUMMARY.

(Erase heading not required.)

Place	Date	Hour	Summary of Events and Information	Remarks and references to Appendices
TRENCHES Subsec 2nd 2.C. near RICHEBOURG L'AVOUE	6/9/15	7 p.m.	A Company relieved "B" Company in 1st line trenches & supports and at 8.30 p.m. "C" Company relieved "D" Company, B & D Companies taking up Reserve Trenches.	
	7/9/15	10.30 a.m.	A. L.G.V. German Biplane flew over trenches from West to East.	
		3 p.m.	Lieut Nash accidentally wounded in "Staffords" Trenches by bursting of a trench mortar.	
		11 p.m.	Capt Fry & Lieut Hastings accidentally wounded in revolver accident.	
"	8/9/15		Our artillery fired at intervals all day on german lines.	
"	9/9/15	9 a.m.	german guns very active, & shelled front line & reserve trenches with high explosive. One man wounded in Reserve Trench. At 6 p.m. one man of D. Coy & one of C. Coy were wounded by german anti aircraft guns whilst walking up CADBURY Trench. B & D Companies relieved A. & C. in 1st line trenches.	
"	10/9/15		Capt Byers & Lt Fitzgerald & 1 man D. Coy patrolled towards german lines in the morning. Brought back useful report, and various articles of german equipment. A. "B" Coy Officers Patrol reported working party between F^me DU BOIS & F^me COUR D'AVOUÉ at 5.30 p.m. & reported germans advancing their line of trench between these farms. Rapid fire on working party at 7 p.m. resulted. At 4 p.m. a german biplane was hit by our anti aircraft & seen to fall near BOIS DU BIEZ. At 3.30 p.m. germans fired machine gun on trenches from a point S 16.C.16. in advance of their trench line.	

INTELLIGENCE SUMMARY

(Erase heading not required.)

Instructions regarding War Diaries and Intelligence Summaries are contained in F.S. Regs, Part II. and the Staff Manual respectively. Title pages will be prepared in manuscript.

Place	Date	Hour	Summary of Events and Information	Remarks and references to Appendices
TRENCHES Subsec 2nd II C. near RICHEBOURG L'AVOUÉ	11/9/15	11pm	Our working parties in front of 1st line trenches, were fired on by "whiz bangs" machine gun & rifle fire, but suffered no casualties, otherwise quiet day.	Ly
	12/9/15	2 a.m.	Aircraft heard passing over the trenches between 2 & 3 a.m, suspected to be hostile.	
		3 a.m.	Germans from near F me COUR D'AVOUÉ were heard shouting. One of them shouted "Come over & finish it". Our machine gun silenced them.	
		7.50 a.m.	A german standing on hostile parapet, was shot by "B" Coy. sniper.	
		9.15 a.m.	A german biplane passed over our trenches, travelling high from W. to E. probably one of ours.	
			head going out during the night.	
		9.30 a.m.	A few hostile shells burst near our reserve trenches.	
	13.9.15	9.45 a.m.	Our sniper hit a german periscope	Ly
		8 p.m.	"D" Coy, on left 1st line trenches, opened rapid fire on enemy heard moving in Ridge. S.15.d.1.5	
		9 p.m.	Enemy fired 19 shells behind Reserve trenches, & finally set fire to haystack 100x S of CHOCOLATE POST.	
		11 p.m.	Having handed over our section of trenches to the South Lancashire Regt, we evacuated, marched to billets. Ly	
LOCON X.1	14.9.15	3 a.m.	Arrived in billets near LOCON	Ly
do	15.9.15		Two companies went to baths at LESTREM. Cleaning up, and issuing new clothes	Ly
	16.9.15		Two companies went to baths at LESTREM. "A" + "D" Coys went digging at night on communication trenches near GIVENCHY.	

INTELLIGENCE SUMMARY.

(Erase heading not required.)

Place	Date	Hour	Summary of Events and Information	Remarks and references to Appendices
Near LOCON	17.9.15		Company route marches, physical training, issuing of new clothing etc. C.O visited new trenches near GIVENCHY	
- do -	18.9.15		- ditto -	
- do -	19.9.15		- ditto - 50 men of "B" Coy working during the night on communication trenches near FESTUBERT.	
"	"	9.a.m.	The four company Commanders went round their section of new trenches near GIVENCHY.	
- do -	19.9.15	9.30 a.m.	Church Parade at H.Q.	
- do -	20.9.15	4.p.m.	550 men working at HAYSTACK POST, ARGYLE ROAD communication trenches and also near GIVENCHY during the night. also 10 N.C.O.s & 30 men B. Coy occupied posts & keeps near LE TOURET	
- do -	21.9.15		Company parades.	
- do -	22.9.15		Company route marches etc	
- do -	23.9.15		Company route marches etc	
- do -	24.9.15		Fitting kit etc preparatory to departure	
LE HAMEL	25.9.15	3 a.m	Moved from billets at LOCON and marched to bivouac at LE HAMEL	
MARAIS.	- do -	9.15am	left LE HAMEL and marched in Brigade to MARAIS via GORRE. The advance on the enemy's trenches East of GIVENCHY having been withdrawn, the 57th Brigade remained in Army Reserve at MARAIS, till late in the afternoon, to be employed in the event of a hostile counter attack, & subsequently the Battalion occupied the Labour trenches	

INTELLIGENCE SUMMARY.

(Erase heading not required.)

Place	Date	Hour	Summary of Events and Information	Remarks and references to Appendices
	25th		S of the BETHUNE - FESTUBERT Rd, just West of MARAIS. The North Staffordshire Regt being in the same line of trenches North of the Road, both battalion in reserve to Warwicks & Worcesters, holding a parallel line of trenches 1/4 mile to the East in support to the troops near GIVENCHY	4
do.	do.	10.30 pm	The 5⟨⟩th Btt withdrew to vicinity of LE HAMEL and the Battalion occupied billets immediately East of the road junction of LA COUTURE - LE TOURET Roads and the RUE de BOIS Road. Rain fell heavily all the afternoon and evening but weather cleared up on the march back at night.	4
LE TOURET	26th		Remained in billets as Army Reserve. A reinforcement draft of 5 N.C.Os and ten men arrived today.	4
- do -	27th	5.45pm	Orders received for Battalion with 1st line transport to proceed at once and concentrate with remainder of Brigade at LE HAMEL. Battalion arrived there at 7.20 p.m. Raining hard. - On arrival orders were received from Brigade to return to billets & be prepared to concentrate again at LE HAMEL within one hour of the order being received at Bttn H.Q. - Battalion arrived at billets at 8.30 pm in heavy rain.	4
- do -	28th		Remained in billets.	4

INTELLIGENCE SUMMARY.

(Erase heading not required.)

Place	Date	Hour	Summary of Events and Information	Remarks and references to Appendices
TRENCHES In front of rear.	29th		Orders received re going into trenches. C.O. went round the subsection to be taken over, in the morning, and Company Commanders in the afternoon. Rained all day.	T.G.
		5.30 p.m.	The Battalion left billets and marched to ESTAMINET CORNER where platoon guides of 9th Cheshire Regt took platoons into trenches. Trenches taken over from 9th Cheshires by 10.30 p.m. A Coy took over front line trenches from Bay 1 to 34 and C Coy from Bay 35 to 58. B Coy took over support line, and D Coy & H.Q. Reserve line along Grouse Butts. The trenches were in a very muddy condition owing to the rain which fell all the time.	T.G.
FESTUBERT				
-do-	30th		Fine day. Spent most of day in cleaning up trenches. Everything quiet.	
		5.30 p.m.	A Coy extended their line to Bay 38, and C took on from 39 to 73. A Coy employed parties during the night in burying dead men of the Welch Regt in front of the 1st line parapet. These men were killed in action of 25th Sept 1915.	T.G.
-do-	1st October	5.30 a.m. to 9 a.m.	Enemy shelled the trenches west of CRATER, and between 12 noon & 4 p.m. shelled between No 5 Communication Trench & YELLOW ROAD in vicinity of Reserve Trenches, but no damage was done. Men were employed by day in making dug outs in new Support Trench & clearing up GRENADIER Communication & during the night the front-line companies buried dead men of the Welch Regt killed in trench & action of 25th Sept.	T.G.

INTELLIGENCE SUMMARY.

(Erase heading not required.)

Instructions regarding War Diaries and Intelligence Summaries are contained in F. S. Regs., Part II. and the Staff Manual respectively. Title pages will be prepared in manuscript.

Place	Date	Hour	Summary of Events and Information	Remarks and references to Appendices
TRENCHES Ind II near FESTUBERT	Oct 2nd	8 a.m.	Hostile aeroplane flew from German lines as far as Support Trenches, but was driven back by anti-aircraft fire. During morning, Germans were seen busy working at their trenches, & our Snipers had shots at them. Officers of 2nd Gurkhas arrived in morning to take over trenches, and at 8 p.m. the relief commenced and our last company filed out about 11 p.m. Marched to bivouac at LE HAMEL, arriving there by 1 a.m.	
LE HAMEL	Oct 3rd	5.30 p.m.	Marched from LE HAMEL. B & D companies marched and took up posts round CHOCOLATE POST & occupied reserve trenches along RUE DeBOIS between Albert and Edward Roads in S.Q.C. — A & C Companies & H.Q. went into billets near LACOUTURE. The Battalion thus went into	
LACOUTURE	Oct 4th	5 p.m.	C. Company marched to prolong trenches occupied by B & D companies and B. Coy took over 9 posts & keep by CHOCOLATE POST, leaving C & D Companies in the Rue de Bois Reserve Trenches. ⚹ One Officer & 58 men of A. Coy left at 5.30 p.m. and occupied 3 posts near RICHBOURG St VAAST. leaving about 100 men of A Coy and H.Q. still at LACOUTURE.	
–do–	Oct 5th		The 58 men of A Coy spread out over three more redoubts near RICHBOURG St VAAST.	

INTELLIGENCE SUMMARY.
(Erase heading not required.)

Instructions regarding War Diaries and Intelligence Summaries are contained in F.S. Regs., Part II. and the Staff Manual respectively. Title pages will be prepared in manuscript.

Place	Date	Hour	Summary of Events and Information	Remarks and references to Appendices
LACOUTURE	Oct 6th		100 men from B & D companies employed digging communication trenches by night.	EG
-do-	Oct 7th	5 p.m.	A Coy at H.Q. being relieved by a company of Worcesters, marched to billets in VIELLE CHAPPELLE into Divisional Reserve, followed shortly by B Coy who had been relieved of their posts. C & D followed about 8 p.m. and H.Q. was relieved	EG
VIELLE HA CHAPELLE	Oct 8th		at 12.30 a.m. 8th inst. 200 men of C & D Coys working at communication trenches arrived back in billets at 2.30 a.m.	EG
-do-	"		All Companies were billeting at LA GORGUE Battn today.	EG
-do-	Oct 9th		All Companies route marching, refitting, rifle exercises etc	EG
-do-	Oct 10th		Church parade near H.Q. at 9.30 a.m.	EG
-do-	Oct 11th	5 p.m.	Companies paraded & marched off separately at ½ hour interval in the order A B C D via RICHEBOURG ST VAAST and EDWARD ROAD & took over 2nd & 4th Gr. Trenches from 8th N. Staffs from FARM CORNER to VINE STREET. Fire Trenches A on right, B in centre, C Coy on left with 2 platoons per company in support. D Coy and H.Q. in Reserve Trench. D Coy holding PALLMALL KEEP with 15 men. Relief completed by 9.10 p.m.	EG
2nd & 4th Gr. Trenches. FARM CORNER to VINE STREET -do-	Oct 12th		Enemy normal. One man of A + 1 man of C Coy both seriously wounded by shrapnel & machine gun.	EG

INTELLIGENCE SUMMARY.

(Erase heading not required.)

Place	Date	Hour	Summary of Events and Information	Remarks and references to Appendices
TRENCHES IN IV b. FARM CORNER & VINE STREET	Oct 13	3 a.m.	Two men of "C" Coy in front line trenches accidentally wounded by premature explosion of bomb.	
		9 a.m.	One man of "B" Coy slightly wounded by bayonet periscope being shot.	
		5 a.m.	Hostile mortar bombs fell between RANGERS and Support Trenches. No damage done.	
		6.30 a.m.	Several Rifle Grenades fell all round Officers Mess near BOARS HEAD, some "blind". No damage. We retaliated with double the number.	
		12 noon	Heavy bombardment from our guns on right & left of Ind IV commenced and continued for three hours. Smoke bombs were also thrown during that time which completely blotted out the enemy's trenches, some of the smoke penetrating our front line. Our section of guns commenced bombardment of enemy's trenches and support & reserve lines at 1 p.m. & continued for one hour. The enemy retaliated with shrapnel and H.E. shells spread all over our section of the trenches. One H.E shell knocked down a piece of "C" Coy's front line parapet near VINE STREET and another damaged the reserve parapet of "D" Coy. and smashed three rifles. Minenwerfer, rifle grenades, bombs were thrown near Officers Mess near BOARS HEAD, but no damage was done. Result of enemy's bombardment was three men of "D" Coy wounded by shrapnel in Reserve Trench. All day heavy bombardment from our guns was observed and heard in the distance towards the South in the direction	

INTELLIGENCE SUMMARY.

(Erase heading not required.)

Instructions regarding War Diaries and Intelligence Summaries are contained in F.S. Regs., Part II. and the Staff Manual respectively. Title pages will be prepared in manuscript.

Place	Date	Hour	Summary of Events and Information	Remarks and references to Appendices
TRENCHES	Oct 13th		of HULLUCH. This continued through the night. Otherwise afternoon & night all quiet on our front.	
2nd IV b.				
FARM CORNER	Oct 14th	10.a.m.	Misty morning upto 10.a.m. As soon as mist cleared at 10.35 a.m. a german minenwerfer commenced enfilading our front line trenches in the vicinity of BOARS HEAD from a point in the german trenches located opposite VINE and BOND STREET. It fired regularly every three minutes and the fire lasted till 12.5.p.m. The holes made by the shells were of an immense size and a large amount of damage was done to the parapet, which was breached in several spots, and communication stopped between A & B Companies. In the hour and a half thirty minenwerfer burst. Air 11 a.m. 4 H.E. shells burst near Junction of RUE DU BOIS and PALL MALL Trench. Between 11.50 a.m and 11.55 a.m. ten pip's squeaks burst over the trenches on the left of our line. Our artillery gave us very little support during the bombardment. From 3.30 p.m to 4 p.m. our artillery fired shells (H.E.) on F^{me} du BOIS. All quiet in the afternoon and evening. During the bombardment our casualties, chiefly due to minenwerfer were:- A Coy. 1 killed 1 missing (believed killed) 5 wounded. "B" Coy. 1 killed, 9 wounded. "D" Coy. 3 wounded. Several men were buried in dugouts, chiefly due to minenwerfer and had to be dug out. During the night "B" Coy & "A" Coy worked continuously to repair damage done	
VINE STREET				

Instructions regarding War Diaries and Intelligence Summaries are contained in F. S. Regs., Part II and the Staff Manual respectively. Title pages will be prepared in manuscript.

INTELLIGENCE SUMMARY.

(Erase heading not required.)

Place	Date	Hour	Summary of Events and Information	Remarks and references to Appendices
TRENCHES Ind IV b. FARM CORNER to VINE STREET.	15/4/15	7:30am	A german walking along his parapet, thinking the mist sufficient cover, was "dropped" by one of "C" Coy Snipers.	
		8:15am	A "C" Coy patrol in the mist got within 100 yds of german party working in front of their parapet, the patrol opened rapid fire and three germans fell and more were hit. Enemy working had all day at the spot from whence the Minenwerfer was seen to be firing's from yesterday. This spot was located to be the 160° magnetic from head of VINE STREET & 153° magnetic from head of BOND STREET.	
		12.45pm	Hostile "pipsqueaks" burst near front parapet, no damage done. Rifle grenades were sent near trenches by BOARS HEAD during the night, doing no damage. Work by day & night chiefly on front parapet which was breached in several places by the minenwerfer on the 14th.	LG
	16/4/15	7am	Two of our machine guns fired from "C" Coy Trenches on german working party in the mist, the mist prevented our seeing the result.	
		2.40pm	Our Artillery dispersed a german party working in their support trenches. One sniper was active. During the night seven trench mortars minilla fell behind RANGERS TRENCH, but they failed to explode, and there is no trace of them.	LG

1577 Wt. W10791/1773 500,000 1/15 D.D. & L.   A.D.S.S./Forms/C. 2118.

INTELLIGENCE SUMMARY.

(Erase heading not required.)

Place	Date	Hour	Summary of Events and Information	Remarks and references to Appendices
TRENCHES Int IV b FARM CORNER to VINE STREET	18/7/15		Misty morning and quiet all day. Enemy had no work on their defences. Our snipers active. There missiles were sent over during the evening the near Pt S 16 a 5.8 the report being slightly louder than a rifle. Enemy fired rifle grenades on trenches near BOMB HEAD during the night, to which we vigorously retaliated.	
		11 A.M.	A german in dark green uniform was spotted on german parapet for a second or so. Shrapnel & H.E. Shells fell about trenches, starting near H.Q. & then assuring back by degrees to front trenches. One Shrapnel burst near EMBANKMENT TRENCH and at the same time a catapult bomb from which there were 3 casualties, and EMBANKMENT TRENCH blocked up. Our guns vigorously retaliated and enemy's fire ceased.	
		3 p.m.	Our "heavies" bombarded the spot from which the minenwerfer fired a 14" round and made very good shooting.	
		4 p.m.	Our snipers fired on german working party at S 16 a. 5.8 and dropped three men, & a fourth was dragged over the parapet.	
		9 p.m.	A trench mortar (minenwerfer) bomb exploded between the two front trenches, no damage	

INTELLIGENCE SUMMARY.

(Erase heading not required.)

Instructions regarding War Diaries and Intelligence Summaries are contained in F.S. Regs., Part II and the Staff Manual respectively. Title pages will be prepared in manuscript.

Place	Date	Hour	Summary of Events and Information	Remarks and references to Appendices
TRENCHES Ind IV & FARM CORNER & VINE STREET	19/15	7 am	A patrol had through the night on german party working in front of parapet & dispersed them rapidly with loss. A german Sniper post located at S.16.a. 3.5-7.5. Enemy are continually working at S.16.a.5.8 where a strong redoubt is being made in the german front line. At 6.45 p.m. our rapid fire & machine gun fire dispersed a working party of enemy at S.16.a.5.8. Enemy's fire of maxims along top of parapet very active during the night. One man of "D" Coy killed whilst working on parapet at 7 p.m.	
-do-	20/15	6.30 am	Our snipers from BOARS HEAD observed a german looking over parapet of Stein Boars Head Salient. He wore a stiff grey cap like ours. As a bomb had just been thrown & exploded on the post from whence he appeared, it is suspected that the salient has a bomb-proof shelter at its end. Enemy's Snipers very active during the morning, & broke three of our box periscopes.	
		12-2 pm	Eight Catapult bombs were fired at our trenches near BOARS HEAD. 6 fell outside the parapet & exploded and 2 burst inside, but no damage done. Catapult was located at S.16.a.6.5. A portion of RANGERS TRENCH was damaged by shrapnel at 1.30 pm.	
		6 pm	One company 8ᵗʰ Gurkhas and 3 companies Garhwal Rifles came in and relieved the Battalion in Ind. IV to trenches. Relief completed by 8 p.m. Battalion marched	

INTELLIGENCE SUMMARY.

(Erase heading not required.)

Instructions regarding War Diaries and Intelligence Summaries are contained in F.S. Regs., Part II. and the Staff Manual respectively. Title pages will be prepared in manuscript.

Place	Date	Hour	Summary of Events and Information	Remarks and references to Appendices
LE HAMEL	20/10/15	8 p.m.	to billets at LE HAMEL and settled into billets at 10 p.m.	&.
- do -	21/10/15		In Brigade Reserve. Companies employed in cleaning up.	&.
- do -	22/10/15		Company route marches, physical drill etc. Bad boots exchanged etc.	&.
- do -	23/10/15		All Companies had baths at LOGON from 9 a.m. to 6 p.m. Rain at night.	&.
- do -	24/10/15	9.30am	Church Parade in field near "B" Coy billets. Slight rain all day, heavy rain all night.	&.
- do -	25/10/15		Wet all day. Companies route march in the morning. Bombers practised with live bombs.	&.
- do -	26/10/15		Companies route marching & physical drill. Bombers practising with live bombs.	&.
- do -	27/10/15		— Ditto — Having received orders to relieve 10th Warwicks on 28th inst, Major Moore went round	&.
- do -	27/10/15		IND.1.A. trenches in the afternoon preparatory to taking over tomorrow.	&.
- do -	28/10/15	2.30pm	Companies in order of B.D.A.C.&H.Q. marched at half hours interval, and went into trenches IND.1.A. just north of GIVENCHY, and went up by YELLOW ROAD & FIFE TRENCH. Relief completed by 6 p.m. Very heavy rain all the afternoon and trenches in a very bad state indeed. B Coy took up the right section of front line, from GRENADIER ROAD to the LOOP and D. Coy from the LOOP to just beyond STUART Road, and one platoon of "A" Coy extended B's left. Three platoons of "A" Coy in Support in GEORGE STREET, and "C" Coy.	

INTELLIGENCE SUMMARY.

(Erase heading not required.)

Place	Date	Hour	Summary of Events and Information	Remarks and references to Appendices
INDIA Trenches first north of GIVENCHY			and H.Q. in Reserve along GROUSE BUTTS. Rained heavily all night, & several dugouts fell down, and in the front line the supervision and in some cases the parapet fell down in several places owing to the rain. Enemy sent up several green flares during the night, but nothing unusual occurred after these flares were sent up.	
-do-	29/10/15	9.45a.m.	Enemy fired half a dozen H.E. shells on junction of YELLOW and FESTUBERT Roads which killed a Sergeant of S.W.B. working party. Otherwise enemy were very quiet, and did practically no sniping. Our guns retaliated very strongly in the morning & afternoon. No rain today, so a lot of work was done clearing up mud, and clearing trenches especially in front line where the supervision trench & parapet had collapsed. Sounds of water being pumped out of the enemys trenches were heard opposite our right.	
-do-	30/10/15	6.30a.m.	After one of our snipers fired from the loop, a cry was heard in enemys trench denoting that a man had been hit. Last night the enemy sent up several red & green flares but nothing resulted.	
		10 a.m.	Enemy again shelled YELLOW ROAD with 4 H.E. Shells. One bomber wounded whilst drawing water. Our guns fired with great effect practically all day.	

INTELLIGENCE SUMMARY.

(Erase heading not required.)

Instructions regarding War Diaries and Intelligence Summaries are contained in F.S. Regs., Part II. and the Staff Manual respectively. Title pages will be prepared in manuscript.

Place	Date	Hour	Summary of Events and Information	Remarks and references to Appendices
IND.1.a Trenches just North of GIVENCHY	30/10/15	11 a.m.	"B" Coy Snipers fired on german working party of 5, working near CRATER. One man fell, and remainder bolted.	
		12 noon	Enemy fired 6 H.E shells at our parapet near GRENADIER trench. All fell short at 5 out of the six were 'bling'.	
		7 pm	16-7-30 pm, a steady light was visible on ridge 250 yds S. of CRATER.	
		7.45 pm	Our M.G. opened fire on enemy working at their parapet opposite LOOP, work ceased at once and cries of 'hurrah' were heard. The enemy appeared very exuberant during the night, I shouted a lot.	
		9.15 pm	Sentries report hearing one long blast of whistle then pause, then one long & one short which was followed by red flare after which occasional fire was opened on our parapet. No rain today, trenches drying up, and men were at work all day Cleaning up and repairing damage done by the rain.	tkp.
-do-	31/10/15	9.45 a.m.	A hostile biplane flew high over our trenches from West to East, and when it passed over hostile trenches, it dropped a silver spray. Our snipers were active during the day. During the morning one of our batteries fired several H.E shells which pitched very short, a burst close in front of our parapet and	

INTELLIGENCE SUMMARY.

(Erase heading not required.)

Instructions regarding War Diaries and Intelligence Summaries are contained in F. S. Regs., Part II. and the Staff Manual respectively. Title pages will be prepared in manuscript.

Place	Date	Hour	Summary of Events and Information	Remarks and references to Appendices
IN D. 1.A Trenches just N. of GIVENCHY	31/1/15	10.45 p.m.	One burst just on our wire entanglement. From A.3 a.7.6. enemy threw over a fire ball which fitted near our wire & burnt for 3 minutes. At 11 p.m. another was sent over which burnt for 40 minutes, making slight explosions every 10 minutes. It rained occasionally to day. All men employed in cleaning up & repairing trenches.	

G.T. Nelmes, Major.
Com'd'g 5(Sv) Bn Gloucestershire Reg't

57th Inf.Bde.
19th Div.

WAR DIARY

8th BATTN. THE GLOUCESTERSHIRE REGIMENT.

A U G U S T

1 9 1 5

INTELLIGENCE SUMMARY.

(Erase heading not required.)

Instructions regarding War Diaries and Intelligence Summaries are contained in F. S. Regs., Part II. and the Staff Manual respectively. Title pages will be prepared in manuscript.

Place	Date	Hour	Summary of Events and Information	Remarks and references to Appendices
CAUDESCURE	1st Aug		Physical Training etc.	K.10.a. Sheet 36a.
- do -	2nd Aug		- do -	
ESTAIRES	3rd Aug	8-30 am	Marched from CAUDESCURE to billets near ESTAIRES L.21.b. — L.27.b.1.6. — L.28.c.9.d. sheet 36 a.
ESTAIRES	4th Aug		Physical Training etc.	
- do -	5th Aug	4.30 pm	2 officers 15 men went to Estaire for 3 days grenade course. 1 officer 9.5 men for 3 days French Mortar course.	
- do -	"	9 a.m.	Battalion Route march.	
- do -	6th Aug	7 a.m.	All companies washing in baths at LA GORGUE 7 a.m to 5 p.m.	
- do -	7th		Company Route marches & Physical Training.	
- do -	8th		(Sunday) Church Parade,	
- do -	9th		Company Route marches & Physical Training.	
- do -	do	5 p.m.	"A" Company marched to LAVENTIE and went into "A" Subsection Trenches in relief of one company 10th Worcesters, at 9 p.m.	
- do -	10th	5 pm.	Battalion less "A" Coy, marched to billets in LAVENTIE	
LAVENTIE	"	8 p.m.	"B" Company went into "B" Subsection Trenches in relief of a company 10th Worcesters	
- do -	11th	9 p.m.	"C" Company went into "A" Subsection Trenches in relief of "A" Company.	
- do -	11th	9 p.m.	"D" Company employed all night in making parapet trench behind "C" Subsection Trench.	

Instructions regarding War Diaries and Intelligence Summaries are contained in F.S. Regs., Part II. and the Staff Manual respectively. Title pages will be prepared in manuscript.

INTELLIGENCE SUMMARY.
(Erase heading not required.)

Place	Date	Hour	Summary of Events and Information	Remarks and references to Appendices
LAVENTIE	August 12	3 p.m.	Pte Goodfield "C" Company killed in action in trenches	
"	"	8 p.m.	"D" Company went into "B" Subsection Trenches in relief of "B" Company	
"	"	9 p.m.	"A" Company employed all night in making support trench in "C" Subsection Trenches	
"	13 "	9 p.m.	"B" Company employed all night in digging support trenches in "C" Subsection Trenches	
"	14 "	7 p.m.	Battalion less "D" Company marched to former billets near ESTAIRES.	
"	"	9 p.m.	"D" Company relieved from "B" Subsection Trenches, marched to former billets near ESTAIRES	
ESTAIRES	16 "	9 a.m.	Battalion marched to former billets at CAUDESCURE near MERVILLE.	
CAUDESCURE	17 "		Company route marches etc.	
"	18 "	10 a.m.	C.O. 2 Company Commanders, 10 men attended "gas" demonstration near MERVILLE, remainder route marches	
"	19 "	"	Route marches by Companies, physical training etc.	
"	20 "	9 a.m.	The Company Commander & three platoon Commanders of "B" Coy went into trenches for 48 hours instruction attached to Tulloch or Brigade. Remainder Company route marches & physical training	
"	21 "		Company route marches - physical training	
"	"	4 p.m.	C. Company 2 18 men 7 officers with one Company 8th N. Staff Reg.t marched to billets at CROIX-BARBES under Major D.M. Moore, for entrenching work.	M 2 b d sheet 36.SW.1.
"	22 "	9 a.m.	The Company Commander and three Platoon Commanders of "D" Coy went into trenches for 48 hours instruction, attached to SIRHIND Brigade.	

INTELLIGENCE SUMMARY.

(Erase heading not required.)

Instructions regarding War Diaries and Intelligence Summaries are contained in F. S. Regs., Part II. and the Staff Manual respectively. Title pages will be prepared in manuscript.

Place	Date	Hour	Summary of Events and Information	Remarks and references to Appendices
CAUDESCURE	23/8/15	—	Company Route Marches, bombing practice etc.	££
-do-	24/8/15	9 am.	A Company Commander & 9 Platoon Commanders went into trenches for 48 hours instruction	££
-do-	do		Company Route Marches etc.	££
-do-	25/8/15	2 pm.	"C" Company returned from entrenching work at CROIX-BARBÉS. Casualties Nil	££
-do-	26/8/15		A, B, & C Companies route march & physical training etc	££
-do-			A, B, C & D Coys. route march & physical training. C.O. went to inspect reserve trenches which the battalion will occupy shortly.	££
-do-	27/8/15	3:30 pm.	Battalion marched to billets at MARMUSE prior to entering the trenches.	££
MARMUSE	28/8/15	5:30 pm.	Battalion marched to trenches near RICHEBOURG-L'AVOUÉ, taking over the reserve trenches from 2 companies 2nd Batt. The Queen's Regt; all four companies taking up a section of the reserve trench, being connected up.	££
TRENCHES	29/8/15	4 pm.	Enemy fired a few round shrapnell which burst near the trenches, but did no damage.	
		7 pm.	A & C Companies relieved the companies of 10th Worcesters in the first line trenches between PIPE Communication Trench & EMBANKMENT Communication Trench. A Coy's place in Reserve trench being taken over by one company Worcesters. B & D Companies spread out & thus held the line vacated by C Coy.	££

INTELLIGENCE SUMMARY.

(Erase heading not required.)

Place	Date	Hour	Summary of Events and Information	Remarks and references to Appendices
TRENCHES	30th	11.a.m	One Private A. Coy, wounded by bullet through head in front line. Men employed in repairing & improving trenches. Situation Normal. One sergeant wounded by shell while digging by night in front party.	
do	31st	12 noon	Our artillery bombarded farm COUR D'AVOUÉ where enemy's working party. Their head 1st line trenches shelled at 10 a.m. but no damage last night. C. Company's	4
		10.30pm	A & C Companies, working in front of first line parapet, were obliged to return to trenches on account of hostile maxim and artillery fire. No casualties however.	4

J.H. Potts Lt Col.
Con.dg 8th Gloucester Regt V.

57th Inf.Bde.
19th Div.

Battn. disembarked
Boulogne from
England 18.7.15.

WAR DIARY

8th BATTN. THE GLOUCESTERSHIRE REGIMENT.

J U L Y

(17.7.15 - 31.7.15)

1 9 1 5

Jan '19

War Diary.

8th (Su) Bn. Gloucestershire Regt.

From 17th July to 31st July (inclusive) 1915.

Volume I.

INTELLIGENCE SUMMARY.

(Erase heading not required.)

Instructions regarding War Diaries and Intelligence Summaries are contained in F.S. Regs., Part II and the Staff Manual respectively. Title pages will be prepared in manuscript.

Place	Date	Hour	Summary of Events and Information	Remarks and references to Appendices
Tidworth	17/7/15	7.a.m	3 officers, 107 men, and all 1st line Transport left Tidworth by train.	—
Havre	18/7/15	3.30am	Above advance party, moving via Southampton, disembarked at Havre, & proceeded to No 5. Rest Camp.	—
Havre	18/7/15	1.30pm	Advance Party left No 5 Camp & entrained for the front.	—
Tidworth	18/7/15	2.55pm	Remainder of Battalion, 27 Officers including Chaplain & Medical Officer and 838 rank & file left Tidworth by two trains, and arrived BOULOGNE 10.30 p.m. & proceeded to K. Rest Camp	—
BOULOGNE	19/7/15	8.30pm	Battalion left Rest Camp and marched to PONT à BRIQUE's Railway Station.	—
PONT à BRIQUES	do	12.am	Entrained in train in which 1st line Transport arrived from HAVRE	—
WATTEN	20/7/15	3.30am	Arrived WATTEN and detrained. Marched to billets at NORTLEULINGHEM	—
NORTHLEULINGHEM	do	9.30am	Battalion & 1st line Transport arrived and were billetted	—
do	21/7/15	9.a.m	Route march and Physical Training	—
do	22/7/15	9.a.m	Route march, etc.	—
do	23/7/15	9.am	Left NORTLEULINGHEM & marched to billets in vicinity of RENESCURE	—
RENESCURE	24/7/15	8.30am	Left RENESCURE and marched to billets at ISBERGUES	—
ISBERGUES	25/7/15		Rested	—

INTELLIGENCE SUMMARY.

(Erase heading not required.)

Instructions regarding War Diaries and Intelligence Summaries are contained in F. S. Regs., Part II. and the Staff Manual respectively. Title pages will be prepared in manuscript.

Place	Date	Hour	Summary of Events and Information	Remarks and references to Appendices
ISBERGUES	26/7/15		Physical Training etc	
do	27/7/15		do	
do	28/7/15		do	
do	29/7/15		do	
do	30/7/15	9.30 am	Marched from ISBERGUES to billets at HAVERSKERQUE	
HAVERSKERQUE	31/7/15	1. p.m.	Marched from HAVERSKERQUE to billets at CAUDESCURE near MERVILLE	

J.H.G.H. Lt Colonel.
Comdg 8th (Ser) Bn Gloucestershire Regiment

St. Petersburg
Vol: 6
Tan

19

C. M.
18 sheets

WAR DIARY

INTELLIGENCE SUMMARY.

Army Form C. 2118.

8th Gloucester Regt

Place	Date	Hour	Summary of Events and Information	Remarks and references to Appendices
LES LOBES Billets	Jan 1st 1916		Companies went for short routemarch this morning, and 100 men of "A" Coy batted at VIELLE CHAPELLE	
"	2nd		Sunday. C.O. went round the trenches occupied by 6th Wilts whom we are to relieve. Companies went for route march in the morning, & "C" Coy beat Div: Cyclists by 4-3 goals at association football in the afternoon.	
"	3rd		Companies route marched in morning, and Company Commanders went-round their section of trenches they are to occupy.	
"	4th		Companies left billets at ½ hour intervals beginning from 1:30 p.m. in order of B. D. C. & H.Q. and A. Coy, & marched via VIELLE CHAPELLE - LACOUTURE - CROIX BARBEE, to rest-house No 8 where gum boots were put on, then via WINDY CORNER to the trenches. "B" Coy went straight from CROIX BARBEE to their line holding LA BASSÉE ROAD to OXFORD STREET with 3 platoons and one platoon in reserve on EDGEWARE RD. with 30 men of "C" Coy in PORT ARTHUR KEEP. This part of the line was taken over from 4th King's Liverpool Regt.	

WAR DIARY

Army Form C. 2118.

8th Gloucester Regt.

INTELLIGENCE SUMMARY

(Erase heading not required.)

Place	Date	Hour	Summary of Events and Information	Remarks and references to Appendices
	4th	5 p.m.	"D" Coy took over line from COPSE ST. to 200 yds N. of PLUM ST. "A" continued the line northwards to LA BASEE Road, and "C" Coy has 30 men in PORT ARTHUR took over Reserve line where HQ was also situated. All three were taken over from 6th Wilts. Relief commenced 5 p.m. and finished 12.45 a.m. There was great delay owing to insufficient gumboots, and only COPSE ST. Com. Trench to use. "C" Coy/Welch Regt was attached to Bn today for instruction. Our line now extends from COPSE ST. (inclusive) to OXFORD ST. exclusive. Trenches South of our line are held by 56th Brigade, and on left of our line A/Bg 10th Worcester of our own Brigade.	
TRENCHES COPSE ST. to OXFORD Street.	5th		During the afternoon the enemy shelled our front line with shrapnel but did no damage. This was in retaliation for C.87 Battery breaking up wire N and S. of LA BASEE Road. early in afternoon. From dusk till 10. p.m. enemy were very active with machine gun & rifle fire along front parapet & again at 6.30 am 6"Mort. Four officers Patrol were sent out to reconnoitre German damaged wire, but trenches were	

Army Form C. 2118.

WAR DIARY
or
INTELLIGENCE SUMMARY.
(Erase heading not required.)

8th Gloucester Regt.

Place	Date	Hour	Summary of Events and Information	Remarks and references to Appendices
TRENCHES COPSE STREET to Oxford Street.			found strongly held and germans were not found working on wire. "C" Coy 16th Welch Regt left the trenches tonight, ceased to be attached to the Battalion.	
	6th		Enemy shrapnelled the centre of our front line (A Coy) during the morning and did some damage to the parapet. PORT ARTHUR was also shelled but no damage was done. They employed a lot of sniping and machine guns traversed the parapet during the night. An officers patrol (2 Lt Hawker) went out at midnight to Pt S.10.d.3.6 but could not get to the wire as a large working party was active on german parapet. The patrol returned & reported the fact, and 3 machine guns & rifle fire were directed on the working party. Another officers patrol (b Coy) went out towards Pt S.11.a.3.3. but found germans working on the wire. Machine guns & rifle fire was therefore similarly directed on the spot. A third Officers patrol got up to the wire in Pt S.10 to 8.1. (from Key) and found the german wire was good.	

Army Form C. 2118.

8th Gloucester Regt

WAR DIARY
or
INTELLIGENCE SUMMARY.
(Erase heading not required.)

Place	Date	Hour	Summary of Events and Information	Remarks and references to Appendices
TRENCHES COPSE STREET to OXFORD STREET just South of NEUVE CHAPELLE	Jan 7th	11 a.m.	GUARDS TRENCH in Local Reserve, occupied by D. Coy, was shelled by H.E and Shrapnel from 11 to 11.45. a.m, 3 dug outs were destroyed and parapet breached in 5 places, but there were only two slight casualties. The steel helmets saved some men from injury.	
		5:45 p.m.	An Officers patrol (A Coy) reached enemy's wire opposite S.10.b.6.4½ & crossed some low trip wire, ~10 yds further, barbed wire on corkscrew iron pickets, and at foot of parapet chevaux de frise of strong barbed wire. The wire was not damaged. At point where ditch meets German Parapet pt 7.9. there is a post strongly held. Patrol as it retired was fired on by machine gun, but escaped injury. Enemy active every night with searchlight, & machine gun fire. Our Snipers active during the day. On the right of our line by COPSE STREET the trenches are only 60 yards apart, and the enemy's Snipers are very active on any of our periscopes. We are constructing Sniper posts along here.	
	8th	2:30 p.m.	Our howitzers shelled enemy front line till 3.15 p.m, and enemy immediately	

WAR DIARY

INTELLIGENCE SUMMARY.

Army Form C. 2118.

8th Gloucester Regt.

Place	Date	Hour	Summary of Events and Information	Remarks and references to Appendices
	January			
			retaliated by traversing with H.E shells from COPSE STREET to PLUM STREET along the RUE DU BOIS and Bn H.Q. at 3.30 pm. No damage was done however except the holly line was breached about 100 yds from terminus. Four H.E shells also exploded near Bn. H.Q. at 7.30 p.m. in addition to some 'duds'. The Battalion was relieved by 8th North Staffordshire Regt. Relief completed by 9 p.m. One company (D. Coy) remained in Reserve Trenches, and the other three went in billets near CROIX BARBÉE, C. Coy finding 1 Officer and 50 men for LANDSDOWNE POST and 1 Officer and 30 men for S. VAAST POST.	
Billets CROIX BARBÉE	9th Sunday		"B" Coy. & 75 men of "C" Coy had baths at CROIX BARBÉE today. Inspection of kit.	
"	10th		A Coy & 80 men of "C" Coy had baths. "B" Coy was out on R.E work.	
"	"	5pm	"C" Coy relieved "D" Coy in Reserve trenches, & "D" returned & occupied "C" Coy billets & placed 1 officer & 50 men in LANDSDOWNE and 1 officer and 30 men in S. VAAST POSTS.	

WAR DIARY 8th Gloucester Regt

INTELLIGENCE SUMMARY

Army Form C. 2118.

Place	Date	Hour	Summary of Events and Information	Remarks and references to Appendices
CROIX-BARBEE BILLETS	January 11th		80 men of D Coy batted at CROIX-BARBEE. A Coy found 60 men for R.E. work in the morning and 50 men in the evening. B Coy were employed in repairing and draining reserve line of defense trenches, morning and afternoon.	
"	12th		The Battalion relieved 8th North Staffords in trenches from COPSE STREET to OXFORD STREET. Relief commenced 6.30 p.m. from billets, and was completed by 10.15 p.m. "C" Coy which was in Reserve line moved up into front line trenches during the day & relieved a Company of North Staffs. "B" Coy took up the line COPSE STREET to LA BASSEE ROAD. "D" Coy from LA BASSEE ROAD to OXFORD STREET. "A" Coy in Reserve in GUARDS TRENCH and one company 8th North Staffords in Local Reserve along RUE DU BOIS. Very pretty quiet during the night except for occasional rifle & machine gun fire.	
		11.30 p.m.	Machine gun & rifle fire was directed on enemy found working opposite MOLE STREET.	

Army Form C. 2118.

WAR DIARY
INTELLIGENCE SUMMARY. 8th Gloucester Regt

(Erase heading not required.)

Place	Date	Hour	Summary of Events and Information	Remarks and references to Appendices
TRENCHES from COPSE STREET to OXFORD STREET just South of NEUVE CHAPPELLE	January 13th		Enemy quiet today except for sniping. PORT ARTHUR Redoubt was shelled as also fire trench in advance between 12 & 1.15 p.m. Machine guns traversed our parapet from 6.30pm to 8.30pm. Patrols sent out during the night. One patrol found enemy working on wire of S.10.d.7.9. with two evening parties out 70 yards on either flank. A volley of & rifle grenades followed by rifle & machine gun fire was directed onto the party & was repeated after a minute. The enemy are apparently doing a lot of work on their parapet all along the line. A lot of work is necessary & being done gradually on our trenches.	
"	14th		Snipers active on both sides all day, otherwise enemy very quiet. Patrols went out during the night and near PLUM STREET reported enemy very cheerful and all along the line a lot of work was going on, and the enemy very alert.	
"	15th		Our field guns bombarded the enemy's wire near pt. S.10.d.7.9. during the morning and the enemy retaliated on our trenches and Bn H.Q. with	

WAR DIARY

INTELLIGENCE SUMMARY

8th Gloucester Regt. Army Form C. 2118.

Place	Date	Hour	Summary of Events and Information	Remarks and references to Appendices
TRENCHES from COPSE STREET to OXFORD STREET			H.E. Shrapnel. A heavy 8" howitzer fired 20 shells during the afternoon of which 8 were duds and most fell short of their mark which was the enemy's parapet at S.10.d.7.9 & enemy's Pope's Nose. During this it cannot be ascertained what damage was done. During this shelling, the enemy retaliated on our trenches just South of LA BASSEE ROAD, and made three breaches in the parapet. Our machine guns and rifles were directed on the enemy's parapet on which our heavy gun had fired, and kept up a constant fire all night. Patrol went out but had nothing much to report.	
"	16th	12.30pm	"A" Coy on right near COPSE STREET fired 12 rifle grenades on parts of enemy parapet where smoke was seen. Our field guns fired in direction of S.11.a.4.9, just in front of our left Coy at 2.30 pm on some German works being erected. The shooting was very good, and one machine gun emplacement was demolished. At 3.p.m. our heavy 8" Howitzers fired 20 shells on pt S.10 d.7.9. Five shells fell	

Army Form C. 2118.

WAR DIARY
or
INTELLIGENCE SUMMARY.
(Erase heading not required.)

Place	Date	Hour	Summary of Events and Information	Remarks and references to Appendices
TRENCHES from COPSE STREET to OXFORD STREET		11.30 a.m.	blind and several fell in "no mans land" short of the mark, and as far as we can see, no breach in the parapet has been made. Enemy shelled GUARDS TRENCH with a few shrapnel shells, and again at 4 p.m. Shells were also distributed along PORT ARTHUR - RUE DUBOIS and OXFORD STREET. No damage was done however. Rifle and machine gun fire was directed on pt 7.9 during the night to prevent the enemy repairing any damage that may have been done by our heavies. Early in the night an officers patrol made its way towards German Parapet at 7.9. They got within 30 yards of the parapet at their point and then went 20 yds Northwards, being fired on. No breaches could be seen in the enemys parapet. Another patrol went out the reported gap in enemys trenches 30 yds South of LA BASSÉE Rd. They could see no gap there but found a large party working on their parapet & wire. The patrol reported this whereupon we "strafed" them with artillery, rifle & m.g. fire. The usual work of improving parapet, making dugouts & improving trenches generally was carried out	

WAR DIARY of 8th Gloucester Regt

INTELLIGENCE SUMMARY

Army Form C. 2118.

Place	Date	Hour	Summary of Events and Information	Remarks and references to Appendices
TRENCHES between COPSE STREET and OXFORD ROAD Just South of NEUVE CHAPELLE	January 17th	11 a.m. to 2 p.m. 12 p.m. to 2 p.m.	Our field guns shelled the enemy's wire with a view to cutting lanes through it. During the bombardment our Trench mortars, from direction of PLUM STREET fired several shots apparently with good effect, as the germans were heard shouting after some of the shots had fallen in their trenches. One shell appears destroyed, as a piece of corrugated iron was seen sticking up over the parapet. While the Trench mortars were firing our right (A) + our centre (C) Companies fired several rifle grenades into the german trenches apparently with good effect. The enemy retaliated with H.E./Shrapnel on our front trenches without doing much damage. They also fired several H.E. shells about Battalion H.Q on the RUE DU BOIS at 1 p.m. and one shell burst direct on a dug out, in the Orchard by H.Q, killing three men + wounding two others who were in the dugout at the time. They were 5 of the 8 Worcestershire Reserve Company. The bodies of the dead were terribly mutilated. The Battalion was relieved by 8th North Staffs. Relief commenced 5 p.m. + was completed by 7.30 p.m. "B" Coy were left in Reserve Trenches	

WAR DIARY or INTELLIGENCE SUMMARY

Army Form C. 2118.

Place	Date	Hour	Summary of Events and Information	Remarks and references to Appendices
Billets near CROIX BARBEE.	18th		with Works Staffs and remaining Companies went into Brigade Reserve billets at CROIX BARBEE. "A" Coy furnishing 1 officer and 30 men for ST VAAST POST and one officer and 50 men for LANDSDOWNE POST. "C" Coy & 50 men of D. Coy had baths at No 40 Rest House CROIX BARBEE Fday. One officer + 25 men of A. Coy + 1 officer and 25 men of D. Coy were working under R.E. at redoubts near hutches during the evening.	
-do-	19th		"D" Coy + H.Q. had baths at No 40 Rest House. "C" Coy relieved "A" Coy in LANDSDOWNE and ST VAAST POSTS during the afternoon. "D" Coy + "A" Coy found one officer + 25 men each for R.E. work.	
-do-	20th	8.45 a.m.	60 men from "D" Coy under an officer started working under R.E. in LORETTO Rd.	
		10 a.m.	A. Coy had baths at No 40 Rest House.	
		3 p.m.	A. Coy commenced relieving "B" Coy in Reserve trenches. Relief completed by 5 p.m. "B" Coy occupy billets vacated by A. Coy.	
		6 p.m.	One officer and 25 men from C & D. Coys each, went for R.E. work.	

WAR DIARY
INTELLIGENCE SUMMARY

Army Form C. 2118.

Place	Date	Hour	Summary of Events and Information	Remarks and references to Appendices
	January 1916			
CROIX BARBEE	21st	10 a.m.	Battalion less A Coy in Trenches and men of C. Coy in LANSDOWNE and ST VAAST POSTS, marched by platoons & collected at VIELLE CHAPPELLE and marched from there at 12.20 p.m. and via LE CORNET MALO to the Canal, & along canal bank to HAMET BILLET which was reached at 4.15 p.m. Companies went into billets in barns, and the pl.ts of C. Coy marched in about 10. P.M.	
BILLET	22nd		The Battalion is now with the 19th Division in Corps Reserve.	
HAMET			Cleaning up.	
BILLET	23rd	5 p.m.	A Coy arrive from trenches and went into billets.	
"	24th	2.30 p.m.	Inspection of billets & men in fatigue dress by G.O.C. 57th Brigade.	
"	25th			
"	26th		Cleaning & smartening up.	
"	27th		57th Brigade training programme commenced. Platoon marches, drill smartening up, lectures to young officers and	
"	28th		N.C.O.'S.	
"	29th			
"	30th	11 a.m.	Church Parade	
"	31st		As on 27th 6 29th inst	

M Lawson Lt Col.
Comdg 8th Gloucester Regt.

SECRET.

8th Gloucestershire Regt Order No 1   Copy No 1.

Reference BETHUNE   20th January 1915
Combined Sheet.

INTENTION. 1. The 57th Bde will be relieved in the present left Sector of the 19th Division front by the 114th Brigade. The Battalion less (A Coy) will march to HAMET. BILLET. to-morrow, and be relieved in its present billets by the 10th Welch Regt.

ORDER of MARCH. Companies will march off from billets by platoons at
A. Q. Coy   400 yds distance commencing at 10 am in order of march
D   "   and take the route, via, LACOUTURE and along the
B   "   road North of LOISNE River to Pt LEVIS in R.34.a.7.9.
C   where the Battalion will close up, and packs will be
Transport   taken off. The Battalion will move off from this point at 11.52 am. via VIELLE. CHAPELLE. LES. LOBES. LE CORNER MALO to HAMET BILLET.

A rear party of 1.NCO and 6 men from C. Coy will march in rear of the transport. Starting point Road Junction in M.31.b.3.1.

Dress. Marching order with fur coat and waterproof cape wrapped up in waterproof sheet and worn in place of the pack.

BAGGAGE Blankets and packs to be stacked ready by 10-15 am at the Store House in M.31.b.3.1. A loading party from D Coy will then load them as follows:-

   Blankets on 4 G.S. Wagons.
   Packs   on 3 G.S. Wagons.

All officers mess and officers kits to be ready stacked on the road by their billets at 9.15 am, with loading parties ready.

2.

(Continued) The 100 rounds in bandoliers to be collected and loaded on ammunition limbers at 9.45 am as follows:—
  One limber for HQ Coy & D Coy
  One limber for B Coy & C Coy

4 BILLETING PARTY

A billeting party of 1 billeting N.C.O. per Company and the Interpreter under 2/Lieut Poole will leave HQ on bicycles at 8 am. to take over new billets from 10th Welch Regt.

5 GARRISONS of POSTS

The garrisons of LANDSDOWNE and St VAAST POSTS. will march to HAMET. BILLET. independently as soon as relieved

6 REPORTS Up to 11 am. at HQ billet. After that to head of Battalion.

Issued 2.pm.
Copies No 1 and 2 War Diary.
  3 D Coy
  4 C "
  5 HQ "
  6 Transport Officer
  7 Quarter Master
  8 H.Q. Mess.

H C Greenstock. Capt.
Adjutant 8th Bn Gloucestershire Regt.

SECRET.

8th Gloucestershire Regt Order No 1   Copy No 2.
Reference BETHUNE   20th January 1915
Combined Sheet.

INTENTION. 1. The 57th Bde will be relieved in the present left Sector of the 19th Division front by the 114th Brigade. The Battalion less (A Coy) will march to HAMET. BILLET. to-morrow, and be relieved in its present billets by the 10th Welch Regt.

ORDER of MARCH.
H.Q Coy
D "
B "
C "
Transport

Companies will march off from billets by platoons at 400 yds distance commencing at 10-am in order of march and take the route, via, LACOUTURE and along the road North of LOISNE River to Pt LEVIS in R. 34. a. 7. 9. Where the Battalion will close up, and packs will be taken off. The Battalion will move off from this point at 11-52 am. via VIELLE. CHAPELLE. LES. LOBES. LE CORNER MALD to HAMET BILLET.

A rear party of 1. NCO and 6 men from C. Coy will march in rear of the transport. <u>Starting point</u> Road junction in M 31. b. 3. 1.

<u>Dress</u>. Marching order with fur Coat and waterproof caps wrapped up in waterproof Sheet and worn in place of the pack.

BAGGAGE Blankets and packs to be stacked ready by 10-15 am at the Store House in M. 31. b. 3. 1. A loading party from D Coy will then load them as follows:-
　　　Blankets on 4 G.S. Wagons.
　　　Packs on 3 G.S. Wagons.

All officers mess and officers kits to be ready stacked on the road by their billets at 9-45 am, with loading parties ready.

2.

(Continued) The 100 rounds in bandoliers to be collected and loaded on ammunition limbers at 9.45 am as follows:—

    One limber for HQ Coy & D Coy
    One limber for B Coy & C Coy

4 BILLETING PARTY

A billetting party of 1 billetting N.C.O. per company and the Interpreter under 2/Lieut Poole will leave HQ on bicycles at 8 am. to take over new billets from 10th Welch Regt.

5 GARRISONS of POSTS

The garrisons of LANDSDOWNE and St VAAST POSTS will march to HAMET BILLET independently as soon as relieved.

6 REPORTS Up to 11 am. at HQ billet. After that to head of Battalion.

Issued 2.pm.
Copies No 1 and 2 War Diary.
    3 D Coy
    4 C "
    5 HQ "
    6 Transport Officer
    7 Quarter Master
    8 H.Q. Mess.

H. Cheesewright Capt:
Adjutant 8th Bn Gloucestershire Regt.

3ᵈ Gloucester
Vol 8

S. M.
10 sheets

WAR DIARY

Army Form C. 2118.

8th Gloucester Regt

Place	Date 1916	Hour	Summary of Events and Information	Remarks and references to Appendices
Billets in	February 1st to		In corps Reserve, route-marching daily and cleaning up; weather fine. 1st week Company marches, Lectures, N.C.O.s. 2nd week Battalion marches, 3rd week Brigade marches.	
HAMET BILLET 19	18th		Battalion marched from billets at 8 a.m. via St VENANT – St FLORIS South Bank of LYS Canal, + Skirted MERVILLE, arriving at LA GORGUE at 12 P.M., + went into billets, being now in Divisional Reserve. Took over billets from 3rd Grenadier Guards. The Battalion is finding the Brigade Church Parade in theatre.	
LA GORGUE	20th		and Town Guard. Baths at LA GORGUE Baths. Route-marching + Physical training.	
"	21st 22nd 23rd		C.O. visited trenches which we are to take over, on 22nd inst. Snow fell yesterday + today, + is lying.	
"	24th		Company Commanders went to their sections of the trenches in the morning. Companies left billets commencing at 4 p.m. at intervals of 5 minutes, in order D. B. A. C. and took up one platoon per company, of 16th West Yorkshire Regt at RIEZ BAILLEUL, per	

WAR DIARY
or
INTELLIGENCE SUMMARY
(Erase heading not required.)

Army Form C. 2118

8th Gloucester Regt.

Place	Date	Hour	Summary of Events and Information	Remarks and references to Appendices
TRENCHES from SIGN POST LANE to MOATED GRANGE STREET	24		instruction in Trench Warfare. Found guides at ROUGE CROIX, & relieved the 9th B Cheshire Regiment in trenches just North of NEUVE CHAPELLE. Relief completed by 9.30 p.m. the Battalion held the right of the 59th Brigade Division line, being the trenches from 56th Brigade 38th Division SIGN POST LANE to MOATED GRANGE STEET, with the 10th Worcestr Regt on our right by NEUVE CHAPELLE & the 10th Worcestr Regt on our left. The Battalion also holds LAFONE, PUMP and SOUTH TILLELOY POSTS, all just behind the front line trenches, and Battalion H.Q. is at EBENEZER FARM.	ALP
"	25		The enemy were very quiet during the night, except for occasional bursts of machine gun fire along the front line parapet. Officers patrols went out during the night to examine the craters in front of our line and found them unoccupied by the enemy, & no enemy patrols were seen. This is probably due to the snow on the ground, which made patrolling very difficult. All companies worked at improving the wire along our front during the night. They were able to work without being seen owing to a thick mist which hung about all night. Enemy shelled support trenches, which are not occupied, in retaliation for our shell fire at 2.30 p.m. and a few shrapnel shells were sent on EBENEZER FARM at the same time, otherwise enemy very quiet.	

WAR DIARY
INTELLIGENCE SUMMARY

Army Form C. 2118
8th Gloucester Regt.

Place	Date	Hour	Summary of Events and Information	Remarks and references to Appendices
TRENCHES SIGN POST LANE to MOATED GRANGE STREET	January 26th	3 p.m.	Snipers on both sides active during the morning. Battalion H.Q. at EBENEZER FARM was shelled with about 30. 4.2. H.E shells till 4 p.m. Shells were very accurately placed but some damage was done to the building, and one shell demolished a corrugated iron structure holding 25 men, who were out of it by this time, and another shell wrecked the C.O.'s dugout. Considering the number of shells which fell in the farm, it was wonderful that there was only one slight casualty, that was a machine gunner of the 8th North Staffords, who was taking over.	
		6.30 pm	Companies of 8th North Staffordshire Regt commenced relieving the Battalion; Relief completed by 9.30 p.m. & the Battalion marched to billets in RIEZ BAILLEUL.	
RIEZ BAILLEUL Billets.	27th	10 a.m.	X. company 19th West Yorkshire Regt (Bantams) who arrived for instruction in trench warfare, marched off this morning to LE SART.	
	28th	4.15	Capt Greenhill, Adjutant, 19th West Yorkshire, 10th Durham L.I. 2nd Lt Poole and Attramed acting Adjutant, 19th West Yorkshire. The Battalion moved from billets at 4.45 p.m. to relieve the 8th North Staffordshire Regt in the trenches. The relief was completed by 9.40 p.m. The Battalion occupied the same line as before. 40 hours from 24th – 26th inst. The night very quiet. Officers L.Ts. W. Terrell was slightly wounded in side. W Coy of 19th Durham Light Infantry coming in as officers falser went out from DUCK'S BILL and reported enemy working; coming in as officers were attached to us	
TRENCHES SIGN POST LANE to MOATED GRANGE STREET				

Army Form C. 2118

WAR DIARY
or
INTELLIGENCE SUMMARY
(Erase heading not required.)

Instructions regarding War Diaries and Intelligence Summaries are contained in F.S. Regs., Part II. and the Staff Manual respectively. Title Pages will be prepared in manuscript.

Place	Date	Hour	Summary of Events and Information	Remarks and references to Appendices
TRENCHES SIGN POST LANE TO MOATED GRANGE STREET	Feb. 1916. 28th		for instruction. One platoon was attached to each of our Companies.	
	29th	6pm	Very quiet during the day. Between 6-7pm Rockets were sent up at Bray two minutes by Coys in front line in order to test efficacy of Rockets. The results were satisfactory. The Brigade on our right	
		8.40pm	made a demonstration with rifle & machine gun fire at about 8.40 pm & the enemy replied with heavy fire and rifle grenades. Patrols went out during the night. They reported the German lines strongly held, a good deal of work going on inside their Trenches, hammering sawing &c. No hostile patrols or listening posts were encountered. A new piece of work was observed during the day in the shape of a pile of new sandbags at M.36 a.1½.4½. The tarp seemed to be laid enclosing some sides of a square & might form as a listening post or an advanced post for the use of rifle grenades &c. Lewis gun opened fire upon it but in conjunction with Rifle grenades. Wiring, draining trenches, cleaning trench boards & building dugouts was continued.	

Concdg [signature] 8th Glouc. Regt.

SECRET. 1st Worcestershire Regt. Order No. 2.
Copy: 1st
Reference Map sheet 36a   25th February, 1916.
and combined sheet.

I. INTENTION.

The Battalion will relieve the 9th Cheshire Regt. in the trenches to-morrow night. Companies will hold the line in the following order from right to left: D. B. A. C. (less garrisons of posts).

II. ORDER OF MARCH.

D Coy Companies will move off at intervals
B " of 5 minutes, the leading Coy to move off
A " at 11 PM. After the first halt the march will
C " be by platoons at 3 minutes intervals.
HQ " After arrival at ROUGE CROIX the march
      will be by sections at 2 minutes intervals.
      Guides for each platoon, HQ & Coys will be
      at ROUGE CROIX at 6 PM.
      The garrisons of LAFONE — PUMP —
      STILLERY posts, Battn Bombers, and
      HQ will move off from billets in above
      order after C Coy.

III. LEWIS GUNS.

The L.G.O. will arrange to relieve the
L.G. detachments of 9th Cheshire Regt.
in the front line by 1 PM tomorrow.
He will send one Lewis Gun detachment
to report for orders to the officer of 10th Worcester
Regt.

2.

Capt. ___ who will be in command of DREADNOUGHT KEEP. The L.G. and detachments will march from billets with 13th Bn. as instructed by & under the orders of the above ___ officer.

IV. DRESS. Greatcoats, skin coats and waterproof capes will be taken into the trenches, also 5 sandbags per man.

V. BAGGAGE.
Packs, blankets and waterproof sheets will be stacked ready at 8 A.M. tomorrow and loaded on transport under arrangements by Company Commanders.

VI. BOMBERS.
The Battn. Bombing Officer will make all arrangements for the getting of the Battn. Bombers guns as to per establs to stores.

VII. MISCELLANEOUS
All men of the M.G. Platoon who are not doing duty in the front line will parade with the HQ detachment.
One Pioneer per Coy will be sent to his Coy for duty, the remainder with the Pioneer Sergt. will remain at HQ.
Regimental Scouts will do duty with their Companies.

VIII. BILLETS.
The Qr. Master will take over all Company billets clean by 1 P.M. tomorrow and hand

3.

them over with billet stores to the incoming Unit.

IX RATIONS.

Two days rations will be brought up to the trenches tomorrow night.

X ATTACHMENT.

A Platoon of "B" Coy W. York's Regt from 25th Div: will be attached for instructions to each Coy as under:-

    "D" Coy   No 5 Platoon.
    "B" Coy   No 6 Platoon.
    "A" Coy   No 7 Platoon.
    "C" Coy   No 8 Platoon.

These platoons will be met at RIEZ BAILLEUL and distributed amongst the Company and taken on into the trenches from there.

XI REPORTS.

Up to 7 pm to H.Q. after that hour to Battn H Quarters EBENEZER FARM.

Issued at 4.40 P.M.
No 1 Order Book
2 War Diary
3 "A" Coy
4 "B" "
5 "C" " & M Gun
6 Diary

F. C. Crewsturt
Capt.
Adjt. 8th Bn Gloucestershire Regt.

SECRET.   No 3

Operation Orders by Lieut Col G. D. M. Moore

I INTENTION

The Battalion will relieve the 8th North Staffords Regt in the trenches to night

II ORDER OF MARCH

1 D Coy   Coys will march in order as per margin
2 C "   from billets by Platoons at distance of
3 B "   200 yards the leading platoon to move at
4 A "
(less Keeps) 4-45 PM.

5 LAFONE KEEP
6 PUMP KEEP
7 SOUTH TILLELOY KEEP
8 H Quarters

III GUIDES

Guides for Keeps will be at ROUGE CROIX at 6 PM

IV POSITION

Companys will take up the same position in the trenches as vacated on the night of 25/26th. The Commanders of A & C Coys will proceed to trenches this afternoon and arrange their Division of the left portion of the line

V ATTACHMENT

"X" Coy of 19th Durham Light Infantry will join the Battalion at 1 PM 28th instant for instruction

V ATTACHMENT, Continued.
   Platoons will be attached to Coys as follows:—

   No 5 Platoon   To A Coy
   " 6   "   To B "
   " 7   "   To C "
   " 8   "   To D "

VI FATIGUE PARTY.
   A party from "A" Coy will load transport for the trenches

VII AMMUNITION.
   Coy. Commanders will complete from Regimental SAA reserve up to 100 rounds in pouches and 50 rounds in one bandolier

VIII BOMB STORES
   The bombing officer will arrange for the following Depôts in the trenches—
   A bombing party complete and a reserve store of bombs & rifle grenades to be at each Depôt
   (a) In PUMP KEEP (b) LAFONE KEEP
   (c) In DUCKS BILL

IX LEWIS GUN
   The L.G.O. will have the four Lewis Guns at his disposal

Issued at 19-20 28.2.16

A.L. Poole 2nd Lt
Adjutant. 8th Batt Gloucester Regt

No 1 Order Book
   2 War Diary
   3 A Coy
   4 B Coy
   5 Coy & M Gun
   6 D Coy

WAR DIARY or INTELLIGENCE SUMMARY

8th GLOUCESTER REGT — Army Form C. 2118

Place	Date March 1916	Hour	Summary of Events and Information	Remarks and references to Appendices
TRENCHES: SIGN POST LANE – MOATED GRANGE STREET	1st	7.30pm	The weather being much milder relief in present for another 48 hours. The day proved quietly. Enemy working parts was dispersed by our M.G. fire. Enemy fired some rifle grenades which fell short. Our snipers active to day. Several patrols went out. They report the German lines strongly held. There are a large number of dead bodies in "no mans land", both German & British. Enemy was continuous in front of our parapet, also much work done in the trenches, draining, laying & clearing trench boards, constructing fire-step.	
	2nd 3rd		German Snipers very active this morning. Two men being killed. The Divisional order of no firing between 7-10 pm was cancelled from today. Batt. exclusive [3rd March]. The Battalion was relieved in the trenches by the 8th NORTH STAFFORDSHIRE REGT. The relief was completed by 10.50 pm. The Battalion went into billets [Rietz] Brigade Reserve at Billets at Riez Bailleul. Two platoons of B. Coy went into Keeps ROUGE CROIX EAST & ROUGE CROIX WEST.	
BILLETS RIEZ BAILLEUL	4th 5th 6th 7th		Coys cleaning up & kit inspections.	
REGNIER LE CLERC	8th	8.30. 10.30.	Moved into Divisional Reserve at REGNIER LE CLERC nr MERVILLE. Battalion moved off at 8.30 am and was in the new billets by 10.30 am. The 18th (S) Battalion H.L.I., 106th Bde. took over the billets at [Rietz] RIEZ BAILLEUL.	
	9th	11am	The Brigadier visited the billets. 300 men per Battalion sent on working parties to L'EPINETTE FARM on 11.50 am & returned at 10.30 pm. 2nd Lt T.W. Aylife reported his arrival & was posted to "D" Coy.	
	12th 13th		2nd Lt Thomas & 2nd Lt Watson reported their arrival & were posted to "A" & "C" Coys respectively. Coys made a route march to the Assembly point in case of alarms from in the Divisional Defence scheme.	
RIEZ BAILLEUL	14th		The Battalion moved to billets at RIEZ BAILLEUL in relief of the 13th Battn. Royal Scots. The Battn. in took over the orders of the 106th Bde. The Ducks Bill was blown up by enemy mine at 6.15 am - 6 am Bomb. Bombers were called upon to man the trenches & hold the crater which is abt 100 ft in (orders for mine attached)	

WAR DIARY / INTELLIGENCE SUMMARY

Army Form C. 2118

Place	Date	Hour	Summary of Events and Information	Remarks and references to Appendices
RIEZ BAILLEUL	14th		Brewelti. Between also called upon to relieve LAFONE & PUMP HOUSE KEEPS. Our working parties were engaged all night in constructing a new trenchwork in DUCK'S BILL.	
TRENCHES 15th SIGN POST LANE to MOATED GRANGE STREET	15th		The Battn moved to Trenches in relief of 18th H.L.I. The Frontage is the same as before held and so out. The disposition is as follows:— D Coy on the right, A Coy in the centre, C Coy in the left. B Coy garrisons S TILLELOY, LAFONE & PUMP HOUSE KEEPS, the remainder of B Coy remains at H.Q. EBENEZER FARM to provide ration parties, fatigues &c. The 10th Worcestershire Regt is on our right & the 9th Royal Welsh Fusiliers on our left. The night was quite quiet.	(orders for wire attached)
	16th	7 am	At 7am we exploded a small mine under the Southern Crater about 150ft east of head of Colvin Street. Throughout the day the enemy was active with trench mortars & rifle grenades.	
	17th	5–7:30 am	The enemy bombarded the Crater with minenwerfer bombs. Between 30 and 40 were sent over, doing considerable damage to the work done since the explosion of the mine.	
	18	12 midnight	About midnight 17/18 the enemy made a small bombing raid on the DUCK'S BILL Crater which was easily repulsed. The enemy continued to be very active with minenwerfer bombs & rifle grenades.	
	19	5.45	A German of the 13th Bavarian Regiment came over to our lines & gave himself up. This is the third German prisoner captured by this Regiment.	
	20	5 pm 10 pm	A small mine was successfully exploded, a German mine getting time blown in. At 10 pm 3 mines were fired at M.30.a Central Rapid fire was kept up for 3 minutes & then at intervals of 3 minutes for the minute till 11 p.m. In the meanwhile a bombing raid was made by a Company of the 8th North Staffords. Their Regiment answered our fire. At 12.45 am the enemy retaliated	

WAR DIARY or INTELLIGENCE SUMMARY

Army Form C. 2118

Place	Date	Hour	Summary of Events and Information	Remarks and references to Appendices
TRENCHES SIGN POST LANE to MOATED GRANGE STREET	March 22	10.45 am -1.30 am	by firing a mine just outside our wire opposite COLVIN STREET & firing machine gun & rifle fire on our front line. At the same time the enemy shelled STILLE LOY C.T. & flooded it in 3 places. The bombardment did little damage & cost only had 5 casualties of which were slight. Capt CM Childe was killed by a bullet wound through the head. At 10.45 am enemy opened an intense bombardment of our front line with shrapnel & H.E. This shells appeared to come from the direction of the BOIS DE BIEZ, enfilading our line. MOATED GRANGE STREET considerable damage was done. The parapet was breached in several places & the supervision trench was in parts destroyed. Heavy rifle & machine gun fire was kept up. The retaliation bombardment lasted till noon. Re-lation was difficult to get & when obtained was weak & ineffective. At 12.15 NEUVE CHAPELLE was bombarded. many of the shells were lachrymatory & produced their effect.	
RIEZ BAILLEUL	23	5.30 pm	This battalion was relieved by the 8th North Staffordshire Regt, the relief being Completed by 9.30. The battalion marched back to billets at RIEZ BAILLEUL.	
	24		The C.O. went on leave to-day & Major Hudson assumed command of the Battalion in his absence. Drain was supplied in the evening & received in 2nd & 12 the Brain platoons.	
	26		Heavy rain fell in the night. 275 men of the Battn employed in working parties.	
TRENCHES SIGN POST LANE to MOATED GRANGE STREET	27 28		The Battalion moved to the Trenches in relief of the 8th North Staffordshire Regt. B Coy was posted from right to left 13 A&C. Day garrisoned the posts. At Weekly reported his arrival & were posted to billets C Coy. Very quiet night.	Operation orders attached.

WAR DIARY
or
INTELLIGENCE SUMMARY

Army Form C. 2118

Place	Date	Hour	Summary of Events and Information	Remarks and references to Appendices
RIEZ BAILLEUL	29		The Battalion was relieved in the trenches by the 8th North Staffordshire Regt. The relief was completed by 8.50 p.m. The Batt'n moved into its former billets at RIEZ BAILLEUL.	
	31		The Battalion moved into billets at REGNIER LE CLERC near MERVILLE starting at 11 a.m. his Battalion reached MERVILLE & was billeted by 12.45 p.m. Companies occupy the same billets as they occupied when in Divisional Reserve 7th-14th inst.	

31/3/16

C. H. Hardeng Major
Comdg 8th Gloucester Shire Regt

SECRET.   Operation Orders by Lieut Col: G.D.M. Moore.   Copy № 2
               Comdg: 8th Battn Gloucestershire Regt. 6/3/16
_____

I MOVE.   Battalion will move to billets at REGNIER LE CLERE tomorrow.

II ORDER OF MARCH.

Pioneers & Signallers
"A" Coy
        Mouth Organs
"B" Coy
"C" Coy
        Band
"D" Coy
        Mouth Organs
Lewis Gun Detn
Bombers
Transport.

The Battalion will fall in, "A" Coy facing South, remaining Companies facing North, closed up Pioneers head of "B" Coy on junction of roads near Depôt ready to march off at 8-30 AM, in order as per margin.

Companies will detail parties of 6 men under a N.C.O. to load their blankets Etc & to act as baggage guards. Bombers & Machine Gun in proportion.

III FATIGUE PARTY.

"C" Coy will find a party to load ammunition, tools Etc at Depôt

IV KIT.

The 2 blankets per man of "A" Coy, the H.Q Coy: & the Lewis Gun Detn will be loaded in a G.S. wagon under the orders of the Qr. Master, & will be taken to LA GORGUE to be washed. A party of 4 men from "A" Coy & 2 from the Lewis Gun Detn, & 2 from H.Q Coy: under an N.C.O. from "A" Coy will accompany this wagon. This party will take haversack rations

V POSTS.

The posts at ROUGE CROIX. E & W. will be relieved at 3-30 AM on the 6th & 7th 3/16 & will rejoin their Company

VI KITS FROM POSTS.

The O.C. "B" Coy will arrange for the conveyance of skin coats & waterproof sheets of above posts to the Depôt to enable them to be taken to REGNIER LE CLERE today.

Issued at 12-40 AM

№ 1. Office Copy
   2. War Diary
   3. A Coy
   4. B Coy
   5. C Coy
   6. D Coy
   7. Machine Gun
   8. Officers Mess
   9. Depôt Coy
  10. Sergt: Major:
  11. Bombers

                                                A.L. Poole 2nd Lieut
                                        Adjutant. 8th Bn Gloucestershire Regt:

SECRET.   Operation Orders by Batt. Cdr. T.D.H. Moore
          Comdg: 8th Bn. Gloucestershire Regt. 12/3/16.

1. INTENTION.

The Battalion will move to RIEZ BAILLEUL & relieve the 17th Royal Scots at that place tomorrow.

2. ORDER OF MARCH.

Pioneers
Signallers
"B" Company
"C" "
"D" "
Bombers
Lewis Gun Detl.
Transport.

The Battalion will be ready to move off in order as per margin at 9.30 A.M. The head of the regiment will be on the railway crossing on the BEAUPRÉ road about 600 yards East of railway station. DRESS.— Marching order. Shrapnel helmets to be worn by all ranks who are in possession of them. The Bugle Band will march in rear of "B" Company.

3. BILLET WARDENS.

One man from each Coy. & H. Quarters will be detailed as billet wardens to hand over billets to relieving troops. "D" Coy. will detail a L/Cpl to march these men to RIEZ BAILLEUL on morning of 13/3/16.

4. KITS.

Blankets, skin coats & officers kits to be ready for loading at 8.30 A.M. Each Coy. will detail a loading party of 1 N.C.O. & 5 men. These parties will form a baggage guard to the Transport on the march.

5. FATIGUE PARTY.

"D" Coy. will find a party to load ammunition, tools, etc. under arrangements to be made by the Regimental Transport Officer.

6. F.S. CAP

The field service cap of those who wear shrapnel helmets will be carried under the flap & on top of the pack.

7. BILLETING PARTY.

Companies will occupy the same billets at RIEZ BAILLEUL as before. Company Qr. Mr. Sergts & billetting parties of 3 men per Coy. will proceed to RIEZ BAILLEUL & take over billets in advance of the Battalion starting from their billets at 7 AM tomorrow.

8. BILLETS.

The Qr. Master will hand over these billets to the relieving unit. He will be responsible that all billets now occupied by Companies are clean before companies move off to the starting Point.

A L Poole 2nd Lt
Adjt 8th Bn Gloucestershire Regt

SECRET.   Operation Orders by Lieut Col: E.D.M. Moore
           Comdg: 8th Bn Gloucestershire Regt   14/3/16

1 INTENTION

The Battalion will move into the trenches tomorrow evening in relief of the 18th H.L.I.

2 ORDER OF MARCH

D Coy:
C "
B: Lin Keeps
H.Q. Party
LAFONE Keep
PUMP House Keep
S. TILLELOY Keep
H. Quarters
& ½ Platoon D Coy

In order as per margin Companies & Parties will move off from their billets so as to be clear of the point M.19.d.6.7., at intervals of 5 minutes, the leading Coy: to be clear at 5 PM.

3. INTERVAL

After pass ROUGE CROIX troops will move by sections in single file at distances of 200 yds

4 KEEPS

The O.C. "B" Coy will detail a ½ platoon to remain at H. Quarters. 1 officer and a platoon for PUMP KEEP. 1 officer & No 8 platoon for South TILLELOY KEEP, & 1 NCO & 20 men for LAFONE KEEP.

5 KITS.

Packs & blankets will be stored under Coys arrangements, 2 men per Coy being left in billets to guard them.

6 LEWIS GUN.

The Lewis Gun Detacht will march from billets at 2 PM. & take over the L. Gun emplacements in the trenches

7. OC COYS VISITING TRENCHES.

Company Commanders, the Signalling Officer & Sergt: Major will proceed to the trenches tomorrow afternoon to take over stores Etc

8 GUIDES

The OC "A" Coy: will detail guides for PUMP & SOUTH. TILLELOY KEEPS & the OC "D" Coy will detail a guide for LAFONE KEEP.

9 BOMBERS

The Bombing officer with 12 bombers will remain at H.Q.

10 LEWIS GUN.

The men of the L. Gun Det: not doing duty with the guns will rejoin their Companies for duty. They will be given stations on the parapet as near the L. Gun emplacements as possible

A.W. Toole 2nd Lieut
Adjutant 8th Bn Gloucestershire Regt

SECRET.

Operation Orders by Major C. H. Harding
Comdg. 8th Bn. Gloucestershire Regt. 26/3/16

1. INTENTION.

The Battalion will move into trenches this evening in relief of the 8th North Staffordshire Regt.

2. ORDER OF MARCH

LAFONE KEEP
B Company
C "
PUMP KEEP
TILLELOY KEEP
H. Quarters
Remainder of B Coy

Companies will move off in order as per margin at 5-minutes intervals leading Coy to be clear of Point M.19.d.6.7. by 5 P.M. After passing ROUGE CROIX troops will move by sections in single file at distance of 200 yards.

3. KEEPS

The O.C. "D" Company will detail 1 Officer & 30 men for PUMP KEEP. 1 Officer & 20 men for ST. TILLELOY KEEP. 1 Officer & 20 men for LAFONE KEEP. Remainder of the Coy will be attached to H. Quarters.

4. GUIDES

The party for LAFONE KEEP will guide "B Coy" via SIGN POST LANE into the right portion of the line. O.C. "B Coy" will detail guides for PUMP & S. TILLELOY KEEPS.

5. KIT.

Packs & Blankets will be stored under company arrangements. Two sick men per company being left in Billets to guard them.

6. LEWIS GUN.

The L.G.O. will arrange to relieve during the afternoon. The men of the L.G. detachment not doing duty with the guns will rejoin their companys for duty. They will be given stations on the parapet as near to the Lewis Gun emplacements as possible.

7. OC COYS: VISITING TRENCHES

Company Commanders. Signalling Officer and Sergt. Major will proceed to the trenches this afternoon to take over stores etc.

8. TRENCH KITS.

Officers kits for trenches & mess stores will be left outside billets under the charge of Officers servants to be loaded on ration limbers at 6-15 P.M.

A. Poole 2nd Lt.
Adj: 8th Gloucestershire Regt.

Lieut Priestley

Army Form C. 2118

8th GLOUCESTERSHIRE REGT
VOL 4

WAR DIARY
or
INTELLIGENCE SUMMARY
(Erase heading not required.)

Place	Date April 1916	Hour	Summary of Events and Information	Remarks and references to Appendices
REGNIER LE CLERC	1		Rest Billets. Division at Reserve. Kit inspections by Coys.	
	2		Batts at LA GORGUE allotted to the Battalion.	
	3-5		Training under Company arrangements.	
	6		Moved into Brigade Reserve at RIEZ BAILLEUL.	
RIEZ BAILLEUL	7		Moved into Right Sub-Section of MOATED GRANGE SECTION in relief of 4/5 BLACK WATCH. Relief was carried out by 8.50 A.M. Machine guns were active & there was a good deal of rifle fire.	
	8		Trenches which were wet & require a considerable amount of draining. During the day there was very little artillery activity. Work was done amplifying roofs of dug outs. Revetting & thickening parapets + building traverses. Dug out 37 was cleaned. Patrols were sent out at night & they report going good in "No Man's Land". Enemy wire appears to be quite strong. A special patrol was sent out to inspect the outer lip of the DUCKS BILL CRATER. They neither heard nor observed any work on the part of the enemy nor encountered any enemy patrols. Our snipers near C6, VIN ST claimed that they smashed 6 enemy periscopes. A machine gun emplacement was located and the Artillery blew it in. Enemy machine guns were on active up to midnight but were very quiet during the day. Work done on parapets.	
	9		Wiring & raising thinkbands, cleaning of trenches and making new Battalion HQ. Twice were taken head N of PUMP KEEP & thinned were successful in drawing enemy attention. They were shelled in the morning. On the whole the enemy were very quiet along the whole front. Our Trench Mortars fired on Machine Gun emplacement apparently with good effect. Listening Post along SIGN POST LANE reports enemy hard at work on his trenches at night. Work was done clearing up trenches & building T.M. & M.G. emplacements. Barbed wire put out between DUCKS BILL and SIGN POST LANE.	
	10			
	11		Our snipers claim to have hit a German Officer. Enemy very quiet all day. Work was done wiring trench front, building of knife-rest & parados. Relief was carried out by 10-0 P.M. when night outposts was taken over by 8th York Staffs. Battalion moved to billets in Brigade Reserve at RIEZ BAILLEUL	

G.M.

WAR DIARY or INTELLIGENCE SUMMARY

Army Form C. 2118

Place	Date	Hour	Summary of Events and Information	Remarks and references to Appendices
RIEZ BAILLEUL	11		One Officer and a platoon were furnished for garrison of ROUGE CROIX EAST and also same for ROUGE CROIX WEST. Relief was carried out without casualties.	
	12		Balks were allotted to Battalion at PONT DU HEM. Several working parties provided. Grenades Companies were at disposal of Company Commanders to battalion.	
	13.		Church parades and cleaning up generally. This unfortunate.	
	14.		Court of Enquiry re death of Pioneer William caused by rifle grenade which had failed to explode when fired by our Bombers when billeted at HAMET BILLET. Working parties provided at night.	
	15.		Relieved 8th NORTH STAFFS in right sub Section. Trenches carried out without casualties by 9 p.m. Our patrols report enemy very quiet and no encampment was encountered. Work was done on parapet & parados. Regular Rifle & M.G. fire on unparapeted part of our trenches.	
TRENCHES SIGN POST LANE to MOATED GRANGE STREET.	16		Our Snipers did very good work & they claim two enemies. A listening post was established & fire to arm all unmanned house S. of DUCK'S BILL which unsupported was listening post. The enemy were very quiet & suffered no casualties upon this M. Gun. Work was done wiring Traversing trench boards, repairing parapet, parados & traverses. Shelters made for bombs & Vermorel Sprayers.	
LA GORGUE	17		Relieved in trenches by the 17½ Welsh Regt 38th Division. The relief was completed by 10 p.m. The Battalion marched back to billets at LA GORGUE.	
HAMET BILLET	18		The Battalion moved to Billets at HAMET BILLET starting at 9 p.m. route via MERVILLE. CALONNE, & ROBECQ. Marching Billets at 1.15 p.m. owing to the Battalion moving light - a large amount of surplus kit & stores was dumped at Divisional Dump MERVILLE.	
	20		Battalion moved to 1st Army Training area & billeted at CRESQUES S.W. of AIRE. Starting at 10 a.m billets were reached at 4 p.m. Battalion marched as Brigade and lead, the 20 N. Staff Regt following.	

WAR DIARY or INTELLIGENCE SUMMARY

Army Form C. 2118

2nd Gloucestershire Regt

Place	Date	Hour	Summary of Events and Information	Remarks and references to Appendices
CRESQUES	21		Platoon Training Programme	
		8.30 am	Close Order drill to include:- inspection in marching order as proved by Coy; to training area, practice musketry discipline, marching at regulation pace of 3 miles an hour; extending from column of route	
		10/10 am	Physical training – running, jumping etc. 10.45 movement in extended order. 12.15 – 1 chinning.	
		10 am	Fire Discipline & rapid firing. 1.30 – 2.15 pm steady drill. 2.30 pm march to billets.	
	22	8.30 am	Platoon Training continued. Programme – 8.30 am – 10 am march to area. C Coy practices S.A.	
		10	Advanced guard. 10 – 11 am intercommunication during battle. 11am – 12 noon supply of S.A.A. in the field.	
		12 noon	Dinners 12.45 – 1.45 Steady drill. 1.45 – 2.30 pm Fire Discipline & rapid loading & firing	
	23		Easter day – Holiday.	
	24	8.30 am	Company training Programme 8.30 – 10 am	
		10.45 am	movements. 10.45 – 12 noon organization of Coy for outposts; placing & captured villages or localities in state of defence; Done practically as regards trench digging + by C.O. The in the ground as regards defence of same. 12 – 12.45 Dinners. 12.45 – 12.30 pm advancing over open country under shell fire. Rifle Range 8 Coy 12 noon – 2.15 pm C Coy 2.15 – 4 pm A Coy 4 – 7 pm Practice 5 rounds rapid at targets 1/8 figures 300 yds.	
		12 noon	lying Bombing Regimental Bombers 7am – 10 am. A Coy bombers 10am – 1 pm under Capt Bombing Officer. Signallers & Lewis gun section work under their respective commanders.	
			Capt H.P. LESCHALLAS reported his arrival 22nd with the 1st taken over command of B Coy from Mr F. He. Capt E.H. Crocke is transferred to A Coy as 2nd in command.	
	25	8.30 am	Company training continued. Programme 8.30 – 10 am march to area. 10 am – 12 noon	
		12 noon	Company in Attack – Supply of S.A.A. in the communication etc. 12 noon – 12.45 pm Dinners.	

WAR DIARY
INTELLIGENCE SUMMARY

1st Gloster Regt.

Army Form C. 2118

(Erase heading not required.)

Place	Date	Hour	Summary of Events and Information	Remarks and references to Appendices
CRESQUES	25	9 pm	Night march from billets along road leading through 1 of NIELLES. Men in 4 platoons of each Company with 50 paces at intervals & compass bearings from 16 pace platoon to a point of assembly on the NIELLES-DELETTE and Rifle range.	
		9.30 am		
		11.30 am	to B. Coy 11.30 - 1.30 pm: Bombing B Coy & C Coy bombers under Batt. Bombing officer. Lecture by Major of B² + H/s Coy R.E. on Defence of village at 5.20 at School House BLESSY.	
	26	8.30 am	Battalion training begins. Parade at 8.30 to Scheme of Battalion in the attack. In evening	
		9 pm	night marching on a compass bearing.	
	27	9 am	Battalion parades for practice in outposts. Listening party of 1 officer & 40 men sent to MRE for intending coal. This Listening continues for 3 days & each day there shifts.	
		11.45 pm		
	28	8.30?	Battalion in attack & retirement. Bombing parade A Coy 8 - 9.30 am B.Coy 9.30 - 11 am	
		till 2 pm	C Coy 11 am to 12.30 pm " Sey 1.30 - 3 pm. S Coy on the Rifle range in afternoon.	
	29	9-10 am	Musketry. 12 noon kits inspection by Coy Commanders. Bombing A Coy 1-4pm B Coy 4-7pm	
		10 pm	Brigade Training. Night operations moved off at 10 p.m. 1st LINC. R.Lp. 8th N. Staff Regt. 8th Gloc. Regt. 1st Royal Warwickshire Regt. advance across country in Column of platoons and attack at Dawn. Return to billets at 6 am.	
	30			

J.B.Hooll, Lt Col
Comg 8th Gloc Regt.

8th Gloucestershire
XIX 8th Glos Regt Vol. 9

WAR DIARY
INTELLIGENCE SUMMARY 8th Glos Regt

Army Form C. 2118

(Erase heading not required.)

Instructions regarding War Diaries and Intelligence Summaries are contained in F.S. Regs., Part II. and the Staff Manual respectively. Title Pages will be prepared in manuscript.

Place	Date MAY	Hour 1916	Summary of Events and Information	Remarks and references to Appendices
CRESQUES 1ST ARMY TRAINING AREA	1	5.30 am	Brigade Training left billets at 7.30 am. to point of assembly at PONCHE - ERNY ST JULIEN road where Regt formed up in masse. Practice. Advance Guards.	
	2	10.30 am	Brigade and Cap hostility. Bayonet fighting. Brigade training moved from billets 10.30 am to point of assembly on road ENGUIN LES MINES - ERNY ST JULIEN. Practice Brigade in attack. Heavy Thunder storm	
	3		Companies paraded for musketry, bayonet fighting, bombing etc.	
	4	7.15 am	Divisional training. moved from billets at 7.15 am to Divisional point of assembly. Practice Division in attack. Supper in reserve.	
	5		Parades under Coy arrangements - Musketry, Bayonet fighting, Bombing + Billeting party sent forward to new area.	
	7	4.37 am	Left billets at 1.50 am & detrained at AIRE at 4.37 am. Reached LONGEAU SE of AMIENS which was reached 8.20 pm	
	8	12.30 pm	12.30 pm on 8th where Batt detrained. marched to billets at VIGNACOURT. From there July 1st 19th	
VIGNACOURT			Division is attached to IIIrd Corps 4th Army.	
	9	11.30 am	Parades for musketry under Company arrangement	
	10		Coy musketry, physical drill, rapid marching &c.	
	11	8.30 am	Batt Route march	
	12	7.30 am	Battalion paraded for musketry on range at DOMART	
	13		Coy parades for musketry, drill &c.	
	14	11 am	Battalion Church parade	
	15		Very wet and Battalion parade cancelled. work carried out by Companies - musketry, drill &c	
	16	8 am	Batt paraded for practice in the attack west of the FORET DE VIGNECOURT. Form mass devro	

WAR DIARY

INTELLIGENCE SUMMARY

8th Glouc. Regt.

Army Form C. 2118

(Erase heading not required.)

Instructions regarding War Diaries and Intelligence Summaries are contained in F.S. Regs., Part II. and the Staff Manual respectively. Title Pages will be prepared in manuscript.

Place	Date	Hour	Summary of Events and Information	Remarks and references to Appendices
VIGNACOURT	16		Return as Regimental Chaplain to-day. The Regimental Scout's from Stockmust is thereupon broken up from his Batt and 2 guns with a team of 12 men are attached to each Coy. Capt R.K. Byam of his regiment is appointed Brigade Scout Officer.	
	17		Musketry parades by Coys. afternoon practice on range near BOIS DUCROQUET.	
	18	3.30	In morning Bombing and musketry. At 3.30 pm Batt'n parade for Outpost scheme on line ½ mile N.W. of FREMONT to a point 1 mile N.E. of ST VAAST.	
	20	8.55 am	Brigade Training in the attack: parade at 8.55 am training ground VIGNACOURT WOOD. Brigadier spoke. Batt'n team successful	
	21	10 am	Church Parade. Blankets withdrawn from men & returned to midhead. In Assaulting Competition	
	22		C.O., 2nd in Command & 6 other officers attend a Divisional scheme for testing signalling with Aeroplanes by mirrors. Hostile and general signal.	
	23		C.O. & 2nd in Command attend a staffride under G.O.C. Division. Battalion had talks on HAVERNAS	
	24	7.30 am	Parade for musketry at DOMART Rifle range. Firing stopped by heavy rain at midday	
	25		Parade under 2nd in Company arrangements. C.O. Major Thomas & Capt Loveridge attend Bombs talks at STOKES MORTARS at VALEUREUX. Owing to an accident the ammunition was cancelled.	
	26		Coy parade for musketry on range at DUCROQUET WOOD	
	27	9.30 am	Batt'n paraded at 9.30 am & marched to FLESSELLES to attend Divl Sports.	
	28	10.15 am	Church Parade.	
	30	8 am	Battalion entrained at Vignacourt 575 Brigade marched to Training Area at ST RIQUIER. 8th Gloucs.	
ST RIQUIER	31		First marching 30 to min. Operation orders attached. Musketry & Physical training under Coy Company Commanders.	

J.H.M. Cooke Lt.Col.
Comdg 8th Gloucestershire Regt.

Operation Orders by Lieut Col G.D.H. Moore.   Copy No. 1.
Comdg. 8th Bn Gloucestershire Regt. 7-5-16

1. The Battalion will march to AIRE and entrain there tonight.

2. The Battalion will form up in column of route in order as per margin,
D Coy   the rear of leading company on road junction E of village,
A "   head of column on AIRE-road, ready to move off at 1-50 A.M.
B Coy   Dress - steel helmets to be carried, length ways over pack with rims under
Hd Qrs   cross straps.
C Coy:

3. Signallers, Bombers, Pioneers &c will march with their companies.

4. Blankets rolled in bundles of 10 will be stored under company arrangements
at the Ord. Mr. Stores ready to be loaded in a motor lorry at 6 P.M. this evening.
1 NCO & 3 men will be detailed to load these blankets, accompany them to
AIRE station, unload them there and guard them pending the arrival of the
Battalion. On arrival of the Battalion at AIRE station blankets will be
re-issued to the men. When the Battalion reaches its destination tomorrow,
all blankets will again be rolled and stored at an appointed place
for conveyance to the new billets, the same men accompanying them.

5. The 1st line transport, all officers' horses, pack animals & G.S. wagons will
march to AIRE station at 12 mid-night under the Battn Transport Officer
The S.A.A. will be withdrawn from the pack animals and loaded in S.A.A. limbers.
2 Platoons from "B" Coy, the L.G. Detn & "B" Coy stretcher bearers will march
with the transport and load the wagons on the train.

6. Baggage wagons to be loaded by 11-30 P.M. tonight. "B" Coy. will furnish a loading
party of 1 NCO & 6 men to be at Ord. Mr. Stores at 11-15 P.M.
Officers' kits & messes will be loaded by officers' servants.

7. When orders are received to entrain Companies will march without noise
to the platform or sidings, parties of 40 men opposite each truck counting from
the front of the troop train. No man will get into a truck until 1 G. has
been sounded; 5 minutes before the time of departure of train the
"Advance" bugle will be sounded and all doors must be closed.

8. At all halts, the Orderly Officer, Regimental Orderly Sergt. & Corporal will alight, see that all is correct and keep men from leaving the trucks.

9. No lights of any description will be allowed during the rail journey.

10. Water will not be obtainable until arrival at destination. Cookers & water carts will be loaded full of water.
2 cooks will be allowed on the trucks with the cookers in the morning to light fires and make tea ready by 12 noon tomorrow.

11. Tomorrow's rations will be carried on the mess.

12. The Quarter Master & one man per Company, H. Quarters, L.G. Detn, Signallers & transport will remain behind for 3 hours in these billets to see that they are left scrupulously clean. They will then proceed to AIRE station & report to the R.T.O. there.

13. Steel helmets will be worn after arrival at the destination tomorrow.

14. From this date all ranks will wear the "Back Badge" on the bunch of the field service cap.

Issued at 1.15 PM.

No. 1 War Diary   No. 7 D Company
. 2. Office Copy   . 8. Lewis Guns
. 3. Second-in-Command .9. Transport
. 4. A Company   . 10. Signallers
. 5 B   . 11. M.O.
. 6. C   . 12 Sergt. Major.

A.L. Poole
2nd Lieut
A/Adjutant 8th Bn Gloucestershire Regt.

8th Gloucestershire Regt: Copy No. I
    Order No. I   29/5/16.

1. The Battalion will move to ST RIQUIER training area tomorrow.

2. The Battalion will be ready to march off at 7-55 AM. in order as per margin. Head of column at junction of main road & POTTEY LANE facing North.

    margin:
    "B" Company
    "C" "
    "D" "
    "A" "
    Bombers
    Lewis Gun Dett.
    1st Line Transport.

3. The O.C. "B" Company will detail a party of 1 NCO & 8 men to load SAA and tools at the Qr Guard & Qr Masters Stores respectively and to form rearguard to 1st Line Transport.

4. Dinners will be cooked on the march & a halt of 1 hour will be made at midday for dinner.

5. Breakfasts tomorrow at 6-30. AM.

6. All stores including tents which are not authorised to be carried on 1st Line Transport will be dumped (at house next door to Qr Ms Stores) by 6-30 PM this evening 29/5/16. One man will be detailed from "B" & "C" Companies respectively to look after the dump, clean up & repair billets. These men will draw their rations daily from 58th Brigade Refilling Point on the VIGNACOURT — FLESSELLES road at 5 PM. daily.

7. The O.C. "A" Company will send two tents to Brigade H. Quarters by 5-45 PM. today to be loaded on a lorry at that place.

Issued at 11-30 AM.

No 1 Copy War Diary
" 2 " 2nd in Command
" 3 " "A" Company
" 4 " "B" "
" 5 " "C" "
" 6 " "D" "
" 7 " Bombers
" 8 " Signallers
" 9 " Transport
" 10 " Office Copy
" 11 " Officers Mess
" 12 " Lewis Gun
" 13 " Sergt Major.

A.J. Poole Lieut
A/Adjt 8th Bn Gloucestershire Regt

Army Form C. 2118

WAR DIARY
or
INTELLIGENCE SUMMARY
(Erase heading not required.)

Instructions regarding War Diaries and Intelligence
Summaries are contained in F. S. Regs., Part II.
and the Staff Manual respectively. Title Pages
will be prepared in manuscript.

Place	Date	Hour	Summary of Events and Information	Remarks and references to Appendices
St RIQUIER	June 1st		Brigade Training. Exercise - the attack	
	2nd		The Spray baths at CAOURS are allotted to the battalion	
	3rd		Brigade Training. Exercise - the attack	
	4th		Church parade.	
	5th		Battn acted as skeleton enemy to the 58th Bde manoeuvres	
	6th		Brigade Training Exercise - the attack.	
	7th		Battn parade for practice in keeping intervals, distances & mks. communication in artillery formation	
	8th		Brigade Training. Exercise - the attack	
	9th		Divisional Training. Exercise - the attack.	
VIGNACOURT.	10th		Battn moved to billets at VIGNACOURT.	
	11th		Battn paraded for Church parade at 10.30 am.	
	12th		Battn paraded for Baths at OLINCOURT.	
	13th		Battn attended memorial service at Bde Hd Q to Lord Kitchener. Lecture at 2.30 pm. by Chemical Adviser 4th Army	
	14th		Battn Training - practice in deploying in lines of platoons in 4's & then extending to 3 paces. "A" Coy practice in using Coys used range at BOIS-DU-CROQUET in afternoon. Programme of Work Major Carton de WIART [Capt L.N. Lunny] acts as Commanding Officer. at 6 & 14	
	15th			
RAINNE-VILLE.	16		Battn moved from VIGNACOURT to RAINNEVILLE.	
	17th		Battn inspected by acting Commanding Officer.	
	18th		Battn paraded for Divine Service at 10 am.	

WAR DIARY or INTELLIGENCE SUMMARY

Army Form C. 2118

Vol 10
8 Gloucesters
June

XIX

Place	Date	Hour	Summary of Events and Information	Remarks and references to Appendices
RAINNEVILLE	June 19th	6.30am - 7am	Physical Drill. 9am Route march. Afternoon Notice in Bayonet fighting.	
"	20	6.30am - 9am	Running Exercise. 9am Bayonet-fighting. Notice under Coy arrangements.	
"	21	6.30am - 7am	Physical Drill. 9am Route march.	
"	22		Battn paraded by Coys for Lt Col Carton de Wiart D.S.O. 7th L North Lancs assumes command of Battn.	
"	23	6.30 - 7am	Physical Drill. 9am "A" Coy Signallers Lewis Gunners & Bombers - tactical exercise "C" & "D" Coys Battn. presentation by Army Commander.	
"	24	6.30 - 7am	Physical Drill. 9am Battn paraded for tactical exercise.	
"	25	10.15am	Battn paraded for Divine Service	
"	26	6.30 - 7am	Physical Drill. 9am Battn paraded for tactical exercise.	
"	27	6.30 - 7am	Physical Drill. 9am Commanding Officer inspected Battalion.	
FRANVILLERS WOOD	27	4pm	Battn moved to FRANVILLERS WOOD & Bivouaced.	
"	28	6.30am	Physical Drill. Rained heavily.	
"	29	6.30am	Physical Drill. 9am Route march under Coy arrangements.	
"	30	6.30am	Physical Drill. 9am Parades under Coy arrangements.	
		8.25pm	Battn moved to Corps Reserve Line E.1.a 2.6 & V.30 d 4.8 [Ref. 57 D S.E.]	

8th Bn Gloucestershire Regt.   Copy No 1
Order No 3.   3/6/16.

Reference Training Area Map.
1. General & Special Ideas Circulated

2. The Battn will parade for practice with the Brigade in the
D Coy   attack today, and will be ready to move off at 12 noon.
A "
B "   Order of march as per margin.   Head of Column at
C "
Bombers
L. Gun Sect Qr: Guards facing West.   Dress: Marching Orders without
1st Line
Transport. packs: pouch ammunition will not be taken

3. The O.C. "B" Company will detail a party of 1 NCO & 7 men to
load S.A.A. Bombs & Tools at the Qr Mrs. Stores at 11-30 a.m.
and to form rear guard to 1st Line Transport

4. NCO's commanding platoons will attend the conference
after the exercise.

5. The position of the front line held by our troops will be held
by 2 Companies of a Battalion from 58th Brigade.
The remainder of that Battalion will represent the enemy,
and barrages.   Before the Assault the enemy
will stand with arms at the slope.
Bayonets will not be fixed for the Assault, as a
safety precaution only.

6 D.P. Smoke Helmets will be taken & will be worn from the
arrival at our own trenches till we rush the enemy
trenches.

2.

7. The lines of trenches will be marked as follows:—
   Assembly trenches & line held by our own troops — White flags.
   Enemy trenches — Red flags.
   Our Artillery barrage — By men waving signalling flags.

8. On arrival at Assembly trenches 1st Line Transport will be Brigaded at A.19.b.9.1. under Brigade Transport Officer. It will be in this position at 1-15 PM.

9. Battalion report centre (a) in Assembly trenches in centre of Battalion (b) in Attack behind centre Battalion.

10. Dinners at 11. PM.   Teas will be cooked ready for arriving on the ground after the exercise.

A L Poole Lieut:
A/Adjt 8: B: Gloucestershire Regt:

Issued at 8-30 AM.

No 1. War Diary
" 2. Office Copy
" 3. H.Q. Mess
4. "A" Company
5. "B" "
6. "C" "
7. "D" "

No 8. Bombing Officer
" 9. L. Gun Officer
" 10. Transport Officer
" 11. Signalling Officer
" 12. Sergt/Major.

Reference Training Area Map 1/20,000

General Idea

The enemy's first line of entrenchments running roughly through the centre of Squares A.2, B and A.4 have been taken by our troops who are at present in occupation of them. The enemy have retired to their second line.

Special Idea

The 19th Division now in Assembly trenches N.E. of MILLENCOURT has been ordered to attack the enemy's 2nd line, lying between A.6.6.6.0. and B.20.a.9.4. close to the B of B. TILLENCOURT. Each Brigade has a frontage of 1,000 yards allotted to it. The 57th Brigade is in the centre and is responsible for taking that part of the line lying between B.7.c.8.9. and B.13.6.8½.1. This Brigade is also responsible for consolidating a position to the N and E of B. GRANDUS on a front of 1,000 yards lying between B.7.b.4.5 and B.14.a.8.6. The troops occupying the enemy's first line have suffered heavy casualties and will therefore be unable to take part in the capture of the 2nd line.

8th Gloucestershire Regt: Copy No 1
Order No 8. 15/6/16.

1. The Battalion will march with the remainder of the Brigade to RAINNEVILLE tomorrow.

2. The Battalion will be ready to march at 7-50 AM.
   D Coy
   A "
   B "
   C "
   L.G. Section
   1st Line Transport.
   in order as per margin. Head of column in line with present Orderly Room facing North.

3. O/C "C" Company will detail a party of 1 NCO & 8 men to load S.A.A., Bombs & Tools at Qr Guard by 7-30 AM.

4. All baggage will be ready loaded by 7-30 am. Officers Mess Stores & Kit to be at Qr: Mr: Stores by that time.

5. The billeting party will proceed as detailed to-day.

6. Capt: Leschallas & 1 man per billet under a NCO detailed by "C" Coy: will remain behind to clear up and burn all refuse.
   The 2nd in Command will report to Brigade Headquarters that billets have been left clean.

7. Breakfast at 6-30 A.M.
   Dinners will be cooked on the road.

8. Sick parade at 5-30 am tomorrow

                W Parkes.
                        Lieut:
        A/Adjutant 8th Bn Gloucestershire Regt:

            Issued at 4 P.M.

Copy No 1 War Diary.   Copy No 8. H.Q. Mess
   "   2 Office Copy.   "   9. L.G. Officer.
   "   3 2nd in Command.   "   10. Signalling Officer.
   "   4 "A" Coy   "   11. Scout Officer.
   "   5 "B" "   "   12. Qr. Master.
   "   6 "C" "   "   13. Sergt. Major.
   "   7 "D" "

SECRET.   8th Bn Gloucestershire Regt   Copy No 1
                   Order No 9.   26/6/16.
               ─────────────

1. The Battalion will march tomorrow with the remainder of the Brigade to
   FRANVILLERS Wood where it will bivouac for the night.

2. The Battalion will march in order as per margin.   Head of column facing
   NE. at the cross roads at the Church ready to move off at 7-15 P.M.
   Dress. Full Marching Order with steel Helmets.
   The Transport Officer will make arrangements for the packs of the band
   to be carried on the transport.

   [margin: Coys / Band / 9 Coy / Bombers / Lewis Gun Section]

3. O/C "B" Company will detail a party of 1 NCO & 8 men to load SAA, Bombs &
   Tools at Quarter Master's Stores by 6-50 P.M.

4. All baggage will be ready loaded by 6-50 P.M. Officer's Mess Stores & Kit to
   be at Qr Masters Stores by that time.

5. The advance bivouacing party will proceed as detailed.

6. Major Harding will report to Commanding Officer & Brigade Headquarters
   that billets have been left clean

7. All 1st Line Transport will march in rear of the Brigade Column.

8. On arrival at Cross roads between MONTIGNY. Chau and Pt 52. The column
   will halt till 9 PM at which hour it will move forward opened out to
   300 yards between units.

9. Battalion will cross the FRENCHENCOURT - BAVELINCOURT road at an
   increased pace & must not interfere with the lorry traffic.

                                                   W. Parker
                                          A/Adjutant. 8th Bn Gloucestershire Regt.

Issued at   Copies to:-
No 1 copy. War Diary   No 7 "B" Company   No 13 Sgt Mess
 " 2 " Office Copy   " 8 "C"   " 14 Lieut Priestley
 " 3 " C.O.   " 9 "D"   " 15 Capt Chambers
 " 4 " 2i in Command " 10 Bombers   " 16 Scouts
 " 5 " Adjutant   " 11 L. Gun Officer   " 17 Depot
 " 6 " "A" Company   " 12 Quarter Master   " 18 Sergt Major

8th Gloucesters
vol: 7

T. M.
10 miles

57th Inf.Bde.
19th Div.

WAR DIARY

8th BATTN. THE GLOUCESTERSHIRE REGIMENT.

J U L Y

1 9 1 6

July 1918
19/57
8 Gloucesters
Vol II

WAR DIARY or INTELLIGENCE SUMMARY

Place	Date	Hour	Summary of Events and Information	Remarks and references to Appendices
MILLENCOURT	July 1st	1:30 AM	Moved forward to Intermediate line N. of ALBERT	
		5 P.M.	Moved forward to valley near ALBERT - POZIERES road	
		10 P.M.	Moved forward to the TARA - USNA line in rear of trenches & remained there for the night	
TARA-USNA LINE	2nd		Battn in trenches TARA - USNA line all day	
	3rd	1:30 AM	Moved forward to attack via St Andrews trench	
		3:15 AM	Attacked LA BOISELLE & consolidated position - remained there all day & night. Officers killed Capt H. Cox Capt F.H. Cooke Capt W.J. Mason 2nd Lt E.G. Evans 2nd Lt F.J. Fadney 2nd Lt J.E.H. Ross	
LA BOISELLE	4th	9 AM	Moved into RYECROFT STREET - Support line	
		5 P.M.	Moved up to LA BOISELLE occupying dug outs in village	
LA BOISELLE	5th		Holding Support line all day - Heavily shelled - marched out via POZIERES - ALBERT road	
ALBERT	6th	2:30 AM	Arrived at ALBERT - Batt in billets near station - Remainder of day passed in cleaning up & reorganising. Official casualties during advance Officers - killed 6 Wounded 14 Other ranks killed, missing & wounded 282	
ALBERT	7th		Under Company arrangements - Baths were arranged for the Battn during the day	
ALBERT	8th	11 am	Battn was inspected by Major General Briggs & complimented on their recent achievements - Remainder of day under Company arrangements	

WAR DIARY or INTELLIGENCE SUMMARY

(Erase heading not required.)

Army Form C. 2118

Instructions regarding War Diaries and Intelligence Summaries are contained in F.S. Regs., Part II. and the Staff Manual respectively. Title Pages will be prepared in manuscript.

Place	Date	Hour	Summary of Events and Information	Remarks and references to Appendices
ALBERT	9th	8.30 am	Battn moved from ALBERT + bivouacked in field N. of MILLENCOURT	
MILLENCOURT	10th	10 am	Inspection of lines by C.O. Remainder of day spent in resting.	
MILLENCOURT	11th	6.30-7 am	Physical Drill – Drafts of 67 other ranks arrived from Royal Fusiliers 7 from Glosters Regt (8th), 35 from 3rd Glosters.	
MILLENCOURT	12th	6.30 am	Physical Drill	
		9.30 am	Church Parade	
MILLENCOURT	13th	6.30-7 am	Running	
		9-10 am	Physical Exercises	Draft of 123 other ranks arrived from 1st Herts
		4-5 pm	Physical Drill by Bayonet Fighting Course	Shewn Pouteney – Commanding 3rd Corps
MILLENCOURT	14th	6.30-7 am	Running	
		9-10 am	Physical Exercise	
		2-3 pm	Bayonet Exercise	
MILLENCOURT	15th	6.30-7 am	Physical Drill	
		8.30-10 am	Route march by Companies	Draft of 18 men arrived from 1st Northants
		11.30 am	"Shoot to"	
MILLENCOURT	16th	11 am	Divine Service	
MILLENCOURT	17th	6.30-7 am	Physical Training	Major C H Hewetson "1st Glosters" reported for duty
MILLENCOURT	18th	6.30-7 am	"	"Shoot to" during rest of morning – Capt Shewman 1st Glosters reported for duty

WAR DIARY or INTELLIGENCE SUMMARY

Army Form C. 2118

Place	Date	Hour	Summary of Events and Information	Remarks and references to Appendices
MILLENCOURT	19/7/16	10 p.m	Left Millencourt and moved into bivouac S. of Fricourt. Remained under cover on the 20th	
FRICOURT	20/7/16	9 p.m	Moved into the Old German line close to BAZENTIN-LE-PETIT.	
BAZENTIN LE-PETIT	21/7/16	10 p.m	Two companies (A+C) moved into BAZENTIN-LE-PETIT.	
"	22/7/16	9.30 p.m	Relieved WORC. R. (10th) in front line and prepared to attack the German curved line cutting through the wood N. of HIGH WOOD and running S. of MARTIN PUICH with 10th R. War. and 7th S. Lanc. (1 a.m.) Attack failed our casualties being 1 officer killed, 5 wounded, & missing including the C.O. Lt Col de WIART gun shot wound in the neck. 186 casualties among other ranks.	
"	23/7/16	4 a.m	Taken back to support line and remained there all day. Relieved at 7.30 p.m	
BECOURT	24/7/16	1 a.m	Arrived in bivouacs in BECOURT WOOD. Lieut J.H.WRIGHT rejoined for duty from hospital - appointed Major. 8 p.m Major LORD A.G. THYNNE arrived and took over command of the battalion	
"	25/7/16	9 - 12.30	Parades under company arrangements, and refitting	
"	26/7/16 27/7/16	9 - 12.30 9 - 12.30	at 11.30 p.m on the 27th the battalion 'stood to' for half an hour because of a gas alarm. No gas was perceived in the vicinity of the battalion.	
"	28/7/16		Prepared to relieve 6th Wilts in front of BAZENTIN-LE-PETIT. at 4 p.m. Post poned by 24 hours.	

Army Form C. 2118

WAR DIARY
or
INTELLIGENCE SUMMARY
(Erase heading not required.)

Place	Date	Hour	Summary of Events and Information	Remarks and references to Appendices
BECORDT	29/7/16	4 p.m	Marched off from BECOURT and relieved 6th WURS in front of BAZENTIN-le-PETIT. Relief complete at 8 p.m. Cut the wire in front of the English line preparatory to attacking.	
BAZENTIN LE-PETIT	30/7/16	6.10 p.m	Attacked the German intermediate line, A & B coys in front line, C & D coys in second line. Our attack was held up by enfilade Machine Gun fire and concealed snipers from the right. Our men returned to their original front line at 9.30 p.m. Casualties Officers, 3 killed, 3 wounded, 3 missing the C.O. Major Thynne was wounded in the body while urging on the second line. Other ranks 160.	758 c 8/B + S/B
"	31/7/16	8. p.m	Relieved by the 11th Suffolks and arrived in bivouac near BECOURT WOOD at midnight.	
BECOURT	1/8/16 6 p.m		Marched out of bivouac and moved in billets at BRESLE at 7 p.m.	

C. H. Harding
Major.
Comdg 8th Bn Gloucestershire Regt.

57th Brigade.
19th Division.

1/8th BATTALION

GLOUCESTERSHIRE REGIMENT

AUGUST 1 9 1 6:

WAR DIARY or INTELLIGENCE SUMMARY

(Erase heading not required.)

Army Form C. 2118

Place	Date	Hour	Summary of Events and Information	Remarks and references to Appendices
BECOURT WOOD	1/8/16	4:30pm	Marched out of bivouac and went into billets at BRESLE.	
BRESLE	2/8/16	3 pm	Inspected by Commander of 3rd Corps and addressed on leaving it.	
	3/8/16	6:15pm	Marched out of BRESLE and entrained at MERICOURT for LONGPRE-le-CORPS-SAINT. Marched from LONPRE into billets at BOUCHON.	
BOUCHON	4/8/16		Bathing parades under Coy. arrangements. Draft of 34 men from 11th Rifle arrived.	
	5/8/16	11 a.m	Inspection by G.O.C 57th Brigade. Bathing in the afternoon. Draft of 34 men from LONPRE 1:40 a.m. Church parade 10 a.m. Marched out at 11pm and entrained at LONPRE 1:40 a.m.	
BAILLEUL	7/8/16		Detrained at BAILLEUL at noon and marched into reserve billets at AIRCRAFT FM (DRANOUTRE) on Coy at DAYLIGHT CORNER 6 A.B. S. of KEMMEL HILL.	
DRANOUTRE	8/8/16		Inspection of Smoke helmets, goggles etc. Moved coy at DAYLIGHT CORNER to the trenches over on the 15th.	
	9/8/16		C.O. and O.C. Coys visited trenches to be taken over on the 15th.	
	10/8/16	9 pm	Moved into DAYLIGHT CORNER at 9 p.m. and relieved 8th N. Staff. R. in the front line between WYTSCHAETE and MESSINES from N.36 c. 62.62 to N.36.a.4.4 (Messines). On system right of the division. A&C in front, B at R.E. Fm D with two platoons in support in GROUSE BUTTS and 1 platoon in each of two mine shafts.	
	11/8/16		Very quiet except from 4:30 to 5:30 pm when the enemy was active with bombs and rifle grenades on our front line and minenwerfer bombs and trench mortars on our supports. Our Stokes mortars and 18 pdrs. replied.	
	12/8/16		Work on parapet and trench boards carried on. Enemy activity between 4 and 6 pm. TM and Minenwerfer bombs, our artillery replied several times damaging an enemy trench parapet and shifting two casualties. Two patrols heard but saw nothing. Enemy has apparently of few mines in fair condition.	

WAR DIARY or INTELLIGENCE SUMMARY

Army Form C. 2118

(Erase heading not required.)

Place	Date	Hour	Summary of Events and Information	Remarks and references to Appendices
	13/8/16		Parapet repaired and revetted, construction of new latrines. Trailer Comm: Trench moved. Enemy shelling and bombing at 5 p.m. a few rifle grenades fell in our line but a very quiet day. Patrol examined enemy wire and reported it inoccupied. Mine crater examined by another patrol who had nothing to report. Work on parapet continued. Vermorel sprayers and S Frenkus stores tested.	
	14/8/16		Very quiet; between 7 and 8 a few Shrapnel and H.E. fell on our parapets. Enemy reported by our patrols to be working hard in own trenches. Snipers active but in damage performed. Tim?steps put in. Marched into billets on relief by 8th N. Staff R. relief complete by 11 p.m.	
DRANOUTRE	15/8/16	8-12 am	Baths, kit inspection, rifle and gas helmet inspection. Lecture from P.H.G. helmet.	
	16/8/16	9-12	Physical exercises, Arm drill. Movements in close order. Bayonet fighting instruction in rhythmic and carrying enemy's helmet. Lecture by M.O. on sanitation and gas.	
	17/8/16	9-12	Physical exercises steady drill, practice in constructing smoke revetment. Lecture.	
	18/8/16	9-11	Physical exercises. Church parade. Relieved 8th N. Staff R. in the line, moving off at 8.15 p.m. Our front line was heavily bombed at 9 p.m. by T.M.'s and Minenwerfer, parapet knocked in 4 places. Our patrols were active but saw nothing unusual. Work done on trench boards, parapet drainage	

WAR DIARY or INTELLIGENCE SUMMARY

Army Form C. 2118

(Erase heading not required.)

Instructions regarding War Diaries and Intelligence Summaries are contained in F.S. Regs., Part II. and the Staff Manual respectively. Title Pages will be prepared in manuscript.

Place	Date	Hour	Summary of Events and Information	Remarks and references to Appendices
	20/8/16		Enemy front line shelled intermittently by our artillery. Our snipers active. Enemy very quiet but his snipers watchful. Patrol reported enemy at work on his parapet and mine. China gun fired on this when patrol returned. Parapets and paraphs repaired. 750 sandbags used. Front boards cleared. Envelope moved.	
	21/8/16		A very quiet night. Our artillery and TM's heavily bombarded enemy reserve and support trenches 3.30–4.30 p.m. Enemy retaliation started at 4 p.m but caused little damage. Lightning post in front of our line learnt nothing unusual. Work on tunnel borehole continued. Work of strengthening parapet continued, parapet repaired.	
	22/8/16		Quiet. Enemy was reported to be platelety by patrol sent to consist of knife rests iron stakes, and loose wire. Enemy made very light in groups of 3 any 4. Work parapet improved. Trench boards cleared. Relieved by 8th N. Stafford Regt. between 5 and 9 p.m. and went into billets at AIRCRAFT FARM	
AIRCRAFT FARM	23/8/16	8–12 A.M.	Baths at DRANOUTRE. Inspection of feet gas helmet, rifles. Working party of 60 men at 10 p.m. for work in PICADILLY.	
	24/8/16	6–12 A.M.	Parades with company arrangements. Physical exercises, arm drill. WORKING PARTIES— 40 men at 7 a.m. and 60 men at 10 p.m.	
	25/8/16		Physical exercises. Steady drill. Working parties as on 24th.	
	26/8/16		Lecture by Divn gas officer. Enemy artillery sent over the shells in the vicinity of H.Q. Working parties as before.	
	27/8/16		Relieved 8th N Staffords in the Line. Relief complete by 9 p.m. Three companies of 76th Canadians were in the trenches for instruction and remained with the 8th N Staff R. westwards.	

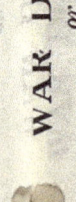

WAR DIARY or INTELLIGENCE SUMMARY

4 Gloucester Regt
Vol 12

Place	Date	Hour	Summary of Events and Information	Remarks and references to Appendices
	28/8/16	12:30 pm	Our T.M's and artillery bombarded enemy mine.	
		10 pm	From 10 pm to 1 am Stokes Mortar fired for 15 mins at ¾ hr. intervals. The section of 78th Canadians in front line relieved those in support. A gap 4 yds. wide was discovered in enemy wire lay out of our portfolio work. Rampet strengthened. Roger emplacements cleaned down for bombs and ammunition inserted in parapet.	
	29/8/16	11 am	Enemy wire again bombarded in same place as yesterday. In rain our rifle grenades and sniperscopes with good effect. The men — archdashapmentmens work carrying parties for Spanner. Brigade R.E. Trench bombs cleaned. Parapet repaired.	
		8 pm	Lewis guns fired on working party on enemy wire. Enemy artillery active and damaged our support line. Machine gun fire than normal from enemy.	
	30/8/16		78th Canadians went out rifle line drainage as to day was very wet. Most work was devoted to local drainage. 40 new trench boards laid.	
	31/8/16	3 pm	T.M's and Artillery endeavoured to cut enemy wire at 2:20 pm and 2:20 pm with bomb and Minnenwfr. enemy way active at 2 am only. Slight damage cannot sort out. Work — Drainage, Cleaning trenches where given way. Cleaning trench boards.	
		10 pm	Relieved by 2nd N. Staffs R. and marched to billets at DRANOUTRE	

C. H. Harding, Major
Comdg. 1/4th Bn Gloucestershire Regt.

Army Form C. 2118

Vol 13

WAR DIARY or ~~Intelligence~~ 2nd Bn Gloucester Rgt. INTELLIGENCE SUMMARY
(Erase heading not required.)

Instructions regarding War Diaries and Intelligence Summaries are contained in F.S. Regs., Part II. and the Staff Manual respectively. Title Pages will be prepared in manuscript.

13 11
4 sheets

Place	Date	Hour	Summary of Events and Information	Remarks and references to Appendices
DRANOUTRE	1/9/16		Cleaning up after tour in trenches. Inspections of rifles, gas helmets etc.	
	2/9/16	9–12 AM	Baths by Coys at DRANOUTRE. Bayonet fighting. Movement in close order.	
	3/9	10.30	Church Parade in Y.M.C.A. hut.	
	4/9	1.30 pm	Marched out by platoons to ROMARIN via NEUVE EGLISE and took over huts from 9th R. Innis killing Fusiliers. Batty sent to occupy post on HILL 63.	
	5/9	9.30 am	C.O. and O.C. Coys went up to front line to reconnoitre the front to be taken over by us. 14th R.I.R. in right subsector. Relief complete at 6.30pm. B Coy in Subsidiary line. In front of MESSINES. 3 Coys in front line.	
	6/9	4 pm	Marched out by 2 Coys to relieve 14th R.I.R. in right subsector.	
	7/9		The night 5/7 and very quiet. Our wire was reported to be very good by patrol. No enemy were encountered by our patrols. A start made on revetting parapet in AVENUE FM. and BARRICADE AVENUE. The enemy artillery was very active. Our artillery retaliated on our support line and the neighbourhood of SEAFORTH FM. and ADVANCED ESTAMINET. Three patrols went out from our front during the night 7/8. The going in NO MAN'S LAND was reported to be good. Enemy cap at U.9.C.20 (Strype) reconnoitred and found to be unoccupied. Enemy wire very thick along his whole front. Enemy sent out a listening patrol in front of right Coy with the following inscription (Translation) 31,000 Roumanians captured. Over 100 guns, hurra, hurra, hurra! Not much artillery activity. Gas alarm raised at 9 pm from the right but found to be false. 2 Patrols out during night. Heard nothing.	
	8/9			
	9/9		Work of draining and repairing parapet continued. Boxes for ammunition and bombs carried to parapet.	

WAR DIARY or INTELLIGENCE SUMMARY

Army Form C. 2118

[Unit:] 8th Bn Gloucester Regt

(Erase heading not required.)

Place	Date	Hour	Summary of Events and Information	Remarks and references to Appendices
	10/9		A quiet day. A further fell on near SEAFORTH FM. no damage done. Patrols reported everything normal. Snipers and concealed in grass in front of German line.	
	11/9		Machine gun very active on both sides during night. Enemy shelling in vicinity of ANTON'S FARM did no damage. Patrols could not approach very close to enemy line because of brightness of night. Enemy was very good apparently from 30 to 50 yards off.	
	12/9		Lt.Col. A. Carton-de-Wiart VC. DSO. rejoined and took over command of the battalion. Relieved by 8th N.Staff R., relief complete at 4.30 p.m. Battalion went into Brigade Reserve at RED LODGE.	
	13/9		Cleaning up. No baths available for men. 2nd Lts. Butter and Steven and 25 men went up to the line and patrolled the ground over which raiding party was to move on the 15th.	
	14/9		Practice for proposed raid. Physical exercises and arm drill.	
	15/9		Physical exercises. Arm drill. Raiding party went over to enemy line. (See Appendix)	
	16/9		Relieved 8th N. Staff R. in night advector, relief complete by 5 p.m.	
	17/9		Enemy shelled our front line lightly. Observation of enemy difficult in the front owing to distance (300-400 yds) between trenches. Work done on parapets – thickened and raised.	
	18/9		A very quiet day. Machine guns more active than usual during night. Enemy very watchful after raid and our patrols were seen and bombed but no casualties inflicted.	

WAR DIARY or INTELLIGENCE SUMMARY

Army Form C. 2118

6th Bn Gloucester Regt

(Erase heading not required.)

Place	Date	Hour	Summary of Events and Information	Remarks and references to Appendices
NEUVE EGLISE	19/9		Relieved by 22nd Manchester R. Relief complete by 1.30 pm. Marched into billets at BULFORD CAMP, 4 mls. S. of NEUVE EGLISE.	
	20/9		Marched out at 9 A.M. via BAILLEUL and went into billets in OULTERSTEENE area. Billets situated between that place and DOULIEU, and very scattered.	
GRAND SEC BOIS	21/9		Moved again at 9 A.M. and marched to Gd Sec BOIS, via VIEUX BERQUIN. Billets again very scattered. Settled in billets 1.30 p.m.	
	22/9		Physical exercise, arm drill.	
	23/9		1 hr route march by companies, arm drill. Lecture to all officers by Brig. Gen. Jefferys CMG at BORRE on discipline.	
	24/9	11am	Church Parade. Roman Catholics attended service in Church at 9.20 a.m. Physical exercise.	
	25/9	7-7.20	1hr. Route march by companies, arm drill.	
		9-12.30	Bayonet fighting and bomb throwing. 2nd Lts F.D Glasgow and J. Lloyd reported for duty from cadet school.	
		2.15-3	Physical exercise.	
	26/9	7-7.20	1hr. Route march, arm drill.	
		9-12.30	Bayonet fighting and bomb throwing, 2.15 – 3 pm Physical exercises.	
	27/9	7-7.20	All officers and 24 N.C.O.s attended lecture at B.H.Q BORRE by Captain Betts on bayonet fighting. Companies route marched under C.S.Ms.	
		9.30		

WAR DIARY
INTELLIGENCE SUMMARY

8th Bn Gloucester Regt

Army Form C. 2118

Place	Date	Hour	Summary of Events and Information	Remarks and references to Appendices
GRAND SEC BOIS	27/9	2.30	Battalion paraded in field near BOIS R E with remainder of Brigade for inspection by General Plumer Commdg. 2nd ARMY. Col. A CARTON-de-WIART V.C. D.S.O. commdg. 8th Glouc. R. presented Silk ribbon for V.C. Brigade marched past the Army Commander.	
	28/9	7-7.30	Bayen Physical Training	
		9-12.30	Batt. route march by companies. Arm drill.	
	29/9	7-7.30	Physical exercises	
		9.15	Battalion route march. Arm drill. Lecture on construction of villages by Lt Colonel 62nd F.C. R.E.	
	30/9	7-7.30	Physical exercises	
		9-12.30	Sandbagging, digging, revetting	
		2.15-3.20	Bayonet fighting, bombing	

Read nothing R Of
Comdg 8th Gloucestershire Regt

WAR DIARY or INTELLIGENCE SUMMARY

Army Form C. 2118

VQ2/4
8th Glouc. R. 19

Place	Date	Hour	Summary of Events and Information	Remarks and references to Appendices
GRAND SEC BOIS	1/10/16	11 am	Church Parade. G.O.C. Brigade present at service. Inspection of billets by G.O.C. 2nd Lt. Colgate joined for duty.	
	2/10/16		7-7.20 am Physical exercise 9-12 am Movements in extended order 2-3 pm Bayonet fighting and bombing.	
	3/10/16	10.30 am	Inspection of Brigade by the King of the Belgians at BORRE after which the Brigade marched past. 2-3 pm Bombing.	
	4/10/16		7-7.20 am Physical exercise. 9-12 am drill, extended order movements 2-3 pm Bombing.	
	5/10/16		7-7.20 am Physical exercise 9-12 Bayonet fighting. Steady drill	
	6/10/16		Marched out of GRAND SEC BOIS at 8.30 am to BAILLEUL and entrained at DOULLENS at 8 pm and marched into billets in huts at AMPLIER. Battn billeted by 11 pm.	
AMPLIER	7/10/16	2 pm	Marched out of AMPLIER into camp in BOIS de WARNIMONT. In billets by 5 pm.	
BOIS de WARNI- MONT	8/10/16	10 a.m.	Church Parade 10 a.m.	
	9/10/16		Parade under Company arrangements for arm drill and bayonet fighting 7-7.20 Physical exercise, 9-12.30 Movement in artillery formation and deploying into line, 2.15-3 pm Bayonet fighting.	
	10/10/16		7-7.20 Physical exercise 9-12.30 as on 10th	
	11/10/16			

WAR DIARY
or
INTELLIGENCE SUMMARY

(Erase heading not required.)

Army Form C. 2118

Place	Date	Hour	Summary of Events and Information	Remarks and references to Appendices
BOIS de WARN- IMONT	12/10/16		Brigade attacked northwards from LOUVENCOURT towards AUTHIE, forming movement in artillery formation, deploying, moving under our own barrage and attacking a line running diagonally across the direction of advance. Similar scheme to above carried out by the Battalion.	
	13/10/16		As on the 12th	
	14/10/16		As on 13th	
	15/10/16	9–11:30 a.m.	Arm drill. Physical training.	
	16/10/16		Arm drill. Physical training.	
WARLOY	17/10/16		Marched out at 10 a.m. with Bde. and went across country to WARLOY. Battalion billeted by 3 p.m.	
	18/10/16		Cleaned up billets. Arm drill and extended order movements. Marched out at 8.15 a.m. with Bde. to go into bivouac outside ALBERT. Order cancelled at 9.20 a.m. and Bde marched back to WARLOY. Physical Exercises. Arm drill. Battalion in afternoon.	
	20/10/16		Marched out at 6.45 a.m. and went into bivouacs on the BOUZINCOURT–ALBERT Rd. (brickfields)	
	21/10/16		Marched out at 9 a.m. and took over the dug outs in the old German front line north of OVILLERS and east of AUTHVILLE WOOD.	
OVILLERS	23/10/16		Preparations for going into the line. Carrying parties of 200 men and 5 officers found.	
	24/10/16	8 a.m.	O.C. Coys reconnaissance line to be taken over by him in the afternoon. Bn. marched off by platoons at noon and relieved the 8th N. Staff R. in front line.	

WAR DIARY or INTELLIGENCE SUMMARY

Army Form C. 2118

Place	Date	Hour	Summary of Events and Information	Remarks and references to Appendices
	24/10/16 25/10/16		East of THIEPVAL. 4th Bn in STUFF REDOUBT. Relief complete at 5.15 pm about line end STUFF REDOUBT heavily shelled. 2Lt Stevens killed and Capt POPE wounded, left of Coy. Patrols reported enemy working on an advanced trench in front of our right. Stray shots but no French developed.	
	26/10/16		Col de Wiart wounded at 6.15am outside STUFF REDOUBT. Enemy artillery very active. the enemy appears to be preparing to counter attack against our left but did not develop. Relieved by 6th WILTS. R. Relief complete at 2 pm. Marched into camp at OVILLERS POST HUTS. east of AVELUY. Major N Godfrey 9th Welch R. reported and took over command of the Bn. Total casualties during tour of Trenches Officers 1 killed, 2 wounded, Other Ranks 16 killed 47 wounded.	
OVILLERS POST	27/10/16		Cleaning up.	
	28/10/10		Voluntary C of E service at 9 AM. Service for Roman Catholics at 6.30 AM	
	29/10/10		View of equipment for forthcoming operations	
	30/10/10	11 am	Marched out and occupied old German dug out N of OVILLERS. Major McMahon reported for duty with the battalion	
	31/10/10		4 Officers & 200 men working on C.T. from GRAVELPIT to STUFF REDOUBT	

W Godfrey Lt Col
8th Welch Regt

Army Form C. 2118

WAR DIARY
or
INTELLIGENCE SUMMARY
(Erase heading not required.)

J.H / E.GLOUC.R / JH/15

15.11
3 sheets

Place	Date	Hour	Summary of Events and Information	Remarks and references to Appendices
OVILLERS	1/11/16		Battalion in reserve in dugouts in Old German Line N. of OVILLERS	
	2/11/16		Relieved 6th N. Stafford R. in STUFF and REGINA Trenches, H.Q. in STUFF REDOUBT. Relief commenced 11 a.m., complete at 7.30 p.m. Trenches very inconvenient due to mud.	
	3/11/16		Relieved by 6th Wilts R. relief complete at 6 p.m. Battalion returned to dugouts N. of OVILLERS	
	4/11/16		2 working parties detail of 2 officers and 180 O.R. found for burying cable from GRAVEL PIT to STUFF REDOUBT.	
	5/11/16		8th N. Stafford R. took over dugouts from the battalion which then moved into Nissen Huts near CRUCIFIX CORNER, east of AVELUY. (Cromwell Huts)	
	6/11/16		Inspection of the battalion by Corps by the C.O. Working party of 50 men for carrying trench boards	
	7/11/16		Working party of 3 officers and 250 O.R. for work in NAB VALLEY Road.	
	8/11/16		Relieved the 7th L.N. Lanc. R. near SCHWABEN REDOUBT. One Coy in front line One in SPLUTTER TRENCH, one in RANSOME TRENCH, one in BATN BRIDGE TRENCH. H.Q. in BULGAR TRENCH. Relief complete 8.30 p.m.	
	9/11/16		Enemy artillery very active, especially on SPLUTTER and BULGAR Trenches. Patrols reported no enemy activity in front of his line, no movement observed.	

WAR DIARY or INTELLIGENCE SUMMARY

Army Form C. 2118

(Erase heading not required.)

Place	Date	Hour	Summary of Events and Information	Remarks and references to Appendices
	10/11/16		Enemy artillery displayed normal activity. Patrol reconnoitred enemy position at point 62. A new trench was discovered which new timber and newthinken was laying about. It was unoccupied. Voices were heard from direction of BEAUREGARDE DOUVECOTE. Search was behind BAINBRIDGE trench. New French armament in front of SPLUTTER. Firesteps cut in parapet. R.E. officers carried up.	
	11/11/16		B.Coy in front line relieved by A.Coy from RANSOME TRENCH. Relief complete at midnight. Enemy artillery was very active during relief. 2nd Lt Junkin killed at 1am on 12th. On snipers shot 2 enemy snipers from shell hole in front of their lines. Trenches dry-ish. French Reports laid in HESSIAN and SPLUTTER.	
	12/11/16		At 12:30 am patrol went out to dry an incomplete point 62 with a view to examining it. Party was bombed and forced to retire. 2 more attempts were made to approach but enemy was very alert. Relieved by 7th L.N.Lancs R. relief complete at 10 pm. Bn moved into CROMWELL Huts East of AVELUY.	
	13/11/16 14/11/16 15/11/16 16/11/16		CROMWELL HUTS. Preparation carried on for forthcoming operation.	
	17/11/16		Marched out of CROMWELL HUTS at 4:30 pm and took over front line trenches from 7th L.N.Lancs.R.	

# Army Form C. 2118

WAR DIARY
or
INTELLIGENCE SUMMARY
(Erase heading not required.)

Place	Date	Hour	Summary of Events and Information	Remarks and references to Appendices
	18/11/16	5.A.M	Formed up in artillery formation preparatory to attack on W. outskirts of GRAND COURT. 6.10AM. Attack launched. First objective reached and gained. The 10th R.War.R. on our right being partially held up our flank was in the air. Casualties. 12 officers, 283 O.R.	
	19/11/16		Were relieved during by 56th Bde. 500 yds in rear of our position. This was reenforced by the 7th King's Own.R. who the battalion were withdrawn. (3am) and marched back to billets in CROMWELL HUTS at 5AM.	
	20/11/16		at CROMWELL HUTS	
WARLOY	21/11/16		Marched into billets at WARLOY.	
	22/11/16		Addressed by General Jeffries. G.O.C. 57th Inf Bde.	
HERISSART	23/11/16		Marched out at 8 am and went into billets at HERISSART	
CANAPLES	24/11/16		Marched out of HERISSART at 10AM. to billets at CANAPLES. Draft of 182 O.R. joined	
ST OUEN	25/11/16		Marched into billets at St OUEN. Battalion billeted at 12 noon	
ST. OUEN.	26/11/16		Kit inspection carried out.	
GEZAIN-COURT	27/11/16		Marched to billets at GEZAINCOURT. Billeted by 3pm. Parades under Company arrangements. Draft of 54 O.R. joined	
	28/11/16			
	29/11/16		Physical exercises from 7 to 7.15 AM. Companies engaged in following exercises for 1½ hrs duration. Squad drill, Platoon drill, Extended order drill, Bayonet fighting, Rifle exercises, Musketry.	
	30/11/16		Parades as 29th inst. 2nd Lt B.E. EASTWOOD rejoined unit.	

W Gray Lt Col.
Comdg 8th Bn Gloucester Regt.

WAR DIARY or INTELLIGENCE SUMMARY

Army Form C. 2118

8 Gloucester R.

8. GLOUC.R.

Vol 16

Place	Date	Hour	Summary of Events and Information	Remarks and references to Appendices
GEZAINCOURT	1/12/16		Bombing, bayonet fighting trenches on training ground. Physical exercise, musketry.	
"	2/12/16		Physical exercise, bayonet fighting, musketry	
	3/12/16		Church Parade at 10 a.m at GEZAINCOURT	
	4/12/16		Work as per programme. Bayonet fighting. Arm drill. Movements in close order.	
	5/12/16		Major starting took over command of the Battalion on the departure of Lt Col Godfrey to 17th command of 9th Welsh R. Arm drill. Movements in extended order.	
	6/12/16		Route march by companies. Bombing. Digging trenches.	
	7/12/16		Marched out of huts at 10.30am to BEAUVAL. Billets billeted by 12.30pm.	
	8/12/16		Batt. at CANDAS. Inspection of rifles and kit.	
	9/12/16		Tactical scheme of an advance on a ridge and notes.	
	10/12/16		Voluntary C of E service at the Marie. First round of Divn soccer football competition. 8th Glouc. v 18th Worc. Result 3 goals to 1 against the Glouc. Lt Colonel Knox Halley rejoined arrival & resumed command of battalion.	

Army Form C. 2118

WAR DIARY
or
INTELLIGENCE SUMMARY
(Erase heading not required.)

Instructions regarding War Diaries and Intelligence Summaries are contained in F.S. Regs., Part II. and the Staff Manual respectively. Title Pages will be prepared in manuscript.

Place	Date	Hour	Summary of Events and Information	Remarks and references to Appendices
BEAUVAL	11/12/16		100 men for working at BOIS FLEURI. Arm drill. bayonet fighting. Musketry. Lt Col Stokes reported his arrival and took over command.	
	12/12/16		Working party of 80 for Amm" dump at VALHEUREUX.	
	13/12/16		Marched into new billets at LA VICOGNE. Completed at 1 pm. 2 Staff of 61 O.R. arrived. 2nd Lt. George, Forbett and Bowden reported their arrival today	
LA VICOGNE	14/12/16			
BEAUVAL	15/12/16		Marched into billets at BEAUVAL Capt K.A.R. Smith reported for duty 15.12.16.	
	16.12.16		Arm drill. rifle exercise. Inspection of kit.	
	17.12.		Voluntary service at Mairie 6 pm. Bath at CANDAS allotted. 250 men 2 officers and 100 men for working at CANDAS station	
	18.12		Physical Training Arm drill Musketry. - 25 yd range prepared	

1875 Wt. W593/826 1,000,000 4/15 J.B.C. & A. A.D.S.S./Forms/C. 2118.

WAR DIARY or INTELLIGENCE SUMMARY

Army Form C. 2118

Instructions regarding War Diaries and Intelligence Summaries are contained in F.S. Regs., Part II. and the Staff Manual respectively. Title Pages will be prepared in manuscript.

(Erase heading not required.)

Place	Date	Hour	Summary of Events and Information	Remarks and references to Appendices
BEAUVAL	19.12		Physical Training, bayonet fighting, arm drill. 2 Coys on 400 yds range at GEZAINCOURT. Lt. James M.A. rejoined for duty 19/12. 2nd Lt. Temple reported for duty 19/12	
	20.12		Physical Training, Bomb Throwing, Musketry, Company drill. Movements in extended order.	
	21.12		Arm drill, Musketry, bayonet fighting	
	22.12		Physical Training, platoon drill musketry, bombing	
	23.12		3 Officers and 300 men for working party at CANDAS station. Tactical scheme for officers under Major McMahon.	
	24.12		Voluntary C of E service in Maire at 9.30 am. Service for R.C.s in church 9am. Military Medal awarded undermentioned for gallantry on the ANCRE in November. 12773 CQMS Johnson CE. 1775h L/cpl Goodway C 13662 Pte Thurston AT 12489 Pte Chandler WT 27725 " Bottom PS 24298 " Hayward EA 17441 " Selwyn C 23309 " Jenkins J	

WAR DIARY or INTELLIGENCE SUMMARY

Army Form C. 2118

Place	Date 1916	Hour	Summary of Events and Information	Remarks and references to Appendices
BEAUVAL	25.12		Xmas Day. – Xmas Paradise – Men had specially prepared Xmas dinners in large marquees. Voluntary C. of E Service at the Mairie BEAUVAL	
	26.12		Physical training – Bomb throwing – Musketry – to company drill 2/Lt. Rogers reported for duty. Physical training – Musketry – Bayonet fighting – Platoon drill	
	27.12		Bombing Aeroplane contact scheme carried out – Novel company Parades	
	28.12		2/Lt A.H. Bloomfield & 2/Lt A.T. Jackson reported for duty. Officers Bombing class commenced – Novel company Parades	
	29.12		One Officer and 200 men for working party at Candas Station. Novel company Parade	
	30.12		Capt. I.H. Wright proceeded to 36th Brigade for duty 2/Lt W.M. Watkins appointed Acting Adjutant	
	31.12		Voluntary services held at the Mairie	

H.M.A. Hawley Lt Col
Commanding 8th Gloster Regt

Army Form C. 2118.

8 Gloucester R¹
8 Glou. R
Vol 17

WAR DIARY
or
INTELLIGENCE SUMMARY.
(Erase heading not required.)

C.B. 17.11.
5 sheets

Place	Date	Hour	Summary of Events and Information	Remarks and references to Appendices
BEAUVAL	1/1/17	9 am	Early morning parade – Platoon leader company arrangements for programme 2/Lt H.N. Worley permitted to sit front of Captain	(R 325 19 4/1) whilst commanding coy
"	2/1/17		2/Lt J.S. Earhart " " " "	" Lieutenant
"			2/Lt J. Lloyd " " " "	"
"			Parades as usual. All Officers attended a Lewis Gun Course Lecture class for NCOs for Bayonet fighting. Men attended bath.	
"	3/1/17		Parades as usual – Remainder of Battn visited the baths 2/Lt Jackson A.S. proceeded to Le Touquet for a L.G. Course	Extract from London Gazette 1/1/17
"	4/1/17		Parades as usual. ⁹⁶²¹⁰ A/RSM J. Burbitt awarded M.C. T/Capt J.H. Wright	Extract from London Gazette 1/1/17
"	5/1/17		T/Capt J.W. Wilson reported for duty + assumed command of "A" Coy 2/Lt F.S. Walton to be transferred to D Coy Parades as usual Capt J.W. Wilson awarded Military Cross	Extract from London Gazette 1/1/17

WAR DIARY or INTELLIGENCE SUMMARY

Army Form C. 2118.

Place	Date	Hour	Summary of Events and Information	Remarks and references to Appendices
BEAUVAL	6/1/17		Parade as usual. Capt K.A.R. Smith left the Battn & was transferred to its 1st Garrison Battn.	
		2.30 pm	Lecture to all Officers at GEZAINCOURT by Div. Commdr.	
		11.30	C. of E. Service followed by Holy Communion.	
	7/1/17	9 am	A voluntary service for Non Conformists.	
		7 pm	A voluntary service to Y.M.C.A.	
			The Divisional Commdr presented ribbons to:-	
			T/Capt. T.H. Wright 6310 A/R.S.M. T. Bishop — Military Cross	
			13602 Pte A.J. Thurston 27723 Pte P.G. Bircom 23309 Pte J Jenkins	
			12489 Pte W J Chandler 17354 Pte C Lockway 24298 Pte S.A. Wignall 17441 Pte J Selwyn — Military Medal	
			A guard of honour under 2/Lt Bloomfield attended the presentation.	
			Extract London Gazette 4/1/17 := Special Mention in despatches Major C.H. Harding 2/Lt F.J. Hawker (since of wounds) 2/Lt. W.N. Woolley C.S.M. T. J. Hopcroft	

WAR DIARY
or
INTELLIGENCE SUMMARY

(Erase heading not required.)

Army Form C. 2118

Instructions regarding War Diaries and Intelligence Summaries are contained in F.S. Regs., Part II. and the Staff Manual respectively. Title Pages will be prepared in manuscript.

Place	Date	Hour	Summary of Events and Information	Remarks and references to Appendices
BEAUVAL	8/1/17		Parade – Company in attack. 2/Lt R.H. Smyth proceeded on leave to England	
"	9/1/17	8.45	Battalion moved to AMPLIER & arrived at 12 noon. 2/Lt Bicketts rather frm	
AMPLIER	10/1/17	10.15	Battalion moved to BAYENCOURT in lorries arriving at 12.30 pm. Billets very good	
BAYENCOURT	11/1/17		2/Lt E.W. Argo reported for duty & posted to L Company. Rifle Inspection by Company – Improving Billets	
"	12/1/17		Entered 19th Division MO A/283/1 Decorations awarded	
			D.S.O. T/Capt & B.E Kingston	
			M.C. T/2/Lt A.H. Britten T 2/Lt R.H. Smyth T Lt J.H. Cochrane RAMC attached 6th SLR and 2421 RSM T.E.P. Vaughan	
			D.C.M. 5702 Sgt W.H. Nott 12172 Cpl A.W. Spencer 12069 Pte H.M. Pugh	
"	13/1/17	9–12	Parade under Company arrangements	
"	14/1/17	10.30am 11.30am	Service at Y.M.C.A. Hut followed by Holy Communion	

WAR DIARY or INTELLIGENCE SUMMARY

Army Form C. 2118.

Place	Date	Hour	Summary of Events and Information	Remarks and references to Appendices
BAYENCOURT	15/1/17	9-12	Parades under Company Arrangements. A fog permitted a working party.	
Trenches	16/1/17	12:35	Moved into trenches at HEBUTERNE relieving 10th Worcesters — Very Quiet	
HEBUTERNE	17/1/17		In trenches — Day & Night Quiet	
	18/1/17		In trenches — one man wounded — Three Officers patrols went out	
	19/1/17		In trenches — Day Quiet — slight shelling at night — relieving company	
	20/1/17		In trenches — one man accidentally wounded	
	21/1/17		In trenches — Day & night quiet	
	22/1/17		Relieved in trenches by 7th S. Lanes & moved to COURCELLES — men's feet rubbed. 2/4th N.M. Church V	
COURCELLES	23/1/17		Day spent cleaning up — 2/5th N. Lan Smith reported for duty. Parades under company arrangements.	
"	24/1/17	10-12	Extract from London Gazette dated Jan 13. 1917	
			2. G/Lt W.N Wooley to be T. Capt July 11th 1916	
			2/Lt B.E Falconer to be T. Lieut July 31st 1916	
			2/Lt J. Lloyd to be T. Lieut Sep 25th 1916	
	25/1/17	10-12	Parades under Company Arrangements. A court of enquiry assembled at 4 o/cp 14hrs to enquire into the course of No 2892 Pte G. Walker being accidentally wounded. Members 2/Lt Welsh — 2/Lt M.A James — 2/Lt E.M Rogers	

WAR DIARY
or
INTELLIGENCE SUMMARY

(Erase heading not required.)

Army Form C. 2118

Place	Date	Hour	Summary of Events and Information	Remarks and references to Appendices
COURCELLES	26/1/17	10-12	Practice in the Attack	
"	27/1/17	10 am	Battalion practised in Attack. 2/Lt E.W. Wingo proceeded on leave to England.	
"	28/1/17	10.30 11.30	Celebration of Holy Communion. Service for Non-Conformists. Major B. Thomas rejoined the Battalion & assumed command of Letter C Coy.	
"	29/1/17	10 am	Battalion took part in a Brigade practice in the Attack	
"	30/1/17	10 am	" " " " " " "	
"	31/1/17	10 am	Battalion took part in a Brigade tactical exercise witnessed by the Army Commander	

J.M.A. Hoskins
Lt Col.
Cmdg 8th Gloucestershire Regt

WAR DIARY or INTELLIGENCE SUMMARY

Army Form C. 2118.

8 Gloucester Regt
1 of 18

Place	Date	Hour	Summary of Events and Information	Remarks and references to Appendices
COURCELLES	1/2/17	10-12	Parades under Company arrangements	
"	2/2/17	10-12	" " "	
"	3/2/17	9-3pm	Baths allotted to the Battn, Lieut & J. Hoggan reported for duty T	
"	4/2/17	8.45am	" Joined to Lewis O. Coy	
		10.45	Church Parade for R.C.	
		11.15	" " for non-conformists	
			" " C. of E. followed by Holy Communion	
Trenches	5/2/17	8.30pm	The Battalion moves to trenches opposite SERRE	
"	6/2/17		Battalion in the trenches 2/Pt Boulton wounded	
"	7/2/17		" " "	
"	8/2/17		" " "	
"	9/2/17		" relieved by 10th Worcesters and marched back to	
			billets at COURCELLES	
COURCELLES	10/2/17		Battn spent day in cleaning up	
"	11/2/17	10 a.m.	Church Parade — YMCA Hut followed by celebration of Holy Communion	18.11. 1 sheet
			"A" F.G.C.M assembled at Headqrs. Members Capt. 13. E. Lalonne P/C. Maj. J.S. McMahon P/C R.K. George	

WAR DIARY or INTELLIGENCE SUMMARY

Army Form C. 2118.

Place	Date	Hour	Summary of Events and Information	Remarks and references to Appendices
COURCELLES	11/2/17		Continued. A Court of Inquiry assembled at Batt. H.Qrs. at 11am for the purpose of investigating the circumstances under which 2/Lt. G.T. Jackson was wounded on the night of 9/10. Members 7/Lt. C.H.N. Clewly (President) 2/Lt. T.M. Chenies	
"	12/2/17		2/Lt. F.B. Owen reported for duty & was posted to letter A Coy 2/Lt. G.H. Portell " " " " " B " 2/Lt. R.J. Joseph granted leave to England — Batt. found working parties for R.E.	
"	13/2/17	7.30pm	Batt. proceeded to trenches & relieved 10th Worcesters — relief complete by 1.45 am	
"	15/2/17		Batt. in the trenches opposite SERRÉ	
Trenches	14/2/17		" " " " " " "	
"	15/2/17		" " " " " " "	
"	16/2/17		" " " " " " "	
"	17/2/17		" Relieved in the trenches by 10th Worcesters — relief complete by 3.45 am	

WAR DIARY
or
INTELLIGENCE SUMMARY.
(Erase heading not required.)

Army Form C. 2118.

Place	Date	Hour	Summary of Events and Information	Remarks and references to Appendices
COURCELLES	18/2/17		Battn rested & spent part of day in cleaning up	
	19/2/17	9 am	Baths allotted to the Battn	
		noon	A Court of Inquiry assembled at A Coy HQrs to investigate the circumstances under which 31589 Pte G Neville D Coy fatally injured himself on the 31st Jan 1917. President Capt J Watson Members 2/Lt T J Neville & 2/Lt L A Pierce	
			Lt Col Hales proceeded on leave to-day 18/2/17. Major D J McMahon assumed command of the Battn	
			The following Officers reported for duty & were posted to Coys: Capt E O Emmet to E Coy 2/Lt T J R Garland to B Coy. 2/Lt W E Hawkins to B Coy 2/Lt W Parker reported for duty & resumed his appointment as Adjutant Capt W T Woosley acting Adjutant resumed command of D Coy.	
	20/2/17	9.30-12	Coys paraded for Kit Inspection	
		3 pm	Capt L G Baker reported for duty & assumed command of E Coy. A/Capt W B Castropo on ceasing to command a company reverts to his temporary rank	

WAR DIARY
or
INTELLIGENCE SUMMARY.

Army Form C. 2118.

Place	Date	Hour	Summary of Events and Information	Remarks and references to Appendices
COURCELLES	24/9/17	6pm	The Batt'n moved to trenches opposite SERRE to relieve the	
	24/9/17		relief complete by 11.30 pm Batt'n in the trenches	
Trenches	24/9/17		" " "	
	24/9/17		" " Orders to advance & occupy trenches evacuated by the enemy.	
	24/9/17		Batt'n advanced & occupied ground to the WEST of SERRE relieved on evening by 8th R.Staffs & marched back to	
BERTRANCOURT			BUS. Col H.M.A. Holes resumed command of the Batt'n	
			Batt'n moved to BUS. 2/Lt E.W. TROTMAN reported for duty & posted to "D" Coy.	
BERTRANCOURT	26/9/17	4pm	Day spent in cleaning of equipment etc. Various working parties provided	
BUS.	27/9/17		Parades under Coy arrangements for cleaning up equipment etc. Also various	
BUS	28/9/17		working parties provided	

H.M.A. Holes
Lt.Col.
Comdg. 13th Bn Gloucester Regt

Army Form C. 2118.

WAR DIARY
or
INTELLIGENCE SUMMARY.

8th Bn. Glouc. Regt.

Nov 19

Place	Date	Hour	Summary of Events and Information	Remarks and references to Appendices
BUS	1.3.17		Batt. remained in billets at BUS	
LOUVEN COURT.	2.3.17		Batt. moved to billets at LOUVENCOURT	
"	3.3.17		Inspection of "A" & "D" Coys by the Commanding Officer. Inspection of Reinforcements by Commanding Officer at 11 a.m.	
"	4.3.17	10.30 a.m	Headquarters, "B" & "D" Coys paraded for Divine Service. "A" & "D" Coys provided working parties for roads etc.	
"	5.3.17		Inspection of "B" & "C" Coys by Commanding Officer. Bombing Instructor under Bombing Officer	
"	6.3.17		Parades under Coy arrangements. "A" & "B" Coys paraded for working parties	
"	7.3.17		Coy Training. One Platoon per Coy carried out Tactical Exercise	
"	8.3.17		Coy Training continued	
GEZAINCOURT	9.3.17		Battalion moved to billets at GEZAINCOURT & was temporarily attached to 56th 13th Group	
FORTEL	10.3.17		Battalion moved to billets at FORTEL & remained temporarily attached to 56th 13th Group	
"	11.3.17		Battalion remained in billets at FORTEL	
CROISETTE	12.3.17		Battalion moved to billets at CROISETTE & remained temporarily attached to 56th 13th Group	
FLORINGHEM	13.3.17		Battalion moved to billets at FLORINGHEM & remained temporarily attached to 56th 13th Group	
"	14.3.17		Battalion remained in billets at FLORINGHEM & remained temporarily attached to 56th 13th Group	
St HILAIRE	15.3.17		Battalion moved to billets at St HILAIRE & remained temporarily attached to 56th 13th Group. 3 sheets	19.11

WAR DIARY
or
INTELLIGENCE SUMMARY.
(Erase heading not required.)

8th Bn Queens R V

Army Form C. 2118.

Place	Date	Hour	Summary of Events and Information	Remarks and references to Appendices
St HILAIRE	16.3.17	—	Battalion remained in billets at St HILAIRE	
STEENBEEQUE	17.3.17	—	Battalion moved to billets at PLAINE HAUTE & PLAINE BAS and reported 57th Bde Group	
MERRIS	18.3.17	—	Battalion moved to billets "D" Coy MERRIS	
"	19.3.17	—	Battalion remained in billets at MERRIS	
"	20.3.17	—	Commanding Officer, 2nd in Command, Adjutant & Officer per Coy visited DIEPENDAAL SECTOR for purpose of 'taking over the line.	
MURRUMBIDGEE CAMP	21.3.17		Battalion moved to MURRUMBIDGEE CAMP. RSM & Coy SM went up to line to take over stores etc.	
DIEPENDAAL SECTOR	22.3.17		Battalion relieved 23rd (S) Batt: The Royal Fusiliers. Relief complete at 8.55 am.	
"	23.3.17		Battalion in line. Works officer instructed. Patrol investigated wire at NAGS NOSE.	
"	24.3.17		Battalion in line. Patrol investigated wire & trenches at NAGS NOSE. 1 O.R. wounded.	
"	25.3.17		Battalion in line. 2 O.R. killed & 2 O.R. wounded. Patrol investigated wire & trenches at NAGS NOSE	
"	26.3.17		Battalion in line. Patrol investigated wire & trenches at NAGS NOSE	
"	27.3.17		Battalion was relieved by 10th Worc Regt. Relief complete at 9.15 am. "B" "C" Coys returned to MURRUMBIDGE CAMP for special training. "A" & "D" Coys to RIDGE WOOD in support under command of Major McMahon	

Army Form C. 2118

WAR DIARY
or
INTELLIGENCE SUMMARY

(Erase heading not required.)

8th Bn. Gloucester Regt.

Place	Date	Hour	Summary of Events and Information	Remarks and references to Appendices
MURRUMBIDGEE CAMP.	28.3.17		2 Coys at MURRUMBIDGEE CAMP. 2 Coys at RIDGE WOOD. Time spent at MURRUMBIDGEE CAMP in cleaning up equipment etc under Coy. arrangements	
"	29.3.17		Lieut E.B. Pope joined for duty. G.O.C. gave lecture to officers & N.C.O.s at MURRUM BIDGEE CAMP on "The History of PRUSSIA".	
MOOLENACKER	30.3.17		Battalion moved to billets at MOOLENACKER. HQ + 2 Coys at MURRUMBIDGEE CAMP were relieved by 9th CHESHIRE Regt. 2 Coys at RIDGE WOOD were relieved by 9th R.W.F.	
"	31.3.17		Battalion remained in billets at MOOLENACKER. Special instruction given to Platoon Commanders in the handling of Lewis Guns.	

J.H. Noakes Lt Col.
Comdg 8th Bn Gloucester Regt.

Army Form C. 2118.

WAR DIARY
or
INTELLIGENCE SUMMARY.
(Erase heading not required.)

8 Gloucs C.B.1

20 20

Place	Date	Hour	Summary of Events and Information	Remarks and references to Appendices
MOOLENACHER	1/4/17		Battalion remained in billets at MOOLENACHER. Divine services were held for all Denominations.	
MOOLENACHER	2/4/17		Battalion moved to billets in HAZEBROUCK area.	
HAZEBROUCK	3/4/17		Battalion moved to billets in LONGUENESS.	
LONGUENESS	4/4/17		Battalion remained in billets at LONGUENESS.	
LONGUENESS	5/4/17		Battalion moved to billets in ZUDAUSQUES.	
ZUDAUSQUES	6/4/17		Battalion commenced training programme:- Organisation of platoon & section in formation of Coy in attack. Company in attack on ground. Musketry: Rapid loading, & firing.	
ZUDAUSQUES	7/4/17		Major S. Thurnes reported for duty from M. Staff Regt (5th Bn.) Battalion training continued. Company arrangement according to Programme. Brigade Canteen opened.	
ZUDAUSQUES	8/4/17		Battalion in billets ZUDAUSQUES. Divine services were held for all Denominations.	
ZUDAUSQUES	9/4/17		Battalion training continued:- Arms drill. Company drill. Battalion Musketry. Training of Specialists. Battalion in attack.	

A5834 Wt. W4973/M687 750,000 8/16 D. D. & L. Ltd. Forms/C.2118/13.

WAR DIARY
or
INTELLIGENCE SUMMARY.
(Erase heading not required.)

Army Form C. 2118.

Place	Date	Hour	Summary of Events and Information	Remarks and references to Appendices
LUDAUSQUES	10/4/17		Battalion training continued according to Programme. The C.O. gave lecture on "Battle Honours" leading by Major Campbell D.S.O. at 2-30 hrs 10 det of Instruction on Bayonet fighting	
LUDAUSQUES	11/4/17		Battalion training continued according to Programme. Bayonet fighting; Musketry was emphasized. Dummy had charming; Physical training; Bayonet ett:	
LUDAUSQUES	12/4/17		Battalion training continued. "A" & "B" Coys attend Range. "C" & "D" Coys as for training Programme.	
LUDAUSQUES	13/4/17		Battalion training continued. "C" & "D" Coys attend Range. "A" & "B" Coys as for training Programme.	
LUDAUSQUES	14/4/17		Battalion training continued. The Battalion in attack; A & B Coys in attack, C & D Coys in reserve — Artillery formation. Brigade Transport Competition held at Quercamps.	
LUDAUSQUES	15/4/17		Battalion in billets LUDAUSQUES. Divine service were held for all Denominations. Brigade Paper Chase took place. Noel. at Guen, Quercamps 3 km	
LUDAUSQUES	16/4/17		Battalion training continued. Battalion in attack as laid down Plat. D S.S.144	

Army Form C. 2118.

WAR DIARY
or
INTELLIGENCE SUMMARY.
(Erase heading not required.)

Place	Date	Hour	Summary of Events and Information	Remarks and references to Appendices
ZUDAUSQUES	17/4/17		Battalion moved to billets – ARQUES.	
ARQUES	18/4/17		Battalion moved to billets in HAZEBROUCK Area	
HAZEBROUCK	19/4/17		Battalion moved to SCHERPENBERG Area & took over CARNARVON CAMP	
SCHERPENBERG CARNARVON CAMP	20/4/17		Battalion in camp. A, B, & D Coys. to move to S.12.c.u.8. (Sheet 28 1/40000) to work with No 262 Coy R.E. (Railway Construction) Coys. relieved by 36th Division. Major B. Thomas in command of the detachment.	Sheet 28.S.9 Sheet 128 1/40,000
"	21.4.17		Battalion remained at CARNARVON CAMP [M.10.d.5.9]. New site for Camp made & renamed OLD BRAGS CAMP.	
"			Working parties provided.	
"	22.4.17		Working parties provided	
"	23.4.17		Working parties provided	
"	24.4.17		Working parties provided	
"	25.4.17		Working parties provided	
"	26.4.17		Working parties provided	
"	27.4.17		Working parties provided	
"	28.4.17		Working parties provided	
"	29.4.17		Working parties provided	

WAR DIARY
or
INTELLIGENCE SUMMARY.

Place	Date	Hour	Summary of Events and Information	Remarks and references to Appendices
CARNARVON CAMP	30.4.17		Battalion moved to G.18.a L Sheet 28 40,000 59th Bde relieved 70th Bde & 19th Division as composed from IX to X Corps in relief of the 23rd Division on the HILL SIXTY and HOOGE sectors	

Signed,
R.O.L
Comdg 9th (S) Bn Gloucester Regt.

Army Form C. 2118.

WAR DIARY
or
INTELLIGENCE SUMMARY.
(Erase heading not required.)

8/Lincs R

Vol 21

Place	Date	Hour	Summary of Events and Information	Remarks and references to Appendices
TORONTO CAMP [G.18.a. NE 40.000]	1917 1.5.17		Battalion remained in billets at TORONTO CAMP (G.18.a.) Officers reconnoitred HILL SIXTY SECTOR.	
RAILWAY DUGOUTS	2.5.17		Battalion relieved the 11th (S) Battalion SHERWOOD FORESTERS in the HILL SIXTY SECTOR and was the Battalion in Bde Reserve.	
do	3.5.17		Battalion remained in Bde Reserve in RAILWAY DUGOUTS. Numerous working parties formed.	
do	4.5.17		Battalion remained in Bde Reserve in RAILWAY DUGOUTS.	
do	5.5.17		Battalion remained in Bde Reserve in RAILWAY DUGOUTS.	
CENTRE SECTOR [HILL SIXTY SECTOR]	6/7.5.17		Battalion relieved the 10th (S) Battalion WORCESTERSHIRE REGT on the night of 6/7 May.	
do	7.5.17		Battalion held CENTRE SECTOR [HILL SIXTY SECTOR]	
do	8.5.17		Battalion held CENTRE SECTOR [HILL SIXTY SECTOR]	
do	9-10 .5.17	At 6p.m on 9.5.15 the following report was received from O.C. 10th R.War.R — the Battalion on our right "Much movement has been observed to-day in enemy's front & support lines. Two officers were seen on the CATERPILLAR with maps and a large sheet of paper on which they appeared to be sketching our lines. This was at 1.50 p.m. They were seen again at 2.57 p.m. and at 5.10 p.m. and are still in position	21.11 5 sheet

WAR DIARY
or
INTELLIGENCE SUMMARY.

(Erase heading not required.)

Army Form C. 2118.

Place	Date	Hour	Summary of Events and Information	Remarks and references to Appendices
CENTRE SECTOR [HILL SIXTY SECTOR]	9/10	5.1F	In front of the CATERPILLAR some sandbags are visible which have a large white blob on. Also two huts are marked in a similar manner. The white faces on huts. Several men were seen carrying planks in front line at 4pm in front of CATERPILLAR. Upon receipt of this report orders were issued to the Battalion to "stand to" for the night. At 9pm the enemy opened a heavy fire on our front line. This fire extended to the Battalions on the right and left. The enemy also opened rifle or machine gun fire on the front line parapet. There appears every probability that he was on the point of reaching the sector. The artillery opened fire on the S.O.S lines and a heavy machine gun a rifle fire was opened from our front line. The raid was completely checked. At 4am the enemy repulsed his tactics his fire of anything being heavier than before. Then indications of a raid were noticeable. What movement was heard behind the enemy's line and the rattle of metal presumably tools was on the S.O.S lines and the raid was again checked before the enemy could get clear of his own lines. Battalion relieved in Sector by 120(S) Battalion Durham Light Infantry	
CENTRE SECTOR [HILL SIXTY SECTOR]	10/10	5.19	and returned to TORONTO CAMP	

WAR DIARY
or
INTELLIGENCE SUMMARY.
(Erase heading not required.)

Army Form C. 2118.

Instructions regarding War Diaries and Intelligence Summaries are contained in F. S. Regs., Part II. and the Staff Manual respectively. Title pages will be prepared in manuscript.

Place	Date	Hour	Summary of Events and Information	Remarks and references to Appendices
TORONTO CAMP	12.5.17		Battalion marched from TORONTO CAMP to DE ZON CAMP [SCHERPENBERG AREA]	
DE ZON CAMP	13.5.17		Battalion remained in billets at DE ZON CAMP. Working parties provided	
"	14.5.17		Battalion remained in billets at DE ZON CAMP. Working parties provided	
"	15.5.17		Battalion remained in billets at DE ZON CAMP. Working parties provided	
"	16.5.17		Battalion remained in billets at DE ZON CAMP. Working parties provided	
"	17.5.17		Battalion remained in billets at DE ZON CAMP. Working parties provided	
"	18.5.17		Battalion remained in billets at DE ZON CAMP. Working parties provided	
"	19.5.17		Battalion remained in billets at DE ZON CAMP. Working parties provided	
			Major J.T.B. McMahon takes command) Befs the Battalion. To take charge of Corps Reinforcement Camp	
			Major B. Thomas takes over duties of 2/n command	
RIDGEWOOD	20/5/17		Battalion relieved 1/1 N Lancs Regiment in RIDGEWOOD. (2 Coys "C" & "D"). "A" & "B" Coys remained at DE ZON CAMP & were attached to 56th Inf Brigade for training commencing 21st inst.	
DE ZON CAMP & RIDGEWOOD	21/5/17		Battalion (less A & B Coys) in Ridgewood. Numerous working parties furnished. A & B Coys at MURRUMBIDGEE CAMP training with 56th Inf Brigade.	
MURRUMBIDGEE CAMP	22/5/17		Major R.B. Umphelby 4th Bn. assumed command of the Battalion	

Army Form C. 2118.

WAR DIARY
or
INTELLIGENCE SUMMARY.
(Erase heading not required.)

Instructions regarding War Diaries and Intelligence Summaries are contained in F. S. Regs., Part II. and the Staff Manual respectively. Title pages will be prepared in manuscript.

Place	Date	Hour	Summary of Events and Information	Remarks and references to Appendices
RIDGEWOOD	23/5/17		Battalion in support in RIDGEWOOD, "C" & "D" Coys relieved by "A" & "B" Coys C & D Coys move to MURRUMBIDGEE CAMP & will come under orders of G.O.C. 56th Inf Brigade for training. Numerous enemy parties prevented	
MURRUMBIDGEE CAMP	24/5/17		Battalion (less C & D Coys) in RIDGEWOOD. Numerous enemy patrols prevented. C & D Coys at MURRUMBIDGEE CAMP training with 56th Inf Bde.	
RIDGEWOOD & MURRUMBIDGEE CAMP	25/5/17		Battalion (less C & D Coys) relieved by 10th R. Warwick Regt & proceeded to MURRUMBIDGEE CAMP. C & D Coys in MURRUMBIDGEE CAMP. Hostile patrols prevented	
MURRUMBIDGEE CAMP	26/5/17		Battalion moved to CARNARVON CAMP in relief 9th Welsh Regt	
CARNARVON CAMP	27/5/17		Battalion remained — lull at CARNARVON CAMP. Divine service held for all denominations	
CARNARVON CAMP	28/5/17		Battalion remained in hutts at CARNARVON CAMP. C.O. inspected Coys. Training by Coys in accordance with programme of work.	

Army Form C. 2118.

WAR DIARY
or
INTELLIGENCE SUMMARY.
(Erase heading not required.)

Place	Date	Hour	Summary of Events and Information	Remarks and references to Appendices
CARNARVON CAMP	29/5/17		Battalion moved to ASCOT CAMP WESTOUTRE in relief of 4th R LANC'S REGT	
ASCOT CAMP	30/5/17		Battalion remained in billets at ASCOT CAMP. Training carried out according to Programme of Work. Working parties furnished.	
ASCOT CAMP	31/5/17		Battalion remained in billets at ASCOT CAMP. Training carried out in accordance with Programme of Work. Working parties furnished.	

P.B. Muntsville
Major
Commandant.
8th (S) Bn. Gloucestershire Regt.
June 1st 1917

WAR DIARY
INTELLIGENCE SUMMARY
(Erase heading not required.)

Army Form C. 2118.

8 Gloucestershire Regt.

Place	Date	Hour	Summary of Events and Information	Remarks and references to Appendices
ASCOT CAMP	1/6/17		Battalion remained in billets at ASCOT CAMP. Training carried out in accordance with Programme of work. Capt. J.H. Wright M.C. rejoined for duty from V Army Head Quarters.	
ASCOT CAMP	2/6/17		Battalion remained in billets at ASCOT CAMP. Inspection of Brigade by Major General Shute (33rd Division) who assumes command temporarily of 19th Division.	
ASCOT CAMP	3/6/17		Battalion remained in billets at ASCOT CAMP. Battalion took part in Bde Tactical s'cheme	
ASCOT CAMP	4/6/17		Battalion remained in billets at ASCOT CAMP. Battalion took part in Bde Tactical scheme	
ASCOT CAMP	5/6/17		Battalion remained in billets at ASCOT CAMP. Battalion took part in 13th Tactical scheme.	
ASCOT CAMP	6/6/17		Battalion moved off at 11.15 a.m. to staging area near LA CLYTTE. was equipped for action.	
LA CLYTTE	9/9/6/17 night		Battalion moved off to take up position of assembly for attack. The IX Corps to which the 19th Division belonged took part in an offensive which had for its objective the Capture of the MESSINES - WYTSCHAETE Ridge.	
WYTSCHAETE BEER	7.6.17		Attack launched at 3.10 a.m. by 19th Division	
	7.6.17	8.10 a.m.	Battalion attacked BLACK LINE in front of ONRAET WOOD & both N.S. objective. Patrol pushed out & line in front of OOSTTAVERNE WOOD also held	

WAR DIARY
or
INTELLIGENCE SUMMARY.
(Erase heading not required.)

Army Form C. 2118.

Place	Date	Hour	Summary of Events and Information	Remarks and references to Appendices
ONRAET WOOD	7/6/17	3.10p.m	Further attack was launched against village of OOSTTAVERNE and ODONTO Trench. Battalion took its objective and consolidated position. The result of the day's operations was' highly successful. During the operations Captain H.B. Hoskings was killed, Lieut. W.E. Hawkens was mortally wounded, Captain J.H. Wright M.C. & 2/Lt. R.S.T. Foskett were wounded	
OOSTTAVERNE	8/6/17		Battalion held portion of ODONTO TRENCH and consolidated position. Patrols were sent out in the morning to obtain with hostile snipers and about thirty German prisoners were captured. In the evening about 4.30p.m S.O.S. signals were sent up on both flanks of the battalion but any attempted hostile counter attack was stopped dead by our artillery barrage	
	Night of 8/9.6.17		Battalion was relieved by the 7th King's Own and the Battalion took up a position in reserve at BLUE LINE which ran in front of GRAND BOIS	
GRAND BOIS	10/6/17		Battalion remained in reserve on night of 10/11. 6.17. Battalion returned to Billets at OE ZON Camp	

Army Form C. 2118.

WAR DIARY
or
INTELLIGENCE SUMMARY.
(Erase heading not required.)

Instructions regarding War Diaries and Intelligence Summaries are contained in F. S. Regs. Part II. and the Staff Manual respectively. Title pages will be prepared in manuscript.

Place	Date	Hour	Summary of Events and Information	Remarks and references to Appendices
DE ZON CAMP	11/6/17		Battalion remained in Billets at DE ZON Camp. Result of operations 7-10/6/17. Two hundred prisoners eleven field guns and 20 machine guns were captured by the Battalion. Casualties 6 officers killed 16 officers wounded O.R. killed 21. Wounded 83. Missing 1.	
DE ZON CAMP	12/6/17		Battalion remained in Billets at DE ZON Camp. Training carried out under company arrangements.	
DE ZON Camp	13/6/17		Battalion remained in Billets at DE ZON Camp. Training carried out under company arrangements.	
DE ZON Camp	14/6/17		Battalion remained in Billets at DE ZON Camp. Training carried out under company arrangements.	
GRAND BOIS	15/6/17		Battalion relieved 1/4 King's Own R. Regt. in the BLUE & GREEN LINES running in front of GRAND BOIS & S.W. corner of ONRAET WOOD respectively.	
GRAND BOIS	16/6/17		Two coys withdrew from GREEN LINE to Old Bnt.7 front line from POPPY LANE to CHICORY LANE. Working parties found by the Battalion.	

Army Form C. 2118.

WAR DIARY
or
INTELLIGENCE SUMMARY.
(Erase heading not required.)

Instructions regarding War Diaries and Intelligence Summaries are contained in F. S. Regs., Part II. and the Staff Manual respectively. Title pages will be prepared in manuscript.

Place	Date	Hour	Summary of Events and Information	Remarks and references to Appendices
GRAND BOIS	17/6/17		Battalion remained in same position as on 16th instant. Working parties were provided by the battalion.	
GRAND BOIS	18/6/17		Battalion remained in same position as on 17th instant. Working parties were provided by the battalion.	
	Night of 18/19.6.17		Battalion relieved 9th R. Welsh Fusiliers on left subsector of IX Corps front. H.Q. at O15.b.3.7 [Sheet 28 40,000 BELGIUM part of FRANCE]	
	19/20.6.14		Battalion was relieved by 11th Royal Inniskilling Fusiliers	
DE ZON Camp	20.6.17		Battalion remained in billets at DE ZON Camp	
M.20.a.1.8 21.6.17 [Sheet 28 40,000]			Battalion moved from DE ZON Camp into Corps Reserve Area	
"	22.6.17		No 14 Battalion remained in Corps Reserve	
"	23.6.17		Battalion remained in Corps Reserve. Inspection of Battn by G.O.C. 19th Division	
"	24.6.17		Battalion remained in Corps Reserve. Battalion paraded for Divine Service	
"	25.6.17		Battalion remained in Corps Reserve. Training carried out under Coy arrangements	
"	26.6.17		Battalion remained in Corps Reserve. Training carried out under Coy arrangements	
"	27.6.17		Battalion remained in Corps Reserve. Training carried out under Coy arrangements	

WAR DIARY
or
INTELLIGENCE SUMMARY.
(Erase heading not required.)

Army Form C. 2118.

Place	Date	Hour	Summary of Events and Information	Remarks and references to Appendices
M 20 a.18. [Sheet 28 400e]	28.6.17 29.6.17.		Battalion remained in Corps Reserve. Training carried out under Coy arrangements. Battalion remained in Corps Reserve. Battalion practised in Tactical Scheme.	
"	30.6.17.		Battalion remained in Corps Reserve. ~~Battalion practised in tactical scheme~~	

McMahon
Major.
Cmdg. 9th Bn Gloucester Regt.

WAR DIARY or INTELLIGENCE SUMMARY

8 Gloster Regt
Army Form C. 2118
No C 23

23/11
4 Annexe

Place	Date	Hour	Summary of Events and Information	Remarks and references to Appendices
Sheet 28 No. 20. M 20 a 18.	1/9/17		Battalion remained in IX Corps reserve until 11-30 a.m. & then moved to camp at N16 C.9.3. Capt. Parker M.C. attached to 19th Div.	
N 16 c 9.3	2/9/17		Battalion relieved 8/Som L.I. in Ridge Defences. Bn. H.Q. ONRAET FARM. Special order of day issued. Military Medal to No 15924 Sergt P. Guillon, No 20619 Sergt H. Bull, No 1291 L/Cpl Q. Jennings, No 29536 Pte J. Paling, Ward No 23290 Pte P. Hannaford, No 12423 Pte A. Curwehr, No 11678 Pte E. Ireland No 30218 Pte N. Smart	
RIDGE DEFENCES	3/9/17		Battalion remained in same position as 2/9/17. Work & parties found	
"	4/9/17		Battalion remained in same position. Working parties found	
"	5/9/17		Battalion remained in Ridge Defences & continued to furnish Working parties	
"	6/9/17		Battalion remained in Ridge Defences & continued to furnish Working parties.	
"	7/9/17		Battalion relieved 10th NORGES Regt no right sub sector OOSTTAVERNE H.Q. IN DE STEERTE CAB.T 0.15.0.5.9.	
Right Sub Sector OOSTTAVERNE	8/9/17		Battalion in line. Work done. Strengthened & reforming trenches & wire.	
"	9/9/17		Battalion attacked enemy position E of OOSTTAVERNE. Objectives gained & firm established & prisoners taken. 2/Lt J.B. Bloomfield 24 E. Yorks killed	

WAR DIARY
or
INTELLIGENCE SUMMARY.
(Erase heading not required.)

Army Form C. 2118.

Place	Date	Hour	Summary of Events and Information	Remarks and references to Appendices
OOSTTAVERNE	10/9/17		Battalion in line. Positions gained night of 9/10 July improved throughout. Relieved by 9th Welsh Regt & moved back to OURAET WOOD — Ridge defence —	
Ridge Defence	11/9/17		Battalion relieved by 9th Cheshire Regt & moved back to ROSSIGNAL WOOD. Camps N=22a. Divisional Reserve.	
ROSSIGNAL WOOD	12/9/17		Battalion remained in billets, re-organising & cleaning up. Special	
"	12/9/17		order of the day awards. D.S.O. to Col. E.B. Umfreville MC. to S.E. Eastwood 2/Lt E. Vergo DCM. No 2664 CSM Brookfield. No 24901 Sergt Kennington W.	
"	13/9/17		Battalion remained in billets. Training & re-organising made toney compact 2/Lt J.H. Vaughan joined Bn 9th and 2/Lt H.F. Kent joined Bn 10th and 2/Lt F.J. R. Probert rejoined from hospital 9th inst. Guards at level crossings formed	
"	14/9/17		Battalion remained in billets. Training & re-organising under Coy arrangements	
"	15/9/17		Battalion remained in billets. Divine service held for all Denominations	
"	16/9/17		Battalion remained in billets, inspected by G.O.C. 57th Inf. Brigade.	
"	17/9/17		Battalion remained in billets, numerous working parties provided	
"	18/9/17		Battalion remained in billets, numerous working parties provided (about 8)	
"	19/9/17		Battalion remained in billets. Working parties forwarded (ditto)	

WAR DIARY
or
INTELLIGENCE SUMMARY.
(Erase heading not required.)

Army Form C. 2118.

Place	Date	Hour	Summary of Events and Information	Remarks and references to Appendices
ROSSIGNAL WOOD	20/4/17		Battalion remained in billets. Working parties founded (whole Bn).	Award -- Sgt Mannion MM224
"	21/4/17		Battalion remained in billets. Working parties founded.	-do- Sgt Mannion MM224
"	22/4/17		Battalion in billets. Divine Service held. Bn left camp 9 p.m. to relieve 9th K.O.R. Kane Regt in line at OOSTTAVERNE	
OOSTTAVERNE	23/4/17		Battalion in the line -- Work done :- Trenches improved & C.T. to 39th Div Command.	
"	24/4/17		Battalion in the line -- Improvements to trenches continued also C.T. 2/Lt Le Brun joined Bn. 2/Lt H.V. Levy wounded.	
"	25/4/17		Battalion in the line. Repair & improvements to trench & C.T. continued.	
"	26/4/17		Battalion in the line. Capt Morley, 2/Lt R Lighthorne, killed. Repair to trenches & work on C.T. continued.	
"	27/4/17		Battalion in the line. Work on trenches & C.T. continued.	
"	28/4/17		Battalion in the line. Enemy made determined raid on front line posts at 1.25 am with a "Sturm Truppe" & were repulsed with considerable loss. 2/Lt Kunkler joined Bn. Relieved in front line by 8th N STAFF Regt & moved to Ridge Defences. Batt Q ONRAET WOOD.	

Army Form C. 2118.

WAR DIARY
or
INTELLIGENCE SUMMARY.
(Erase heading not required.)

Place	Date	Hour	Summary of Events and Information	Remarks and references to Appendices
RIDGE DEFENCES, DOGTTAVERNE	29/4/17		Battalion in support. Bn relieved by 4th S. LANC Regt & moved back to Lilleke at LOCRE. Award: Capt M.A. JAMES awarded Military Cross.	
LOCRE	30/4/17		Battalion remained in huts. Re-organising under Coy arrangements.	
"	31/4/17		Battalion moved at 8am to support area "ROSSIGNAL WOOD" & remained in camp "Standing by".	

P.R. Whitehouse Lt Col
Comdg 8(S) Bn Gloucestershire Regt

E Glouc 6R

WAR DIARY
or
INTELLIGENCE SUMMARY.

Army Form C. 2118.

Vol 24

Place	Date	Hour	Summary of Events and Information	Remarks and references to Appendices
Rossignol Wood	1/8/17		Battn in Divl: Support. Very Wet all day.	
do	2/8/17		In Divl Support Area. Moved back to Doncaster Huts at 4 P.M.	
Doncaster Huts	2/8/17		In Reserve Area at DONCASTER HUTS, Bn moved at 4.30 to Support Area at S.P. 12 KEMMEL relieved 1st Bn KING'S OWN.	
KEMMEL	4.8.14		Bn in Support to 5 yrs 13th 10 Worcs: & N. STAFFS on with 10 R. WARWICKS at G.L.O.O.C. in support. Very wet all day, was shelled with M.V. gun at 4.30 pm to 8 pm	
KEMMEL	5/8/17		In support to 5th Bde. relieved 10th Worc. Regt in DENYS WOOD holding line E of GREEN WOOD A&B Coys front line C Coy support & D Coy Reserve. During relief S.O.S. signal was sent up by 10 Wore. during an attack on HOLLEBEKE. Casualties during relief 3 killed 12 wounded	2B
DENYS WOOD	6/8/17		Bn holding line E of GREENWOOD fairly quiet. 2/Lt Smyth returned from leave. HQrs of BEDFORD REGT reconnoitre line	224 M 4 sheets

8 Glouc. R.

Army Form C. 2118.

WAR DIARY
or
INTELLIGENCE SUMMARY.
(Erase heading not required.)

Instructions regarding War Diaries and Intelligence Summaries are contained in F. S. Regs., Part II. and the Staff Manual respectively. Title pages will be prepared in manuscript.

Place	Date	Hour	Summary of Events and Information	Remarks and references to Appendices
DENYS WOOD	1/8/19		Bn was relieved by 6th BEDFORD RGT: by Coys to RESERVE AREA at M.20.A.1.8. MAJ B THOMAS (wounded) + 2/Lt W V.SMITH (killed during relief).	
ST JEAN CAPPEL	8/8/19		Bn in RESERVE AREA, with 10 R.WAR. — 10th N.STAFF & 10th WORC. in reserve. 2/Lt VIRGO assumes duties 1 A/ADJT. Day spent in cleaning up	
JEAN CAPPEL	9/8/19		Bn in RESERVE AREA. Clothing refitting & general cleaning up.	
—do—	10/6/19		Bn in RESERVE AREA. Capt EMMET + 2/Lt POCKETT leave G.ENGLAND. TRANSPORT & DEPOT left for FROMENTEL	
FROMENTEL	11/8/19		Bn left at 4.30am — Train from BALLEUL & WIZERNES. Halt for meal marched to FROMENTEL, dinners en route. arrived 4 pm. 2/Lt McSCRIBER + SN WATSON joined for duty	
—do—	12/8/19		FROMENTEL. 2/Lt VAUGHAN & Court nt WISQUES. Inspected by ARMY CMDR. of 57th BDE	
—do—	13/8/19		—do—	
—do—	14/8/19		Court of Inquiry on PT SHAYLE (wounded) PRESIDENT, MAJ MCMAHON, Lt POPE & 2/Lt LE BRUN.	

WAR DIARY
or
INTELLIGENCE SUMMARY.
(Erase heading not required.)

Army Form C. 2118.

Place	Date	Hour	Summary of Events and Information	Remarks and references to Appendices
FROMEN-	15/8/17		At FROMENTEL. Inclined scheme for Platoon cmdrs	
TEL	16/8/17		do Scheme with troops carried out	
-	17/8/17		do Medal presentation by G.O.C 19th Division.	
-			Lt Col Umfreville D.S.O, Lt Eastwood M.C. 2/Lt Entwistle M.C. Cpl C.M.A Jarvis M.C.	
-			2 P.T. 6 R=1 D.C.M. 6 M.M. The butterfly cup "A" Coy was addressed by G.O.C.	
FROMEN-	18/8/17		At Fromentel: Bn preliminary heats in preparation for BDE sports	
TEL	19/8/17		do Bde sports held at VERVAL	
-	20/8/17		do Divisional sports held at L'ECALIBE	
-	21/8/17		do Point to Point (DIV) held near FROMENTEL	
-	22/8/17		do Moved into 563Bde area at LE WAAST	
LE WAAST	23/8/17		At LE WAAST Wet all day, men bathing at ECAULT cancelled	
-	24/8/17		do Buses provided for men bathing not available	
-	25/8/17		do 150 men sent to ECAULT to bathe	
-	26/8/17		do Competition on range, field shooting won by 16" Works Pl	
-	27/8/17		do One Field Gun + One Minenwerfer allotted to Bn	
-	28/8/17		do Bn moved by bus to LE NIEPPE area	

WAR DIARY
or
INTELLIGENCE SUMMARY.
(Erase heading not required.)

Army Form C. 2118.

Place	Date	Hour	Summary of Events and Information	Remarks and references to Appendices
LENIEPPE	29/8/17		LENIEPPE – Bn moved to the MERRIS area marching via HAZEBROUCK & STRAZEELE arrived in billets north of STRAZEELE at 1.45 pm.	
STRAZEELE	30/8/17		at STRAZEELE – All Motors troughs ? by lorry, arrived at 3 pm.	
STRAZEELE	31/8/17		at STRAZEELE. Dysentery contacts inspected in the Bn & U.S.A. M.G. examined there.	

Army Form C. 2118.

WAR DIARY
8(S) Battalion Gloucestershire Regt
INTELLIGENCE SUMMARY.
(Erase heading not required.)

WO 25

Place	Date	Hour	Summary of Events and Information	Remarks and references to Appendices
1917				
STRAZELLE	1-9-17		"D" Coy had use of range at NOOT BOOM. Battalion bathed at Bath near STRAZELLE	
	2-9-17		Divine Service for all denominations	
	3-9-17		Tactical Scheme exercised	
	4-9-17		New formation for attack practiced	
	5-9-17		Brigade exercised in New formation for attack. 2nd Lt. C.P. FLEMING joined Battalion for duty	
	6-9-17	9am	Marched to MONT NOIR Area and camped at M.20.a.1.8 (Map BELGIUM & FRANCE Sheet 28)	
MONT NOIR	7-9-17		Training under Company arrangements. Special training for rifle Grenadiers. C.O. and 3 Officers visited line to be taken over	
	8-9-17		Draft of 59 Other Ranks joined	
	9-9-17		Major D.J.B. McMAHON proceeded to 10th Battn Gloucestershire Regt for duty	M
	10-9-17		Battn practised New formation for attack	
	10-9-17		Training on on got out [?]	
	11-9-17	2pm	Battn moved to forward Area at BOIS CONFLUENT. Transport to SIEGE FARM	25. M. 4 sheets

Army Form C. 2118.

WAR DIARY
or
INTELLIGENCE SUMMARY.
(Erase heading not required.)

Place	Date	Hour	Summary of Events and Information	Remarks and references to Appendices
BOIS CONFLUENT	Sept 12th		Draft of 144 Other Ranks joined	
	13th	6pm	Moved into the line and took over the left sector of the 2nd Front in relief of 2nd N. Stafford Regt. and 10th Worcester Regt. 1 Coy in front line at posts from J.31.c.2.9. to J.31.a.75.76. 1 Company J.31.a.75.76. to I.36.d.9.5. 1 Company in close support and remaining Company in the CATERPILLAR.	
KLEIN ZILLEBEKE	14th		Enemy moderately quiet. Relieved at night by 13th Battn. Rifle Brigade and came out to BEAVER CORNER. (N.15.a.)	
BEAVER CAMP	15th		Day spent in cleaning up etc.	
	16th		New Attack formation rehearsed.	
	17th		Brigade rehearsed for New Attack formation. 2nd Lt. G.E. LE BRUN awarded Military Cross & C.S.M. TYE awarded D.C.M. in connection with operations on 31st July 1917.	
	18th		3 Coys preceded by bus to ST ELOI and relieved 13th Battn. Rifle Brigade. 1 Company at Camp N.9.d.8.5.	

WAR DIARY
or
INTELLIGENCE SUMMARY.
(Erase heading not required.)

Army Form C. 2118.

Place	Date	Hour	Summary of Events and Information	Remarks and references to Appendices
KLEIN ZILLEBEKE	Sept 19th		Enemy fairly active	
	20th	5.40 a.m.	Battalion participated in an offensive Zero hour 5.40 a.m. Left front line at points J.31.a.5.3 to J.31.a.25.00. First objective J.31.a.4 & J.31.a.15 reached with imperative ease and this line consolidated. An advance to final objective strong points and snipers dealt with. Objective at points J.32.c.25.35 & P.1.t.85.80 was eventually reached at 7 a.m. Enemy artillery barrage on original front & support lines very heavy. Casualties 2nd Lt R.E. KIMBER & 2nd Lt J.H. HUMPHREY Killed, Lieut F.J. NICHOLAS & 2nd Lt T.M. COLCUTT Wounded - Other Ranks 160 Killed, Missing & Wounded.	
	21st		Both our front line surrendered at intervals. Held line until enemy when Battalion was relieved by 7th South Lancs Regt and returned to BEAVER CORNER.	
BEAVER CAMP	22nd		Cleaning up Etc	
	23rd		Divine Service for all religions held in Camp.	

Army Form C. 2118.

WAR DIARY
or
INTELLIGENCE SUMMARY.
(Erase heading not required.)

Instructions regarding War Diaries and Intelligence Summaries are contained in F. S. Regs., Part II. and the Staff Manual respectively. Title pages will be prepared in manuscript.

Place	Date	Hour	Summary of Events and Information	Remarks and references to Appendices
BEAVER CAMP	Sept 24th		Training under Coy arrangements	
	25th		Adjutant and Coy Comdrs reconnoitred line.	
	26th		Training under Coy arrangements. Special training for Lewis Gunners and signallers.	
	27th		Battalion moved into the line and relieved 11th R Warwick Regt in the Right Sector of the Brigade front. Surplus personnel billeted at KEMMEL Shelters.	
LINE.	28th		Battalion in the line.	
	Night 28/9/		Readjustment of line. Three Companies in the line, one in reserve.	
	30.		Battalion in the line.	

R McM Meakin Lt Col.
Comdg 8(S) Batt. Gloucestershire Regt.

19   8 Gloucester R.   Army Form C. 2118

WAR DIARY
INTELLIGENCE SUMMARY
(Erase heading not required.) O/ C Gen. Res.   Vol 26

Instructions regarding War Diaries and Intelligence Summaries are contained in F.S. Regs., Part II. and the Staff Manual respectively. Title pages will be prepared in manuscript.

26.M.
4 sheets

Place	Date	Hour	Summary of Events and Information	Remarks and references to Appendices
SHREWSBURY FOREST	1.XI.17		Lieut L. B. Pope joined and is present at KEMMEL SHELTERS from F.A.	
	2.XI.17		2/Lieut P.H. Black reported his arrival for duty with the Batt. 2/Lieut J. May's left for F.A.	
			On orders 15 & 3rd Oct the Battalion was relieved in the line by 10th Inniskilling Rifles & moved into Support at HILL 60	
HILL 60	2.XI.17		Capt. H. Allen proceeded on leave	
	3.XI.17		2/Lieut J.H. Batey joined and took at KEMMEL SHELTERS for duty with the Battalion	
	4.XI.17		In the line. Training of reinforcements at KEMMEL SHELTERS.	
	5.XI.17		Relieved by 1st Royal North Lancs R. & moved to Camp at N.6.a.3.3. W.g. BOIS CARRÉ. Capt. K.T. McLeod (R/U.S. F. Rifles) brought to Battn HQrs for instruction in duty in a Battn in line	
BOIS CARRÉ	6.XI.17		Parades under Coy arrangements and baths	
	7.XI.17		Training, Inf. Coys and Lewis gun - all day	
	8.XI.17		Major A.B. Spens of 1st Batt assumed duties of 2 i/c Command of the Batt. from 2/Lt S. Holman 2nd i/c Comd of Batt.	
	9.XI.17		New Sector reconnoitred by O.C. Coys	

A6945   Wt. W1422/M1160   350,000   12/16   D.D. & L.   Forms/C./2118/14.

WAR DIARY
or
INTELLIGENCE SUMMARY.
(Erase heading not required.)

Army Form C. 2118.

Place	Date	Hour	Summary of Events and Information	Remarks and references to Appendices
Bois Carré			The following officers proceeded to gain experience of work of higher rank. Lieut. E.J. Tate, 2/Lt S.M. Cairns, 2/Lt N.M. Clarico, 2/Lt G.W. Vize M.C. Advance party of 1 officer & 4 NCOs per Company proceed to the Line	(19) OK. W. A. 599 d/g. 10. 17
"	11.X.17		The Bath. Sat. in the open Right Sector of Right Brigade Front (BELGIAN WOOD — HESSIAN WOOD — CANAL). Relief by 6th Cheshire Regiment in the Line & 1/15 Cheshire in reserve. Battalion Yeomanry Bath. Relieving Regiment	
			Rops at Trunk Stump & at Koumonly 30, and the personnel	
Line	12.X.17		moved to KEMMEL SHELTERS	
"	13.X.17		Training & recreation & reconnaissance at KEMMEL	
"	14.X.17		2/Lt T. Bishop M.C. rejoined the Battalion for duty. Lieut. E.W. Hingston rejoined from leave. Battalion relieved in Front Line by 10th Worcestershire Regt & moved to STOIL BANK Dugouts	
Stoil Bank	15.X.17		Personal repairs the Battalion	
"	16.X.17		Working parties. Capt. W. Allen rejoined from leave	
"	17.X.17		2/Lt R.B. Churchill rejoined from Course. The Battn relieved the 10th Warwicks in the Right in Front line on Oct 17/18th Oct	
Hessian Wood	18.X.17		Capt. W. Wright M.C. & Lt R.E. Spoon & 2/Lt C. Marshal joined Bn for duty	

WAR DIARY
or
INTELLIGENCE SUMMARY.
(Erase heading not required.)

Army Form C. 2118.

Place	Date	Hour	Summary of Events and Information	Remarks and references to Appendices
HESSIAN WOOD	1917 19/10		Bn. relieved on night 19/20 Oct by 9th Welsh Regt. and moved to Camp at BOIS CARRÉ. 2/Lt. Carrick Ltd rejoined from Course.	
BOIS CARRÉ	20/10		Working parties. Lieut. J.D. Glasgow proceeded on leave.	
"	21/10		Working parties. Lt. Col. R.B. Crompton DSO proceeded on leave. Capt. L.A. Emmet attached to 57th Bde HQrs. Military Cross awarded to T/Lt. T. Seivy, 2/Lt. W.M. Chung and T/2/Lt. S.H. Watson	
"	22/10		Working parties & training	
"	23/10		Capt. B. Tate proceeded on leave	
"	24/10		Working parties & training	
"	25/10		Do. — Lt. B.E. Inchcrow MC proceeded on leave	
"	26/10		Do. — 2/Lt. E.H. Green & 2/Lt. C.A. Hutchins rejoined from Course. 2/Lt. L.B. McLeod from 2nd Army Rest Camp	
"	27/10		Moved into Rossignol Camp (N22 a 2.5) in Bde Reserve Area	
ROSSIGNOL	28/10		Training	

Army Form C. 2118.

WAR DIARY
or
INTELLIGENCE SUMMARY.
(Erase heading not required.)

Place	Date	Hour	Summary of Events and Information	Remarks and references to Appendices
ROSSIGNOL CAMP	1917 29/10		Training	
	30/10		Route march (about 5 miles) and practice of Lt. C.A. Hutchins & Capt. & Adjt. S. Parker M.C. left the Bttn. to join the R.F.C. 2nd Lieut. S. Bayne incurred on leave.	
"	31/10		Training. Lieut. F.D. Glasgow returned from leave.	

[signature] Major
Comdg 8th (S) Bn Gloucestershire Regt.

WAR DIARY
8th (S) Bn Gloucestershire Regt
INTELLIGENCE SUMMARY

Army Form C. 2118.

Place	Date	Hour	Summary of Events and Information	Remarks and references to Appendices
	1917			
ROSSIGNOL CAMP	1.XI		Battalion continued training. Major H.B. Shear evacuated sick and Capt. H. Allen assumed command of the Battalion	
"	2.XI		Battalion continued training. Lieut. Johnston (sick) relieved by Lieut. E.H. Pace. 11.S.O. Moss. Major J. Ryan DSO 6th (Welch Yeomanry) Rt M Welsh Regt took over temporary command of the Battalion	
"	3.XI		Battalion continued training. Capt. E.B. Pope returned from leave.	
"	4.XI		Battalion relieved 7/N. Lancs. Regt in Right Support Sub-Sector (SPOIL BANK and GASTERS CLIFF). 2/Lt F.J. Madlem evacuated to F.A.	
SPOIL BANK	5.XI		Battalion in Support Right Sub-Sector.	
"	6.XI		Reconnaissance Party of 1 Officer and 2 N.C. Officer Cpls proceeded to Front Line	
"	7.XI		On ngt of 7/8 Nov Battalion relieved 10/p.w.r. Regt in R. Sub-Sector (HESSIAN WOOD) Front Line. 2/Lieut I. Ewing M.C. evacuated to F.A.	
HESSIAN WOOD	8.XI		Battalion in Right Sub-Sector Front Line	
"	9.XI		Battalion relieved on ngt 9/10th November by 11/R Warwick Regt	

27.11
H.Week

Army Form C. 2118.

WAR DIARY
8th (S) B. Gloucestershire Regt.
INTELLIGENCE SUMMARY.
(Erase heading not required.)

Place	Date	Hour	Summary of Events and Information	Remarks and references to Appendices
	1917.			
HESSINWOOD	9 XI		and one Company of 6/Bedford Regt, and proceeded to camp at Bois Carré. Lt. Col. Umfreville D.S.O. returned from leave.	
BOIS CARRÉ	10 XI		Battalion proceeded by lorries to billets in MERRIS area.	
MERRIS	11 XI		Battalion remained in billets in MERRIS area. Lieut A.H.Driden MC rejoined. Lieut. B.C.Lockwood MC returned from leave. Capt B. Temple proceeded on leave. 2/Lieuts. H.H.Beaven and C.F.Fleming left to attend courses.	
— " —	12 XI		Battalion proceeded by march route and tram to billets in BLARINGHEM — MONT D'HIVER road area.	
BLARINGHEM	13 XI		Training commenced in BLARINGHEM — MONT D'HIVER road area. Major J.J. Tynan D.S.O. rejoined 6/Wilts Regt.	
— " —	14 XI		Section training and Specialists under Coy. arrangements. 2/Lt. D.S. Chantrell left the Battalion to join R.E. Corps. 2/Lt. G. Ellis evacuated to F.A.	
— " —	15 XI		Training of Companies and Specialists continued in BLARINGHEM — MONT D'HIVER road area.	

Army Form C. 2118.

WAR DIARY
or
INTELLIGENCE SUMMARY.
(Erase heading not required.)

Place	Date	Hour	Summary of Events and Information	Remarks and references to Appendices
BLARINGHEM	16 XI		Training of Companies and Specialists continued in BLARINGHEM - MONT D'HIVER road area. Capts. and Acgt. M. Carter McC returned from leave.	
"	17 XI		do	
"	18 XI		do	
"	19 XI		do	
"	20 XI		do	
"	21 XI		do 2/Lt. L.B. Suchor reported from L.A.	
"	22 XI		do Lt. Col. R.T. Beasley joined the Battalion. 2/Lt W. Vincent returned for duty. 2/Lt L.B. Suchor and Lt Langham proceeded on leave.	
"	23 XI		do	
"	24 XI		do Advance party proceeded by lorry to erect camp near CORMETTE.	
"	25 XI		Sunday - Church parade and Inspections for musketry.	
"	26 XI		Companies marched to Camp to E. of CORMETTE. Signalling & Gunners and Rifle Bombers continued training in BLARINGHEM - MONT D'HIVER road area.	

Army Form C. 2118.

WAR DIARY
8th (S) Bn Gloucestershire Regt.
or INTELLIGENCE SUMMARY.

(Erase heading not required.)

Instructions regarding War Diaries and Intelligence Summaries are contained in F. S. Regs., Part II. and the Staff Manual respectively. Title pages will be prepared in manuscript.

Place	Date	Hour	Summary of Events and Information	Remarks and references to Appendices
BLARINGHEM	1917. 27.XI		Musketry on range (200yards) at TILQUES. 2/Lt. H.H.H.Beaver rejoined from Course.	
"	28.XI		Musketry on range at TILQUES. After firing Companies returned by march route to BLARINGHEM. Capt. B. Temple returned from leave.	
"	29.XI		Marched to new billets at WARDRECQUES.	
WARDRECQUES	30.XI		Training of Companies and Specialists continued in WARDRECQUES area.	

R.B. Winterbotham Lt. Col:
Comm'g. 8th Gloster Regt.

Army Form C. 2118.

WAR DIARY
8th (S) B: Gloucestershire Regt.
INTELLIGENCE-SUMMARY.
(Erase heading not required.)

VII 28

28.11.
6 sheets

Place	Date	Hour	Summary of Events and Information	Remarks and references to Appendices
WARDRECQUES	1917 Dec 1		Training of Companies and Specialists continued in the WARDRECQUES area. 2/Lt. G.B.Ellis rejoined from Hospital.	
"	" 2		Do.	
"	" 3		Do. 2nd Lieuts. H.A Butters & W.S. Vincent M.C. evacuated to Field Ambulance.	
"	" 4		Training of Companies and Specialists continued in the WARDRECQUES area.	
"	" 5		Battalion marched to ST. OMER and entrained for new area.	
BIENVILLERS	" 6		Battalion detrained at MONDICOURT and marched to BIENVILLERS.	
"	" 7		Battalion proceeded by bus and march route to camp near ETRICOURT.	
ETRICOURT	" 8		Battalion moved into Support Tr. of RIBECOURT on night 8/9th Dec.	
RIBECOURT	" 9		In the line. Transport and Depot moved to FINS.	
"	" 10		Do. Moved to trenches in front of RIBECOURT.	
"	" 11		Do. Lt. Col. R.L. Beasley left to take temporary command of 1/E.Lanc.R.	
"	" 12		Do. 2/Lieuts. J.H.Vaughan & L.B. McLeod rejoined from leave. 2/Lieut. T.M. Calvert rejoined from England.	

Army Form C. 2118.

8th (S) Bn. Gloucestershire Regt.

WAR DIARY
INTELLIGENCE SUMMARY.

(Erase heading not required.)

Instructions regarding War Diaries and Intelligence Summaries are contained in F. S. Regs., Part II. and the Staff Manual respectively. Title pages will be prepared in manuscript.

Place	Date	Hour	Summary of Events and Information	Remarks and references to Appendices
WARDRECQUES	1917 Dec. 1		Training of Companies and Specialists continued in the WARDRECQUES area.	
"	" 2			
"	" 3		2nd Lieuts. H.A. Batters + Mr. S. Vincent M.C. evacuated to Field Ambulance. 2/Lt. G. Ellis rejoined from hospital Pt.	
"	" 4		Training of Companies and Specialists continued in the WARDRECQUES area.	
"	" 5		Battalion marched to ST. OMER and entrained for new area.	
BIENVILLERS	" 6		Battalion detrained at MONDICOURT and marched to BIENVILLERS S.	
"	" 7		Battalion proceeded by bus and march route to camp near ETRICOURT.	
ETRICOURT	" 8		Battalion moved into Support Tr. of RIBECOURT on night 8/9th Dec.	
RIBECOURT	" 9		In the line. Transport and Depot moved to FINS.	
"	" 10		Do. Moved to trenches in front of RIBECOURT.	
"	" 11		Lt. Col. R.L. Beasley left to take temporary command of 1/E.Lancs R.	
"	" 12		2/Lieuts. J.Vaughan & L.B. McLeod rejoined from leave. 2/Lieut. T.M. Calvert rejoined from England.	

Army Form C. 2118.

WAR DIARY
8th (S) Bn Gloucestershire Regt
INTELLIGENCE SUMMARY

(Erase heading not required.)

Place	Date	Hour	Summary of Events and Information	Remarks and references to Appendices
RIBECOURT	1917 Dec 13		In the line. 2/Lt. G.R. Le Brun MC left the Battalion to attend Course.	
"	" 14		Do.	
"	" 15		Battalion relieved by Irish Rifles & RIBECOURT.	
"	" 16		In the line.	
"	" 17		Do.	
HAVRINCOURT	" 18		Battalion marched to camp in HAVRINCOURT WOOD.	
"	" 19		Battalion rested and cleaned up in camp. Capt. M.A. Brown ME proceeded on leave to U.K.	
"	" 20		Battalion took over trenches in VALLEY SUPPORT. Transport and Depot moved to NEUVILLE.	
LINE	" 21		In the line. Major E.W. Butler joined the Battalion and assumed the duties of Second in Command.	
"	" 22		Battalion relieved the 9th Bn. R Welch Fusiliers in front line. Capt. E.B. Pope assumed temporary command of "A" Coy.	
"	" 23		Battalion in KHIBER TRENCH.	
"	" 24			

Army Form C. 2118.

WAR DIARY
8th (S) Bn Gloucestershire Regt.
INTELLIGENCE SUMMARY.

(Erase heading not required.)

"Instructions regarding War Diaries and Intelligence Summaries are contained in F. S. Regs., Part II. and the Staff Manual respectively. Title pages will be prepared in manuscript."

Place	Date	Hour	Summary of Events and Information	Remarks and references to Appendices
RIBECOURT	1917 Dec 13		In the line. 2/Lt. G.P. Le Brun MC left the Battalion to attend Course.	
"	" 14		Do.	
"	" 15		Battalion returned to trenches Right of RIBECOURT.	
"	" 16		In the line.	
"	" 17		Do.	
HAVRINCOURT	" 18		Battalion marched to camp in HAVRINCOURT WOOD.	
"	" 19		Battalion rested and cleaned up in camp. Capt. M.A. Johnson MC proceeded on leave to U.K.	
"	" 20		Battalion took over trenches in VALLEY SUPPORT. Transport and Depôt moved to NEUVILLE.	
LINE.	" 21		In the line.	
"	" 22		Major E.W. Butler joined the Battalion and assumed the duties of Second in Command.	
"	" 23		Battalion relieved the 9th Bn: R. Welch Fusiliers in front line. Capt. E.B. Tope assumed temporary command of "A" Coy.	
"	" 24		Battalion in KAIZER TRENCH.	

Army Form C. 2118.

WAR DIARY
8th (S) Bn Gloucestershire Regt
INTELLIGENCE SUMMARY.
(Erase heading not required.)

* Instructions regarding War Diaries and Intelligence Summaries are contained in F. S. Regs., Part II. and the Staff Manual respectively. Title pages will be prepared in manuscript.

Place	Date 1917	Hour	Summary of Events and Information	Remarks and references to Appendices
KAISER TRENCH	Dec 25		Battalion moved to "Support" in FORK AVENUE.	
FORK AVENUE	" 26		In the line.	
"	" 27		Do. 2nd Lieut. C.T. Fleming rejoined from Course.	
LINE	" 28		Battalion relieved the 10th Bn Worcestershire Regt. in left Sub-Sector of Brigade Front. Lieut S.H. Watson M.C. to stage Course.	
"	" 29		In the line. Hon. Lieut & Q.M. L. Evans proceeded on leave to U.K.	
"	" 30		Do. 2/Lt. L. H. Carrick returned from Course.	
"	" 31		Do.	

1.1.18.

R.P.Whitwick Lt Col.
Comdg 8th Glouc. Regt.

Army Form C. 2118.

WAR DIARY

8th (S) Bn. Gloucestershire Regt:
INTELLIGENCE SUMMARY.

(Erase heading not required.)

Instructions regarding War Diaries and Intelligence Summaries are contained in F. S. Regs., Part II. and the Staff Manual respectively. Title pages will be prepared in manuscript.

Place	Date	Hour	Summary of Events and Information	Remarks and references to Appendices
KAISER TRENCH.	1917 Dec 25		Battalion moved to Support in FORK AVENUE.	
FORK AVENUE	„ 26		In the line.	
„	„ 27		Do. 2nd Lieut. C.T. Fleming rejoined from Course.	
LINE.	„ 28		Battalion relieved the 10th Bn Worcestershire Regt. & 11th Sub- Sector of Brigade Front. Lieut S.H. Watson & 2nd Lieut R Cayzer	
„	„ 29		In the line. Hon. Lieut. & Q.M. R. Evans proceeded on leave to U.K.	
„	„ 30		Do. 2/Lt. L.H. Carrick rejoined from Course.	
„	„ 31		Do.	

1.1.18.

40 copies BRH
Hpt. tr MColl
McMurtrie. the Lt Col:
Comdg 8th Glouc: Regt.

WAR DIARY
or
INTELLIGENCE SUMMARY.

(Erase heading not required.)

Army Form C. 2118.

8th (S) Batn. Gloucestershire Regt.

VA 29

Place	Date	Hour	Summary of Events and Information	Remarks and references to Appendices
LINE	1/1/18	—	Battalion in the line. Left Subsector of Brigade Front.	
"	2/1/18	—	— do —	
"	3/1/18	—	— do —	
"	4/1/18	—	— do —	Captain H. Allen wounded.
"	5/1/18	—	Battalion relieved by 9th Welsh Regt. and moved back into HAVRINCOURT WOOD.	
HAVRINCOURT WOOD	6/1/18	—	Battalion in HAVRINCOURT WOOD. Cleaning up and refitting.	
"	7/1/18	—	— do —	
"	8/1/18	—	— do —	
LINE	9/1/18	—	Moved into the HINDENBURG LINE in Reserve.	
"	10/1/18	—	Battalion in reserve.	
"	11/1/18	—	Relieved 7th E. Lanc. Regt. in Brigade Right Subsector. In front line.	
"	12/1/18	—	— do —	
"	13/1/18	—	— do —	
"	14/1/18	—	— do —	
"	15/1/18	—	Lieut. Col. R.M.T. Unfreville DSO proceeded to 5th Corps Reinforcement Camp. 19th Batt Mining	

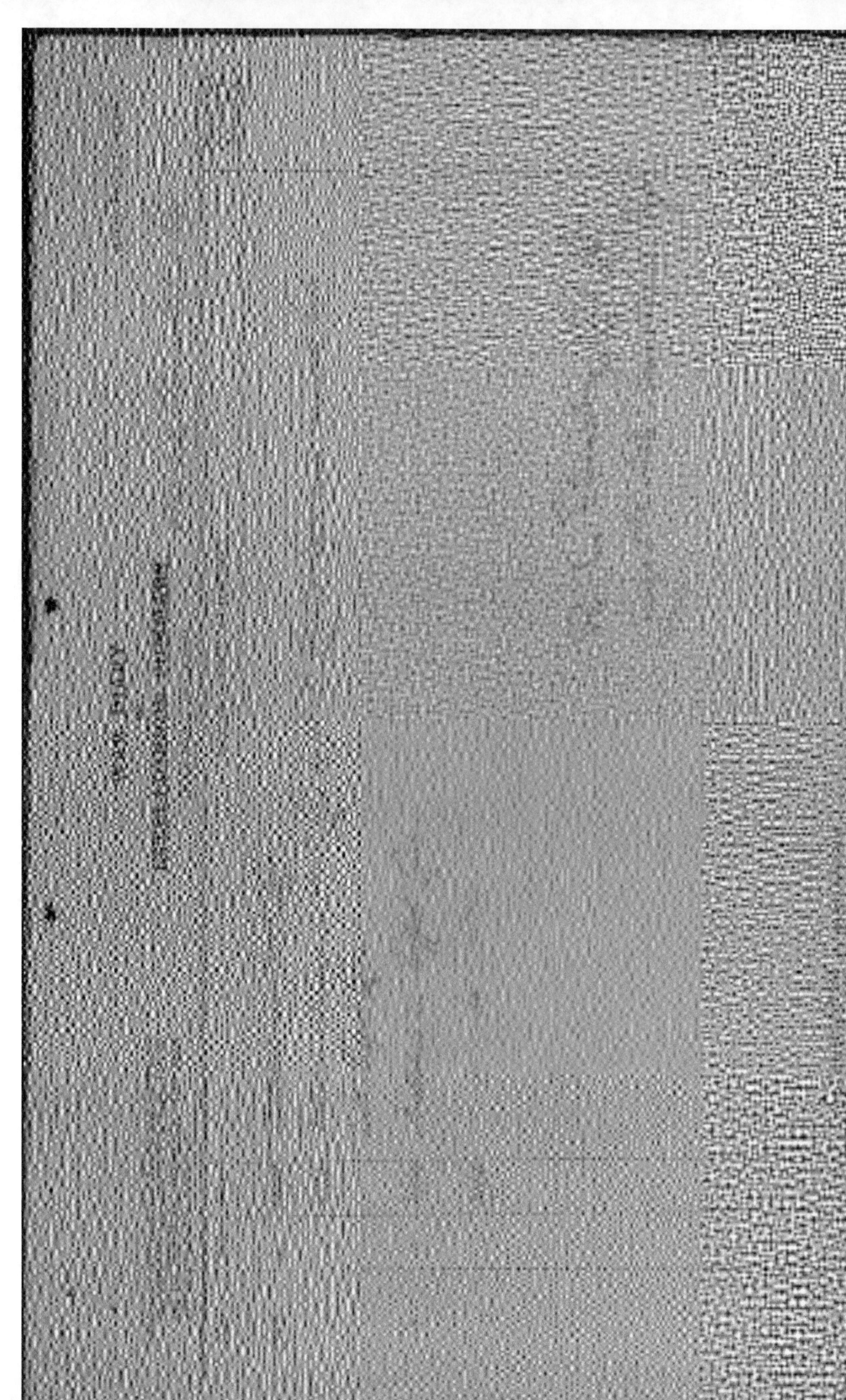

Army Form C. 2118.

WAR DIARY
or
INTELLIGENCE SUMMARY.
(Erase heading not required.)

Instructions regarding War Diaries and Intelligence Summaries are contained in F. S. Regs., Part II. and the Staff Manual respectively. Title pages will be prepared in manuscript.

5th Gloucest R

Vol 30

30. 11.
2 sheets

Place	Date	Hour	Summary of Events and Information	Remarks and references to Appendices
LINE	1/2/18		Battalion in Support Line	
"	2/2/18		Relieved 7th Batty N. Lancs Regt in Front Line.	
"	3/2/18		Battalion in Front Line.	
"	4/2/18		------do------	
"	5/2/18		------do------	
"	6/2/18		Battalion relieved in Front Line by 6th Bt Wilts Regt and moved back to HAVRINCOURT WOOD (EASTWOOD CAMP)	
HAVRINCOURT WOOD	7/2/18		Battalion in HAVRINCOURT WOOD (EASTWOOD CAMP)	
"	8/2/18		------do------	
"	9/2/18		------do------	
LINE	10/2/18		Battalion relieved 6th Bt Wilts Regt in OUILLET TRENCH	
"	11/2/18		Battalion in Front Line	
"	12/2/18		------do------	
"	13/2/18		------do------	
"	14/2/18		Relieved by 7th Batn. Royal Fusiliers and moved back to Reserve Area.	
BEAUCOURT ALMA CAMP.	15/2/18		Battalion cleaning up in ALMA CAMP.	
"	16/2/18		Battalion moved to JERICHO CAMP.	
JERICHO CAMP.	17/2/18		Divine Service for C of E and R. Catholics.	

Army Form C. 2118.

WAR DIARY
or
INTELLIGENCE SUMMARY.
(Erase heading not required.)

Place	Date	Hour	Summary of Events and Information	Remarks and references to Appendices
JERICHO CAMP.	18/3/18		Training by Companies in the vicinity of JERICHO CAMP as per Programme submitted to 57th Brigade.	
"	19/3/18		do	
"	20/3/18		do	
"	21/3/18		Battalion Route March.	
"	22/3/18		Training was carried out by Companies	
"	23/3/18		do	
"	24/3/18		Church Parade for all Denominations. Owing to rain Lectures were given to Companies. Training continued after 11AM.	
"	25/3/18		Training by Companies	
"	26/3/18		Battalion took part in 19th Divisional Scheme.	
"	27/3/18		Training by Companies	

Whitfield Lieut Col.
Comdg: 8th/3rd Gloucestershire Regt.

57th Brigade.
19th Division.

1/8th BATTALION

GLOUCESTERSHIRE REGIMENT

APRIL 1918.

57/9
Army Form C. 2118.
8th Bn Gloucestershire Regt Vol 32

WAR DIARY or INTELLIGENCE SUMMARY.

(Erase heading not required.)

32.M.
3 sheets

Place	Date	Hour	Summary of Events and Information	Remarks and references to Appendices
8th Bn Gloucestershire Regiment	1/4/18		The Battalion relieved the Australians in front of MESSINES.	
	2/4/18		Battalion in front line trenches.	
	3/4/18		do	
	4/4/18		do	
	5/4/18		do	
	6/4/18		do	
	7/4/18		do	
	8/4/18		do	
	9/4/18		do	
	10/4/18		do	
			3.30AM Enemy put up a very heavy barrage which lasted about 5 hours. This followed by a very heavy attack, which resulted in the battalion being out flanked and compelled to fall back to a line traversing STINKING FARM.	
	11/4/18		The 19th Division counter-attacked and the 8th Division (19 & 57 Bde) in support.	
	12/4/18		Units of the 9th Brigade were relieved and took up a position in the Army line between DAYLIGHT CORNER and NEUVE-EGLISE.	
	13/4/18.		Battalion remained in same position	
	14/4/18		Battalion still in same position, but was relieved about midnight and moved back to Rossignol Huts. Battalion Headquarters near SIFES FARM.	

WAR DIARY
or
INTELLIGENCE SUMMARY.

Army Form C. 2118.

(Erase heading not required.)

Instructions regarding War Diaries and Intelligence Summaries are contained in F. S. Regs., Part II. and the Staff Manual respectively. Title pages will be prepared in manuscript.

Place	Date	Hour	Summary of Events and Information	Remarks and references to Appendices
	15/4		Battalion remained at Roggignol HUTS.	
	16/4		The Battalion fell back to trenches near BEAVER CORNER in HUTS.	
	17/4		Remained in same position. Slight enemy shelling.	
	18/4		Orders were received from Brigade to commence to entrain. The Battalion came back to a field near WIPPENHOEK Siding about 2 miles E of ABEELE.	
	19/4		Remained in same position.	
	20/4		do Marching Orders were received from Brigade to move to PROVEN Area on the 21st.	
	21/4		The Battalion moved to the PROVEN Area in PIGEON CAMP.	
	22/4		do	
	23/4		Companies were at the disposal of Coy Commanders for training & reorganization.	
	24/4		Training has carried out under Company arrangement.	
	25/4		Battalion furnished a working party of 400 ranks for work on aerodrome East of POPERINGHE. Orders were received to be prepared	
			to move in 1 hours notice.	

Army Form C. 2118.

WAR DIARY
or
INTELLIGENCE SUMMARY.
(Erase heading not required.)

Instructions regarding War Diaries and Intelligence Summaries are contained in F. S. Regs., Part II. and the Staff Manual respectively. Title pages will be prepared in manuscript.

Place	Date	Hour	Summary of Events and Information	Remarks and references to Appendices
	26/4		At about 3 pm the battalion received orders to move and went into reserve at OUDERDOM.	
	27/4		The battalion moved back to TUNNELLERS CAMP and under orders to move in 15 minutes.	
	28/4		Battalion in TUNNELLERS CAMP	
	29/4		do	
	30/4		About 9.45am orders were received for the battalion to move forthwith to G. H. Q.	

W. C. Vere
Major
8th (S) Bn Gloucestershire Regiment.

19th Division.
57th Infantry Brigade.

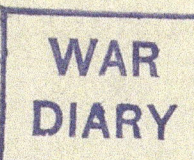

8th BATTALION

THE GLOUCESTERSHIRE REGIMENT

MARCH 1918.

Army Form C. 2118.

WAR DIARY
or
INTELLIGENCE SUMMARY.
(Erase heading not required.)

8 Gloucester R. Vol 31

Place	Date	Hour	Summary of Events and Information	Remarks and references to Appendices
JERICHO CAMP	1/3/18		Training was carried out under Company arrangements in the vicinity of camp.	
"	2/3/18		The Battalion paraded at 3.30pm and took part in 19th Divisional Scheme.	
"	3/3/18		Divine Service for all denominations.	
"	4/3/18		Training under Company arrangements as per Programme of Training.	
"	5/3/18		Coy. to Attack Scheme, as per Programme of Training. Lecture was given to all Officers of the Batt (not at T.M.P.S) Camp. 7 Officers and 7 Serjts were detailed to attend.	
"	6/3/18		Battalion provided 300 O. Ranks working party in the Battalion zone. Renovation of dugouts. Remainder worked at the disposal of Company Commanders.	
"	7/3/18		Battalion moved to SALAMANCA CAMP (O 10.c.3.9)	
SALAMANCA CAMP R.	8/3/18		Tactical Scheme was carried out by the battalion.	
"	9/3/18		Training was carried out under Company arrangements in vicinity of Camp.	
"	10/3/18		Divine Service for all Denominations.	
"	11/3/18		Training was carried out under Company arrangements.	

Army Form C. 2118.

WAR DIARY
or
INTELLIGENCE SUMMARY.
(Erase heading not required.)

Place	Date	Hour	Summary of Events and Information	Remarks and references to Appendices
SALAMANCA CAMP	12/3/18		The Battalion paraded at 7am for test on the Third System.	
	13/3/18		Training was carried out in accordance with training programme submitted to Brigade. Draft of 51 ORs joined the Battalion.	
	14/3/18		Training was carried out under Company arrangement	
	15/3/18		The Battalion paraded at 7.30AM for test on the Second System.	
	16/3/18		The Battalion carried out a Tactical Scheme.	
	17/3/18		Divine Services for all denominations.	
	18/3/18		The Battalion paraded at 7.30am for test on Second System.	
	19/3/18		Training under Company arrangements	
	20/3/18		Conference was at the disposal of General Commander.	
	21/3/18		The Battalion "Stood to" at 5.30 am and moved to assembly positions near VELU WOOD at 1 pm. and secretly attacked the billeting of DOIGNIES at 7pm.	
In the Line	22/3/18		The Battalion issued to 154 Bde as emergency command from 12.1 am. Orders was received by front companies districts from 154 Bde to advance on DOIGNIES at 4 am after suffering casualties. The original battalion were reserved. This was two misleading and later ment for information lot 8 Gloucester.	

WAR DIARY
or
INTELLIGENCE SUMMARY.

(Erase heading not required.)

Army Form C. 2118.

Instructions regarding War Diaries and Intelligence Summaries are contained in F. S. Regs., Part II. and the Staff Manual respectively. Title pages will be prepared in manuscript.

Place	Date	Hour	Summary of Events and Information	Remarks and references to Appendices
	22/3/18		Enemy made 3 separate attempts to counter-attack, and each time was beaten back but heavy loss by MG and rifle fire, but continued to shell Ervillers trenches well directed fire. Our Artillery did not respond to S.O.S. at all, and enemy aeroplanes were flying very low over trenches using MG's on men continuously all day. Favourable targets for tanks were our trenches in the Air. The Balloon Brigade	
	23/3/18		About 7.30 am left flank withdrew quickly leaving the Batts. in the Air. The Batln. Reserve was forced to do the same & was fought a new Guard Action. Machine Gun collapse of the left allowed enemy to get into VELU WOOD. The march from VELU WOOD being quickly and the Brigade was kept from Cahon by pushing up a Company of Gloucesters. Villemoeles in rear of VELU WOOD where they were able to stop the Enemy in the scope, and undoubtedly warned a battery of 18 Pow (2 Ohs.) which was in action in the open firing with open sights on the Enemy advancing over the ridge on the right, all 6th guns which the 18th Gloucester withdrew to BANCOURT, all wounded brought back leaving cases not collected.	
	24/3/18		The Battalion left Combat Sam to hold a reserve line outside of the BAPAUME—CAMBRAI Road about 1 mile E of BANCOURT. Battalion withdrew about 8 pm through BAPAUME closely pressed by the enemy and re-organised at GREVILLERS.	
	25/3/18		Enemy attacked 4th Durham 19th Divn fought a Rear Guard Action from GREVILLERS through IRLES and MIRAUMONT to a line PUISEUX — ACHIET-LE-PETIT	
	26/3/18		Rear Guard Action continued to a line HEBUTERNE — BUCQUOY which was handed over to the early morning and later 19th Divn became stour warre between BAYENCOURT and FONQUEVILLERS.	

Army Form C. 2118.

WAR DIARY
or
INTELLIGENCE SUMMARY.

(Erase heading not required.)

Instructions regarding War Diaries and Intelligence Summaries are contained in F. S. Regs., Part II. and the Staff Manual respectively. Title pages will be prepared in manuscript.

Place	Date	Hour	Summary of Events and Information	Remarks and references to Appendices
	27/3/18		Battalion in Support to ANZACS before FONQUEVILLERS. Enemy held up by fresh troops.	
	28/3/18		The Battalion entrained to neighbourhood of DOULLENS. Casualties Killed 2 offrs 29 ORs. Wounded 9 offrs. 169 OR. Missing 4 offrs. 140 ORs.	
	29/3/18		Entrained for STRAZEELE	
	30/3/18		Battalion proceeded by bus to ROSSIGNOL CAMP.	
ROSSIGNOL CAMP.	31/3/18		Battalion took over line in front of MESSINES.	

Reeve Buxton Major for Lieut. Col.
Comdg. 8" (S) 3" Gloucester Regt.

24/3/18.

The words "1 mile E of Barcourt" should read presumably "1 mile E of Bapaume" (See 57". Bde diary under 24". March and Appendix 10 in 57". Bde file for March 1918.)

[signature]

26/1/26.

277

WO 95/??? 2

May 1915

WAR DIARY
or
INTELLIGENCE SUMMARY.
(Erase heading not required.)

Army Form C. 2118.

8 & 9. 3rd Gloucestershire Regiment

33.11
6 sheets

Place	Date	Hour	Summary of Events and Information	Remarks and references to Appendices
	May 1st/18	9.00	The Battalion in Corps Reserve SE of POPERINGHE.	
	2/5/18		............do............	
	3/5/18		The Battalion relieved the 39th Composite Brigade in the DICKEBUSH line.	
	4/5/18		In the line at DICKEBUSH.	
	5/5/18		The Battalion moved back to the SWISS LINE. Battalion HQ. Farm at H.27.6.18.	
	6/5/18		Battalion again moved to a position at BUSSEBOOM.	
	7/5/18		In reserve at BUSSEBOOM.	
	8/5/18		Battalion moved to a position in reserve near ONTARIO CAMP.	
	9/5/18		In reserve near ONTARIO CAMP.	
	10/5/18		In reserve at BUSSEBOOM.	
	11/5/18		——do——	
	12/5/18		Battalion was relieved and moved back to TUNNELLERS CAMP.	
TUNNELLERS CAMP	13/5/18		In TUNNELLERS CAMP. Cleaning up etc.	
—do—	14/5/18		Training was carried out under Company arrangements.	
—do—			——do——	

Army Form C. 2118.

WAR DIARY
INTELLIGENCE SUMMARY. 8th (S) 3rd Gloucestershire Regiment
(Erase heading not required.)

Place	Date	Hour	Summary of Events and Information	Remarks and references to Appendices
TUNNELLERS CAMP	15/5/18		Training was carried out under Company arrangements in the vicinity of the Camp.	
	16/5/18		Training was carried out under Company arrangements in the vicinity of Camp.	
	17/5/18	2 AM	The Battalion entrained at HEIDBERG SIDING for CHALONS. 3 trains were made	
			during the journey - NOYELLES, POINTOISE and CHATEAULTHIERY.	
	18/5/18		The Battalion arrived at and detrained at CHALONS, and proceeded by road	
			en-route to billets at SARRY.	
SARRY	19/5/18		Voluntary Services were held for Roman Catholics and Non-Conformist.	
"	20/5/18		Training was carried out under Company arrangements.	
"	21/5/18		Training was carried out under Company arrangements.	
"	22/5/18		"A" and "B" Companies training under Company arrangements.	
			"C" and "D" Companies practised the attack West of SOXEN-AUX-MOULINS.	
"	23/5/18		Training was carried out in accordance with Programme of Training	
"	24/5/18		Training was carried out in accordance with Programme of Training	

WAR DIARY

INTELLIGENCE SUMMARY.

Army Form C. 2118.

8 (S) B: Cheshire Regiment

Place	Date	Hour	Summary of Events and Information	Remarks and references to Appendices
SARRY	24.5.18		"MILITARY MEDALS" have Awarded to the following men for gallantry displayed on the SOMME between March 27th to 29th 1918 - To 27509 Pte Harman G, 28554 Pte Dobbs Pte 19008 Pte Wood Hy, 11158 Pte Milton J, 31096 Pte Johnson S, and 15510 Pte Wright E. BAR TO MILITARY MEDAL. - To 9125 Pte West A. M.M.	
	25.5.18		Training two companies out in accordance with Progremme of Training.	
	26.5.18		Divine Service (Voluntary) was held for all denominations.	
	27.5.18		the Battalion carried out Mark practice on ground 1/2M N.E. of Longeveau village.	
	28.5.18		Training two Companies out under Company arrangement. - The "MILITARY MEDAL" with BAR to "MILITARY MEDAL" has awarded to the following:- 20147 L/C Pegram W.R., 24794 Pte Grapp G.H. 11938 A/C Brighton Th, 21091 Pte South A, 19707 Pte Lomas G.A, 27073 Pte Knight R. BAR TO MILITARY MEDAL. 11473 Pte Smith AA M.M.	
	28.5.18	8.30pm	The Battalion embussed for a New Area. Transport moved by road at 12 noon. Surplus Personal remained at SARRY.- (strength 140 O.R.) Busses arrived 10 p.m and moved under recent orders to CHÂLONS-EPERNAY- thence due North.	
CHAMBRECY	29.5.18		Arrived at CHAMBRECY at 4.30 a.m. and Battalion sent out at once to cover the Village as an outpost line whilst remainder of Brigade had	

Army Form C. 2118.

WAR DIARY
INTELLIGENCE SUMMARY

(Erase heading not required.)

8 (S) B. Gloucestershire Regt.

Instructions regarding War Diaries and Intelligence Summaries are contained in F. S. Regs., Part II. and the Staff Manual respectively. Title pages will be prepared in manuscript.

Place	Date	Hour	Summary of Events and Information	Remarks and references to Appendices
CHAMBRECY	29/9/18		Breakfast and rested. No information as to progress of the enemy but most continued had steady left.	
"		9am	Received orders to advance with 8/Gloucs on right, Worcesters and Warwicks in reserve, and security line formed from THERY to TRAMERY — length of advance about 3 miles. Advanced in artillery formation for 2½ miles, then extended over a ridge and came under fire of field guns ("A" Coy. had 5 casualties). In our position by 1 pm, in depth. No bols and had to scratch in. English and French troops observed nicknaming from TRIN CHÂTEAU and woods on either flank, and at 2 pm the Brigade formed the front line — 7th Brigade on left, 58th Brigade on right; 56th in front of SARCY Village. Enemy visible in small numbers, but did not attempt to attack. Rations were late as limbers did not arrive in neighbourhood till midnight, and the long wheel delivered them at Bde H.Qrs, CHAMBRECY, could not get up to us. Quiet night, but enemy massing on my left and advancing to farm	

WAR DIARY
or
INTELLIGENCE SUMMARY.

(Erase heading not required.)

Army Form C. 2118.

Place	Date	Hour	Summary of Events and Information	Remarks and references to Appendices
CHAMBRECY	29.5.18		Took at dusk.	
"	30.5.18		Reliance arrived at Batt: HQ at 8 am, but had to be returned as enemy at that time made an attack in force on the left of the Brigade – the 1/6 Cheshires withdrew and left the 1/4 Wires in the air. After a fight they were driven out of LHÈRY village and the whole line withdrew in good order to the ridge 1000 x west. The enemy made an attack in the line on the left and centre, causing the Worcesters to form an extreme flank and gradually forced into ROMIGNY. The position became untenable and the front line Batt: withdrew at 4 pm to the high ground covering CHAMBRECY covered by 1/4 Warwicks. Casualties – Killed 2/Lt. Gaishpt, Wounded 2/Lt. F. Finch, 2/Lt. R.G. Kitchen, 2/Lt. F. Oakey, 2/Lt. F.D. Glasgow (slight). – Died of Wounds 2/Lt. A.H. Edmonson —— and 60 O.R. A quiet night. Warwicks on left were heavily shelled in VILLE EN TARDENOIS and had heavy casualties, eventually withdrawing, and at night establishing themselves on the left of the Worcesters who were	
"	31.5.18			

Army Form C. 2118.

WAR DIARY
or
INTELLIGENCE SUMMARY.
(Erase heading not required.)

Instructions regarding War Diaries and Intelligence Summaries are contained in F. S. Regs., Part II. and the Staff Manual respectively. Title pages will be prepared in manuscript.

Place	Date	Hour	Summary of Events and Information	Remarks and references to Appendices
CHAULNES	31.5.18		in support. A Batt" of the 22-? Regiment (French) were in support in the centre of the line.	

R M Whitfeuille
Lt. Colonel
Comdg. 8/(S) 63. Gloucestershire Regt.

Army Form C. 2118.

WAR DIARY
INTELLIGENCE SUMMARY.
(Erase heading not required.)

Place: S. Étienne R
June 1915 [likely 1918]

Date	Hour	Summary of Events and Information	Remarks and references to Appendices
1/6/18		Enemy was active all day and attacked 40th French Division on our left, driving them back, and capturing a Battalion complete. He also occupied SAPEY and crept round the right flank of the Brigade. The attack developed here about 4 p.m. and the 9th Cheshires on our right withdrew. My two right Companies found themselves enveloped and all the officers of "A" Coy having become casualties the right withdrew a Company of 3rd Worcesters on my right were all killed or captured — not one general withdrawal onto the village of CHAMBRECY was ordered. Captains — the right Coys "B" & "C" rallied and counter attacked. The 22nd French Regiment joined in and drove the enemy back behind their original line and occupied the casualties on situations of enemies right. Officers – 2 killed and 5 wounded. Other ranks 250.	
2/6/18		Both flanks having been driven in and the rate being weakened by a Coy of the Worc's Div who were astride the VILLE-EN-TARDENOIS ROAD to CHAMBRECY and the Bn had orders to be relieved. The Brigade withdrew at dark to the line of the BOIS D'ÉCLUSE and occupied the high ground – with R.Gloucesters thereabouts thereafter from R.K.L.	

34.M.
5 whls

WAR DIARY or INTELLIGENCE SUMMARY

Army Form C. 2118.

(Erase heading not required.)

Place	Date	Hour	Summary of Events and Information	Remarks and references to Appendices
	3/6/18		A quiet day. 23rd French Infantry relieved by 16th Cheshires in support to 2 R. Battalion.	
	4/6/18		Enemy apparently has brought up more guns and shelled the road and CHAMIZY all day from all sides. Considerable aircraft activity and good visibility.	
	5/6/18		The division received warning of an expected attack, but this did not come off. Enemy movement practically nil. Some shelling of back areas and fresh batteries registering.	
	6/6/18		Enemy put down a heavy barrage at dawn on a front of about 2 miles from the 19th Division left to right of 25th French Division on front - Le Bois d'ECLISSE held by the 59th Brigade was badly gassed, but north End held by Cheshires was lucky. The shelling being confined to the centre clearing which was not shelled. There being on their edge. The Wurschin and Westonfeld suffered most heavily. No infantry attack developed on our front, but about a regiment of Bosch were dispersed by Lewis Gun and Rifle fire.	

"WAR DIARY"
or
~~INTELLIGENCE SUMMARY~~

Army Form C. 2118.

Place	Date	Hour	Summary of Events and Information	Remarks and references to Appendices
	6/6/18		The trench on the Right were driven out of BLIGNY and the 56th Brigade had to withdraw their right flank to conform and the line assumed a right-angle. This was straightened at 2pm by a counter-attack carried out by the 11th K.S.L.I. and the trench retook BLIGNY at 5pm. The shelling of Bois D'ECLISSE lasted from 3am to 11am and undoubtedly the enemy hoped to drive in out by Gas, and the troops encountered were ready to occupy.	
			11th K.S.L.I. Battalion in Front Line.	
	7.6.18		— do —	
	8.6.18		— do —	
	9.6.18	9.30pm	Battalion moved to Brigade Reserve in Bois COURTON. The 19th Division was reorganised temporarily into a Composite Brigade. The Battalion of the 59th Brigade forming the 59th Composite Battalion.	
	10.6.18		Brigade Reserve. The Battalion moved into Divisional Reserve 1 mile before into the Bois COURTON.	
			Divisional Reserve	
	11.6.18		— do —	
	12.6.18			

WAR DIARY
or
INTELLIGENCE SUMMARY.

Army Form C. 2118.

Place	Date	Hour	Summary of Events and Information	Remarks and references to Appendices
	13.6.18		In Reserve Line.	
	13.6.18		— do —	
	14.6.18		— do —	
	15.6.18		— do —	
	16.6.18		— do —	
	17.6.18		— do —	
	18.6.18		Battalion was relieved by the 51st Italian Battalion, on completion of relief moved back to HAUTVILLERS WOOD.	
HAUT VILLERS	19.6.18		Resting in HAUTVILLERS WOOD	
	20.6.18		Moved by route march to billets at SUR OGER.	
SUR OGER	21.6.18		Companies were at the point of entraining when orders and H.Q. convoy lorries arrived at 2.15p.m. and entrained for BROUSSY-LE-PETIT.	
BROUSSY LE PETIT	22.6.18		Companies were at the disposal of Coy Commanders for re-organisation and individual training.	
	23.6.18		Divine Service (Voluntary) in all denominations — Conference was at disposal of Coy Commanders	

WAR DIARY
INTELLIGENCE SUMMARY

(Erase heading not required.)

Army Form C. 2118.

Place	Date	Hour	Summary of Events and Information	Remarks and references to Appendices
	24/6/18		Companies were at the disposal of Company Commanders for individual training.	
	"		Vacated by march route to Camp on the LE-MESNIL - BRUSSY - CONNANTRE ROAD 2½ Kilos N.W. of CONNANTRE.	
	25.6.18		Battalion paraded at 9AM for battalion drill.	
	26.6.18		Training was carried out in accordance with Programme of training.	
	2/7/18		Bath situated at PLEURS were allotted to the battalion. Training was carried out in usual Coy arrangements.	
	28.6.18		Training was carried out in accordance with Programme of training.	
	29.6.18		10	
	30.6.18		Proceeded by march route to new billets at SEMOINE. Capt. MANLEY ANGELL JAMES Awarded the "Victoria Cross."	

R.M. Winfrith Lieut Col
Comdg 8th/3rd Gloucestershire Regiment

Army Form C. 2118.

WAR DIARY

(Erase heading not required.)

8th Bn Gloucestershire Regiment

WA 35

Place	Date	Hour	Summary of Events and Information	Remarks and references to Appendices
GEZAINCOURT	1/7/18		Training was carried out under Company arrangement.	
"	2/7/18		Battalion paraded at 9AM and proceeded by march route to MAILLY. Entrained at MAILLY at about 12 noon for the BRITISH ZONE.	
	3/7/18		Detrained at HEGDIN where Busses conveyed Battalion to billets at REMILLY.	
REMILLY	4/7/18		Cleaning up of kit.	
	5/7/18		Training was carried out under Company arrangements.	
	6/7/18		Training was carried out in accordance with Programme of training submitted to Brigade.	
	7/7/18	AM 10.30	The Battalion paraded for Divine Service. Voluntary Service was held for Non-Conformists and Roman Catholics.	
	8/7/18		Training was carried out in accordance with Programme of training.	
	9/7/18		do	
	10/7/18		do	

35M.
Habunt

Army Form C. 2118.

WAR DIARY
or
INTELLIGENCE SUMMARY.
(Erase heading not required.)

Instructions regarding War Diaries and Intelligence
Summaries are contained in F. S. Regs., Part II.
and the Staff Manual respectively. Title pages
will be prepared in manuscript.

Place	Date	Hour	Summary of Events and Information	Remarks and references to Appendices
RENTY	11.7.18		The battalion paraded at 5.40am and moved by bus to LOZINGHEM XIII Corps Area.	
LOZINGHEM	12.7.18		Training was carried out in accordance with Programme of Training.	
"	13.7.18		do	
"	14.7.18		DIVINE SERVICES Parade Service C of E at 11am. Voluntary Services were held for Roman Catholics and Non-Conformist. Training as for Programme.	
"	15.7.18		do	
"	16.7.18		do	
"	17.7.18		do	
"	18.7.18		Training was carried out in accordance with Programme of Training. The Divisional Gas Officer inspected Gas Equipment of Companies at the Bde Gas hut.	
"	19.7.18		Training was carried out in accordance with Programme of Training.	
"	20.7.18		Battalion moved to a new Area, and proceeded by march route to billets at ST. HILAIRE.	

Army Form C. 2118.

WAR DIARY
INTELLIGENCE SUMMARY.
(Erase heading not required.)

Instructions regarding War Diaries and Intelligence Summaries are contained in F. S. Regs., Part II. and the Staff Manual respectively. Title pages will be prepared in manuscript.

Place	Date	Hour	Summary of Events and Information	Remarks and references to Appendices
St HILAIRE	21/7/18		Voluntary Services were held for all denominations.	
"	22/7/18		The Brigadier commanding 57th Infantry Brigade inspected the battalion by Companies commencing with "A" Company at 11.30 am on ground at 711.t.9.1. The Range situated at T10.A. has allotted to "B" and "D" Companies	
"	23/7/18		Training was carried out under Company arrangements. A Demonstration in the use of the entrenching tool was given at T.17.b.6.9. 2 Officers, 8 NCO's and 6 Privates per Company attended.	
"	24/7/18		Training was carried out under Company arrangements	
"	25/7/18		Training was carried out under Company arrangements.	
"	26/7/18		The Range at B6.d.8.8. has been allotted to Companies. Remainder of training was carried out under Company arrangements.	
"	27/7/18		Training under Company arrangements. In the afternoon PT and BF instructors were at the disposal of Companies. Companies were also exercised in the use of the Entrenching Tool.	

Army Form C. 2118.

WAR DIARY

INTELLIGENCE SUMMARY.

(Erase heading not required.)

Place	Date	Hour	Summary of Events and Information	Remarks and references to Appendices
ST. HILAIRE	29.7.18		Voluntary Services were held for all denominations.	
"	29/7/18		Training under Company arrangement.	
"	30.7		Training Carried out as per Programme. The Baths situated at LA GOULEE was allotted to Headquarters and "B" Company. The Battalion paraded at 8pm and proceeded by march route to billets previously occupied at LOZINGHEM. Battalion was all billeted by 11pm.	
LOZINGHEM	31/7/18		Training was carried out under Company arrangements.	

R.M. Luntzink Lieut-Col.

Comdg. 8.(S) vB Cheshire's Regt.

WAR DIARY / INTELLIGENCE SUMMARY

8th Batt. Gloucestershire Regiment

Place	Date	Hour	Summary of Events and Information	Remarks and references to Appendices
LOZINGHEM	1/8/18	—	Training was carried out under Company arrangements. "A" Coy on ground C.13.a.99. "B" Coy Chateau grounds (C. 7 & 8), "C" & "D" Coys on ground near old Aerodrome.	
	2/8/18	9.30am	The Battalion were inspected by the General Officer Commanding 19th Division, on ground near the old Aerodrome.	
	3/8/18		The Bath situated at HUCHEL have allotted to "A" "B" and "C" Coys. Range No. 10 & 11 situated at C.7.d. been allotted to "D" Coy. The 19th Divisional Horse Show was held at B.15.d.58.	
	4/8/18		Voluntary Services were held in all denominations. Warning Orders received to stand by in relief of 3rd Division.	
	5/8/18		Orders received to move to the Forbord Area. Battalion marched at 4.15pm. and proceeded by road & rail to CHOCQUES Area via MARLES-LES-MINES.	
GOSNAY	6/8/18		The 57th Infantry Brigade relieved the 9th Infantry Brigade, holding route of the Divisional Front, 1st, 3rd Wales in right in front line. — 10th Royal Warwicks in Reserve. 8th Gloucesters in Support.	

WAR DIARY
or
INTELLIGENCE SUMMARY.

(Erase heading not required.)

Army Form C. 2118.

Place	Date	Hour	Summary of Events and Information	Remarks and references to Appendices
Lemn 8.	7/8/18	-	Battalion in Support trenches, with 10th Worc. Regt. in front line and 16th R. Warwick Regt. in reserve.	
"	8/8/18		do.	
"	9/8/18		do.	
"	10/8/18		Relieved in the Support Line by 6th Worc. Regt. and moved back to CHOCQUES in Brigade Reserve. 10th R. War. Regt. in front line.	
Chocques	11/8/18		Battalion Cleaning up etc. Coys. were allotted to R. Billets.	
"	12/8/18		No 1. Range situated at Sq.18 was allotted to "A" Company "3" " " " " " " "B" " Frowing are situated at S24 b+d tra-allotted to "C" & "D" Company	
"	13/8/18		No 2 Range tra- allotted to "C" Coy. "5" " " " " " " "D" " Frowing are allotted to No 3 Company.	

Army Form C. 2118.

WAR DIARY
or
INTELLIGENCE SUMMARY.
(Erase heading not required.)

Instructions regarding War Diaries and Intelligence Summaries are contained in F. S. Regs., Part II. and the Staff Manual respectively. Title pages will be prepared in manuscript.

Place	Date	Hour	Summary of Events and Information	Remarks and references to Appendices
CHUIGNES	10/8/18		Coy No. 2 allocated to E.19.b.6.18. transmitted to "A" Company	
		No. 5	" " " " "B" "	
		6	Eig. b. 1. 6	
		No. 3	transmitted to "A+B" Companies.	
	13/8/18		Relieved 10th Royal Warwick Regt. in Front line of Centre Section of Divisional Front. Surplus Personnel moved back to transport lines in Bois-des-Tailles.	
Lam B	16/8/18	Le Front Line		
"	17/8/18		At 3.33 am Patrols sent out to reconnoitre hones at N.6.a. 95.75 and W.6.b.2.5. these were found to be unoccupied. A Platoon of "B" Company pushed forward and took up a position 50 yds. in front of the hones and dug in and patrols pushed forward to WILLOT LANE. At 4.45 p.m. the line was consolidated and patrols pushed forward to WILLOT LANE.	
"	18/8/18			
"	19/8/18		2 Support Platoons were pushed through to WILLOT LANE and took up a position 150 yds. in front. Line was consolidated at 9.15 pm and patrols working on our front.	

WAR DIARY or INTELLIGENCE SUMMARY

Army Form C. 2118.

(Erase heading not required.)

Instructions regarding War Diaries and Intelligence Summaries are contained in F. S. Regs., Part II. and the Staff Manual respectively. Title pages will be prepared in manuscript.

Place	Date	Hour	Summary of Events and Information	Remarks and references to Appendices
LINE	20.8.18		2 Platoons advanced at 1.10 a.m. and had not much difficulty in reaching their objective and at 2.30 a.m. the two consolidated in front of HYACINTH LANE. At first day the left flank were in touch with the SEAFORTHS who sat at R.31.b.3.3. At 1 p.m. 2 platoons took up a position as follows R.32.b.56.0 to right at R.32.a.5.3 to LOCON ROAD.	
"	21.8.18		The Battalion was relieved by the 3rd Manc. Regt. and moved back to billets at VENDIN.	
VENDIN	22.8.18		Moved from billets at VENDIN to billets at HINGES.	
ANNEZIN	23.8.18		Companies were at the disposal of Company Commanders for Cleaning up etc.	
"	24.8.18		Training Scheme carried out in accordance with Programme of training. Baths at CHOCQUES first allotted to the Battalion.	
"	25.8.18		Divine Service (Sunday) was held for C of E and Roman Catholics.	
"	26.8.18		Training was carried out under Company arrangements.	
"	27.8.18		Training was carried out in accordance with Programme of training.	

WAR DIARY
INTELLIGENCE SUMMARY

Army Form C. 2118.

Place	Date	Hour	Summary of Events and Information	Remarks and references to Appendices
ANNEZIN	28.8.18		Training. Men were put in the vicinity of Lens.	
Lens	29.8.18		The Battalion relieved 9th 2nd London Regt in Support and became Right Support Battalion of the Right Brigade. In Support Line	
"	30.8.18		do	
"	31.8.18		do	

W. Palmer
Major
Comdg. 8th Bn. London Fusiliers Regt.

WAR DIARY
or
INTELLIGENCE SUMMARY.
(Erase heading not required.)

Army Form C. 2118.

8 Gloucesters

37.11.
3 sheets

Place	Date	Hour	Summary of Events and Information	Remarks and references to Appendices
Line	1.9.18		Battalion in Support Line. — Relieved a battalion of the 46th Division in LHERTEUR Sector.	
"	2.9.18		In Front Line System	
"	3.9.18		"	
"	4.9.18		"	
"	5.9.18		The Battalion relieved 9th Royal Welsh Fusiliers in the Left Brigade	
"	6.9.18		In Front Line System	
"	7.9.18		"	
"	8.9.18		"	
"	9.9.18		Relieved in the Front Line System by the 9th R.W. Fusiliers	
"	10.9.18		On Completion of relief the Battalion moved back to a Camp near LOCON.	
"	11.9.18		Battalion cleaning up etc.	
Locon	12.9.18		The B.M. at AVELETTE DRAWBRIDGE were exhibited to the Battalion. The Battalion Gas Officer inspected all Small Box respirators	84 3
	13.9.18		Training was carried on in accordance with Programme of training.	
	14.9.18		do	

Army Form C. 2118.

WAR DIARY
or
INTELLIGENCE SUMMARY.
(Erase heading not required.)

Instructions regarding War Diaries and Intelligence Summaries are contained in F. S. Regs., Part II. and the Staff Manual respectively. Title pages will be prepared in manuscript.

Place	Date	Hour	Summary of Events and Information	Remarks and references to Appendices
MR LOCON	15.9.18		Divine Service were held for all denominations	
	16.9.18		Training was carried out in accordance with Programme of Training.	
	17.9.18		Battalion relieved 8th & 13th N. Staff Regt. in the Support Line.	
	18.9.18		In Support Line	
	19.9.18		Relieved 6th & 3rd R. Warwickshire Regt. in the Front Line System	
	20.9.18		" "	
	21.9.18		In Front Line System	
	22.9.18		" "	
	23.9.18		" "	
	24.9.18		Relieved by 3rd & 13th Worc. Regt. and moved back to the Support Line	
	25.9.18		In Support Line.	
	26.9.18		" "	
	27.9.18		Relieved 3rd & 13th Worc. Regt. in Front Line System.	
	28.9.18		In Front Line System	

Army Form C. 2118.

WAR DIARY
or
INTELLIGENCE SUMMARY.
(Erase heading not required.)

Place	Date	Hour	Summary of Events and Information	Remarks and references to Appendices
	29.9.18		The Battalion were relieved in the front line System by 9th Polish Fusilier and moved into billets in EGSARD	
EGSARD	30.9.18		The Battalion was inspected by the G.O.C. 67th Brigade on ground near H.Q and Headquarters.	
	30.9.18		Conference at the Orderly of Company Commanders	
			The Battalion paraded at 1.15pm and proceeded by march route to billets at CHOCQ-A-LA-TOUR.	

W. Parker Lieut Col
Cmdg. 8/10 St. Gloucestershire Regt.

579 / 101

Army Form C. 2118.

WAR DIARY
or
INTELLIGENCE SUMMARY.
(Erase heading not required.)

8th Bn. Grenadier Regt.

Vol 38

LB
38. M.
9 mths

Place	Date	Hour	Summary of Events and Information	Remarks and references to Appendices
ESSARS	1/9/18		Battalion Paraded at 1.15pm and proceeded by march route to billets at CAUCHY-A-LA-TOUR.	
CAUCHY-A-LA-TOUR	2/9/18		Paraded at 10am and marched out my march route to billets at BOURS.	
BOURS	3/9/18		Training carried out in accordance with Programme of Training.	
"	4/9/18		Battalion paraded at 2.15pm and billeted at BRYAS - Remained at night at SAULTY and proceeded by march route to billets at ST AMAND.	
ST AMAND	5/9/18		Training has carried out under Company arrangements from 9am to 10am Companies carried out Steady drill – Musketry of the 10am battalion training was carried out in accordance with 19th Division order SB36/5	
"	6/9/18		Training was carried out under Company arrangement. The battalion paraded at 12.45pm and was moved by bus to GRAINCOURT Area.	
GRAINCOURT	7/9/18		Training was carried out under Company arrangements.	

WAR DIARY
or
INTELLIGENCE SUMMARY.

(Erase heading not required.)

Army Form C. 2118.

Place	Date	Hour	Summary of Events and Information	Remarks and references to Appendices
GRAINCOURT	9/10/18		Battalion paraded at 12.15 hrs and marched to bivouac area.	
ANNEUX	10/10/18		ANNEUX. Moved to billets in Eastern Suburbs of CAMBRAI. Major J.G. Laid-Jones to Battalion and took over the duties of 2nd in Command. Captains came at to be observed of Company Commanders. Lieutenant Capt. G.E. Nicholl assumed the duties of was detailed to take "C" Company. 2nd Lt. G.H. Vaughan returned and has gone to to Lets 4th Company. Captains when not to the Medical of Company Commanders.	
CAMBRAI	11/10/18		Battalion stood to at 6 to 12 noon.	
"	12/10/18		At 0.2.30 hrs Battalion paraded and took over bivouac at South Eastern Suburbs of CAMBRAI from the 9th Welsh Regt.	

WAR DIARY
or
INTELLIGENCE SUMMARY.

Army Form C. 2118.

(Erase heading not required.)

Place	Date	Hour	Summary of Events and Information	Remarks and references to Appendices
CAMBRAI	13/10/18		Batt'n & Lt. Infantrie Divin Services were held for all denominations. Band of England and Wesleyans there. Little Retalin in CAMBRAI (a Patrol	
"	14/10/18		The Battalion paraded to Church. A bounty? & carried out advanced Schemes. Lieut. J. Stewart joined the battalion and was posted to letter "B" Company.	
"	15/10/18		Conference of Coy commanders in the new formation of the attack. Special attention was paid to double looking during the advance. Coy tactical scheme. Battalion two billets on the but.	
"	16/10/18		CAUROIR. The battalion moved to billets in CAUROIR and took took on route in a tactical exercise in conjunction with the other units of the Brigade.	

WAR DIARY
or
INTELLIGENCE SUMMARY.

Army Form C. 2118.

Place	Date	Hour	Summary of Events and Information	Remarks and references to Appendices
CARNOY	17/7/16		The Battalion (less transport, stores & surplus Personnel) paraded at 1.30 p.m. and proceeded by march route Mine(?) Carnoy to ST AUBERT, and on arrival became the Support Battalion of the Bde. Scale of transport, stores & surplus Personnel, under command of Major DC Laird proceeded to billets in RIEUX	
ST AUBERT	18/7/16		Battalion remained in billets at ST AUBERT. Training in musketry, Lewis Gun (carried out in the) cellars owing to shell fire.	
"	19/7/16		Training was continued in billets. The Battalion paraded at 2.00 hours to take up assembly positions for the general attack, met nothing - "A" Coy Right front Coy, "B" Coy left front Coy in Railway Cutting Near HAUSSY, "C" Coy in Sunken road W of Railway behind "A" Coy and "D" Coy in Railway Cutting on right of "B" Coy.	

WAR DIARY
or
INTELLIGENCE SUMMARY.

Army Form C. 2118.

(Erase heading not required.)

Place	Date	Hour	Summary of Events and Information	Remarks and references to Appendices
LINE	20/10/18		Attack on the bridge at HAUSSY. RE bridging detachment with "A" & "B" Companies were to standby to lead the attack assault & put up the bridge for the crossing of the river SELLE. Battalion for the night 2 RB Grenade Battalions on the left, 10th R. War. Regt "D" Company were in Reserve. "C" on the Right. of mopping up the village of HAUSSY, which the remainder of the Battalion advanced to the final objective E of Le Right. ground NE of the river SELLE. The attack was entirely successful. Casualties 8 officers 125 other ranks "85 Officers and 25 nominal.	
"	21/10/18		Battalion held the line gained during the previous day	
"	22/10/18		do	

WAR DIARY
or
INTELLIGENCE SUMMARY.

(Erase heading not required.)

Army Form C. 2118.

(Envelope seems to be missing.)

Place	Date	Hour	Summary of Events and Information	Remarks and references to Appendices
LINE	13/4/18		Orders were received at 8.45 hours that the battalion were to make good another objective viz: LA CAPELLE – ST MARTIN ROAD on the battalion front. It was impossible to get orders out to the two foremost Companies owing to heavy hostile machine gun fire. The Coy in support (B Coy) was ordered to push through the two leading Companies and make good this objective. This Coy was however impeded by command of D Stores who was previously commanding the left flank Coy. He was necessary to later officers who knew the ground should be in command. The Coy moved up in artillery formation & big shelled where heavy casualties. Men caught sight— at 14.26 Hours the Coy advanced and gradually worked up to their objective. The assault was pushed home with obstinate determination with the result that the enemy left some Heavy Machine Guns approximately 150 prisoners and approximately 10 wounded Germans.	

WAR DIARY or INTELLIGENCE SUMMARY

Army Form C. 2118.

Place	Date	Hour	Summary of Events and Information	Remarks and references to Appendices
LINE	23/10/18		Same letter. At about 10:20 hours the enemy were reported massing on B27 and B. The trops [troops] immediately fired field guns got on to the area & of quickly and forced to all chance of any counter attack developing. After strong fighting patrols (losses) to find upon the chalk of BERMERAIN to make good the bridge heads over the river ECAILLON. The batln [battalion] met with severe opposition and was unable to make much headway. Barbara had been on and the enemy massing above the R.y.Q. brought fire to also further clemency above Straselry. Cannot [?] No tanks of the brigade. Captures during the day in the line above were as follows — 6 Officers 288 other ranks 35 machine guns	

WAR DIARY or INTELLIGENCE SUMMARY

Army Form C. 2118.

(Erase heading not required.)

Place	Date	Hour	Summary of Events and Information	Remarks and references to Appendices
LINE	23/9/18		Got the Lewis guns and last lot of Machine Guns. Infantry together with the Engineers and were employed against the rehearsal ground. Casualty — 2 Officer — 128 other ranks.	
"	24/9/18		The Battalion was relieved by a battalion of 188th Brigade and moved to billets AVESNES-LES-ST ROBERT.	
AVESNES	25/9/18		Battalion the rest of men allotted to the battalion and conferences were held at the Headquarters of Brigade. Corps were to be ... for cleaning up.	
"	26/9/18		The Battalion paraded at 0930 hours for march to billets CAUROIR and was met. Carried out advanced operations for inspection and other work of the different kinds.	
CAUROIR	27/9/18		Lost inspected. Church parade for C of E only. Training on the vicinity of billets and inspections carried out.	
"	28/9/18		for the battalion.	

WAR DIARY
or
INTELLIGENCE SUMMARY.

(Erase heading not required.)

Army Form C. 2118.

Place	Date	Hour	Summary of Events and Information	Remarks and references to Appendices
CODFORD	1/10/15		Training has carried out in accordance with Battalion Training Programme.	
"	2/10/15		Battalion was inspected in the afternoon. Training was carried out in accordance with Battalion training programme.	
"	3/10/15		Battalion tactical exercise in accordance with scheme issued by 57th Inf. Brigade.	

Comd. 8/(S) Batn. Gloucestershire Regiment.

WAR DIARY
or
INTELLIGENCE SUMMARY

Army Form C. 2118.

8th (S) Bn Gloucestershire Regt

39. 11
10 sheets

Place	Date	Hour	Summary of Events and Information	Remarks and references to Appendices
CAUROIR	1/11/18		The Battalion received orders that the 19th Division would move forward the his preparatory to taking over a portion of the front.	
"	2/11/18		The Battalion moved from CAUROIR to ST HUBERT by cross-country route, an open formation scheme being carried out during the journey. The day being very wet.	
ST HUBERT	3/11/18		The Battalion moved via MONTRÉCOURT across country to VENDEGIES which was reached by night. It was found however that the attack as planned for 05.30 hours of the 4th would not take place owing to further enemy withdrawal. The march was therefore continued to SEPMERIES, where Battalion Headquarters were established in the Chateau.	
SEPMERIES	4/11/18		In the early morning a further move was anticipated, but it did not take place until 11.00 hours, when the 57th Brigade moved to MARESCHES, the 8th (S) Glouc. Regt being quartered in huts on the N.E. edge of the village.	

Army Form C. 2118.

WAR DIARY
or
INTELLIGENCE SUMMARY.
(Erase heading not required.)

Instructions regarding War Diaries and Intelligence Summaries are contained in F. S. Regs., Part II. and the Staff Manual respectively. Title pages will be prepared in manuscript.

Place	Date	Hour	Summary of Events and Information	Remarks and references to Appendices
	4/11/18		The move was much hampered by the considerable traffic on the road. At dusk when it became indeed the advance was less likely to take place before daylight. The Battalion bivouacked & down to the village. Throughout the day the town had been shelled.	
MARESCHES.	5/11/18		The Battalion moved in the morning to JENLAIN. Weather and roads were bad. Three enemy tanks out of action were passed en route, apparently ones which had been captured from the British.	
JENLAIN.	6/11/18		The Battalion moved fairly early in the morning to 65TH Country and the road and most hampered progress considerably. Battalion headquarters was established in the Château together with the headquarters of the 3rd Battalion Worcester Regt. Accommodation was ample and two companies of the Gloucesters were also quartered there. It has been noticed that many articles of value had been damaged, panels had been deliberately cut from a French, and that the lights fittings took all been removed from the Château.	

WAR DIARY
or
INTELLIGENCE SUMMARY.

Army Form C. 2118.

Place	Date	Hour	Summary of Events and Information	Remarks and references to Appendices
	6/11/18		In the afternoon, news had been received that the battalion would relieve the 9th Bn. Devon Regt. An advance party went forward to La. FLAMENGRIE, but on the receipt of subsequent orders the battalion did not move up until after midnight, November 6/7th.	
LA FLAMENGRIE	7/11/18		At. ON. 30 hours Battalion Headquarters were established opposite the Church. LA FLAMENGRIE, and companies were in positions for the attack to be carried out by the 67th Brigade. The 8th Bn. Devon. Regt. were Support battalion to the Brigade. Most of the civilians in LA. FLAMENGRIE have occupied by civilians, who had remained in quarters for a period of eight days. They never had been much exacted by the enemy's (which looks still continuing), but they were apparently on tops at the arrival of our troops. They described many instances of kind treatment of the enemy who had taken away all available and much clothing.	

WAR DIARY or INTELLIGENCE SUMMARY

Army Form C. 2118.

Place	Date	Hour	Summary of Events and Information	Remarks and references to Appendices
	7/11/18		Our attack having proved successful the battalion's headquarters were moved forward to a house at LA PERCHE ROUGE and at dusk to FERTE DE LA TOUR.	
		8 pp.	At dawn the 57th Brigade advanced without artillery support, and found though HOUDAIN, THISNIERES and MA PLAQUET, establishing a line on the whole of BOIS DE LA HAMERE. The are of battle were as follows:—	
			Left front Battalion — 10th Royal Warwick Regt.	
			Support Battalion — 8th Gloucester Regt.	
			Right front Battalion — 30th Worcester Regt.	
			Battalion headquarters were established successively at the cross-roads in HOUDAIN, LA MAISON ROUGE, and at THISNIERES. Much machine-gun opposition was met by the Left front battalion, and a fair advance of the 3rd Worcesters was helped by machine gun fire in the woods until fire was opened by an 18 pdr field gun. After dusk the 57th Brigade pushed forward to the MONS—MAUBEUGE railway running through the Eastern edge of the wood. Orders were received for the battalion to move to MALPLAQUET, but these were cancelled, and the companies were billeted at THISNIERES.	

Army Form C. 2118.

WAR DIARY
or
INTELLIGENCE SUMMARY.
(Erase heading not required.)

Instructions regarding War Diaries and Intelligence Summaries are contained in F. S. Regs., Part II. and the Staff Manual respectively. Title pages will be prepared in manuscript.

Place	Date	Hour	Summary of Events and Information	Remarks and references to Appendices
TASNIERES	9/11/18		At dawn the Battalion up to an assembly position on the MONS–MAUBEUGE railway, passing through the wood. The order of Battle was as follows:– "A" Coy in Support. "B" " Right front Company. "C" " Left front Company. "D" " Centre front Company. The forward two sections of companies were detailed for an advance, and the battalions (through the wood) to the Eastern edge without artillery Support. Enemy machine gun fire at intervals but between directly our line approached forward companies reached their objective on the slope just East of the wood, and consolidated. On the Eastern side of the wood it appeared that many of the enemy, deterred by rifle and MG fire prior to our attack. A large fringe of twelve German own left behind, together look 1 an or two field guns. Units of the 1st & 2nd Divisions forward through our line without delay such continued the advance. Patrols in the morning and Companies were relieved.	

Army Form C. 2118.

WAR DIARY
or
INTELLIGENCE SUMMARY.
(Erase heading not required.)

Instructions regarding War Diaries and Intelligence Summaries are contained in F. S. Regs., Part II. and the Staff Manual respectively. Title pages will be prepared in manuscript.

Place	Date	Hour	Summary of Events and Information	Remarks and references to Appendices
BETTRECHIES	11/11/18		The 59th Brigade moved in the morning to take billets in the vicinity of BETTRECHIES. Had difficulty how ever in moving to the vicinity of heavy bridges demolished by the enemy. All troops were found billets.	
"	12/11/18		Companies were at the disposal of Company Commanders for general cleaning up.	
"	13/11/18		Companies cleaning up.	
"	14/11/18		Companies were at the disposal of Coy Commanders and carried out training on the battalion football field at H9a. from 09.00 hours to 11.00 hours. Lectures 10 to 11. Infantry training was carried out. After 11.00 hours Companies carried on with policing their Company areas.	

Army Form C. 2118.

WAR DIARY
INTELLIGENCE SUMMARY.
(Erase heading not required.)

Instructions regarding War Diaries and Intelligence Summaries are contained in F. S. Regs., Part II. and the Staff Manual respectively. Title pages will be prepared in manuscript.

Place	Date	Hour	Summary of Events and Information	Remarks and references to Appendices
SEMERIES	15/11/18		The Battalion moved by road route to new billets at ST. AUBERT.	
ST. AUBERT	16/11/18		The Battalion moved by road route to billets at CAURIOR.	
CAUROIR	17/11/18		Divine Service for the 69th Infantry Brigade was held at 11:00 hours. Mass was held in the Church CAUROIRONCLES at 09.30 hours for Roman Catholics	
	18/11/18		Companies were at the disposal of Coy. Commanders for the purpose of cleaning up. A Lecture was given in the Concert Hall at 14:00 hours by the Divisional Educational Officer on the two following subjects:- "Demobilisation Scheme" "Educational Scheme"	
"	19/11/18		Companies were at the disposal of Company Commanders for the completion of cleaning up. Baths were allotted to "C" and "D" Companies.	

Army Form C. 2118.

WAR DIARY
or
INTELLIGENCE SUMMARY.
(Erase heading not required.)

Place	Date	Hour	Summary of Events and Information	Remarks and references to Appendices
CHAReRoR	20/1/18		Training was carried out in accordance with Programme of Training. Baths were allotted to the Battalion.	
"	21/1/18		Training was carried out in accordance with Programme of Training. The Commanding Officer inspected "A" Company.	
"	22/1/18		Training was carried out in accordance with Programme of Training. The Commanding Officer inspected "B" Company.	
"	23/1/18		Companies paraded at 09.00 for Salvage Work.	
"	24/1/18		The Battalion paraded at 10.00 hours and marched to the Brick Hall for Divine Service. Service for Roman Catholics was held in the Quiet at 0.30 hours. The G.O.C. 57th Infantry Brigade inspected the Battalion.	

Army Form C. 2118.

WAR DIARY
or
INTELLIGENCE SUMMARY.
(Erase heading not required.)

Place	Date	Hour	Summary of Events and Information	Remarks and references to Appendices
CAVROR	26/11/18		Companies were at the disposal of Company Commanders.	
"	27/11/18		Owing to the move of 59th Brigade being postponed pending further instructions the battalion paraded at 09.30 hours. 1 hour being devoted to Arms drill and ½ hour to saluting drill without Arms.	
"	28/11/18		The 59th Brigade moved by buses to a new area. The Battalion arrived in their new billets at about 20.00 hours. "A","B"& H.Q. Companies were billeted at AUTHEUX, and "C" and "D" Companies at BOISBERGUES.	
AUTHEUX BOISBERGUES	29/11/18		Companies paraded at 10.00 hours on their respective parade grounds. Arms drill, Sect & Sec.42 & 36 infantry training were carried out 10.00 hours to 11.00. Saluting drill without arms from 11.00 hours to 11.30 hours.	

Army Form C. 2118.

WAR DIARY
or
INTELLIGENCE SUMMARY.

(Erase heading not required.)

Place	Date	Hour	Summary of Events and Information	Remarks and references to Appendices
AUTHEUX BOISBERGUES	5/9/18		The Battalion moved from Authieux and Boisbergues to CANDAS. Companies moved off independently at the following times:—	
			Headquarters 12.50 a.m.	
			"A" and "C" Coys 13.00 "	
			"B" " 13.10 "	

[signatures]
Lt Col
Comdg 2/5th Bn Gloucestershire Regt.

WAR DIARY or INTELLIGENCE SUMMARY

Army Form C. 2118.

8 Gloucestershire Regt.

Vol 40

40.11
6 sheet

Place	Date	Hour	Summary of Events and Information	Remarks and references to Appendices
MALTAG.	1/11/18		Companies fell in at 8.0 a.m. for general cleaning up. A Voluntary Service was held for Non-Conformists in the Y.M.C.A. hut at 10.30 hours. Roman Catholics paraded at Batt. H.Q. for service at 10.15 hours.	
	2/11/18		Companies paraded on the respective parade grounds at 08.25 hours. Guard mounted .... Co. Wt. & H. Sgt. Manby, Imm. Sergts & corporal conf.	
	3/11/18		Companies paraded on their respective parade grounds at 08.30 hours. Guard drill with arms Sect 66 & 67 Infan. Tng. Morning parade out from 0930 hours to 1030 hours. Educational scheme was gone into from 10.30 am to 11.60 a.m. All Sergeants and Lance Sergeants paraded for drill under the R.S.M. & the Adjutant.	
	4/11/18		Companies paraded at 08.30 hours on their respective parade grounds. Guard drill with arms was carried out from 08.30 hours to 9.30 hours. Educational schemes were gone into from 10.00 hrs to 10.30 hours. Saluting drill from 11.30 am to 12.00 hours. All Sergeants and Lance Sergeants paraded at 11.30 hours for drill instruction under the R.S.M. & Adjutant.	

Army Form C. 2118.

WAR DIARY
or
INTELLIGENCE SUMMARY.
(Erase heading not required.)

Instructions regarding War Diaries and Intelligence Summaries are contained in F. S. Regs., Part II. and the Staff Manual respectively. Title pages will be prepared in manuscript.

Place	Date	Hour	Summary of Events and Information	Remarks and references to Appendices
FIELD H.Q.	5/12/18		Companies paraded at 09.30 hours on Rec. basketball grounds. Squad drill but after Sec 75 = 80 Infantry Training was carried out from 08.30 hours to 09.30 hours. Educational lectures were given from 10.00 hours to 11.00 hours. All Sergeants and L/cs a Sergeants paraded at 11.30 hours for drill under the Adjutant.	
"	6/12/18		Coys "B" and "D" Companies paraded at 08.30 hours for training as follows:— Physical drill, Arms drill, Squad drill and Saluting drill. "A" and "C" Companies paraded at 09.00 hours for Route March. Training was carried out in accordance with Programme of Training.	
"	7/12/18		Divine Service was held at 11.00 hours, Officers and 100 other ranks by coy attended. R.C. landed at 10.25 hours for Mass in the Church. A lecture was given in the Y.M.C.A. Hut at 14.30 hours by the Revd. R. Little. Subject "Church & Big Ben."	
"	9/12/18		Training was carried out as for Programme of Training.	

WAR DIARY
or
INTELLIGENCE SUMMARY.
(Erase heading not required.)

Army Form C. 2118.

Instructions regarding War Diaries and Intelligence Summaries are contained in F. S. Regs., Part II. and the Staff Manual respectively. Title pages will be prepared in manuscript.

Place	Date	Hour	Summary of Events and Information	Remarks and references to Appendices
CANDAS	10/1/18		Training was carried out in accordance with Programme of Training. Bath at CANDAS was allotted to "B" Coy from 13.00 hours to 14.00 hours.	
"	11/1/18		The inspection of the Battalion ended by the Commanding Officer was cancelled owing to bad weather. Companies were given instruction in their Billets — Musketry etc.	
"	12/1/18		The Commanding Officer inspected the Battalion. Dress:- Drill Order.	
"	13/1/18		Training was carried out in accordance with Programme of Training. The Baths were allotted to "D" Company and a portion of 2nd Company.	
"	14/1/18		Companies were at the disposal of Company Commanders for general cleaning up, and for Inspection. The Commanding Officer inspected the Billets of "A" Coy at 10.30 hours.	
"	15/1/18		Divine Service C of E. 70 Officers and 100 Other Ranks on Company turned out at 09.50 hours for Divine Service. Roman Catholics paraded at 08.50 hours for Mass. The Commanding Officer inspected all Billets.	

WAR DIARY
or
INTELLIGENCE SUMMARY

(Erase heading not required.)

Army Form C. 2118.

Place	Date	Hour	Summary of Events and Information	Remarks and references to Appendices
Cur DHQ	16/9/18		All Signals and Signal Officers paraded at the Drill Hall at 0900 hours for instruction under the Adjutant. Instruction in Musketry etc. under Coy Sergeants. Ammo. given out etc.	
"	17/9/18		All Section Officers paraded at the Drill Hall for Lecture. Battalion Scheme of Rate to March and Entrain moved off in parade at the following times: "A" Coy 0900 hours, "B" Coy 1000 hours.	
"	18/9/18		Draft not yet allotted to the Battalion. Conference carried out 1 hours training in Arms Squad and Saluting drill. Lectures have given on the Concert Hall at 11.30 hours by Col. Sharpe. Subject: Exploration.	
"	19/9/18		Training was carried out in accordance with Programme of Training.	
"	20/9/18		Training was carried out in accordance with Programme of Training.	
"	21/9/19		Companies were at the disposal of Company Commanders for Kit inspection and general cleaning up of arms, equipment, billets etc. The Commanding Officer inspected the Kits of "B" Company at 10.30 hours.	

Army Form C. 2118.

WAR DIARY
or
INTELLIGENCE SUMMARY.
(Erase heading not required.)

Instructions regarding War Diaries and Intelligence Summaries are contained in F. S. Regs., Part II. and the Staff Manual respectively. Title pages will be prepared in manuscript.

Place	Date	Hour	Summary of Events and Information	Remarks and references to Appendices
CANDAS	22/12/18		DIVINE SERVICES. 2 Officers and 100 Other ranks per Company paraded at Battalion H.Qrs at 0955 hours for Divine Service. 2 Officers and Other ranks paraded at 0850 hours for Mass.	
"	23/12/18		Training was carried out in accordance with Programme of Training.	
"	24/12/18		Training was carried out in accordance with Programme of Training.	
"	25/12/18		DIVINE SERVICE. (XMAS DAY.) 2 Officers and 100 Other Ranks per Company paraded at Battalion Headquarters at 09.20 hours for Divine Service. Band sent to Trench and Run.	
"	26/12/18		Training was carried out in accordance with Programme of Training.	
"	27/12/18		Companies were at the disposal of Company Commanders for inspection of kit and general clean up of arms, equipment, and billets.	
"	28/12/18		The Commanding Officer inspected the Kits of "C" Company at 10.30 hours.	

Army Form C. 2118.

WAR DIARY
or
INTELLIGENCE SUMMARY.
(Erase heading not required.)

Instructions regarding War Diaries and Intelligence Summaries are contained in F. S. Regs., Part II. and the Staff Manual respectively. Title pages will be prepared in manuscript.

Place	Date	Hour	Summary of Events and Information	Remarks and references to Appendices
CINBAD	24.9.18		The Batt. were allotted to the battalions.	
"	30/9/18		Training was carried out in accordance with Programme of Training.	
"	3/9/18		Training was carried out as per Programme.	

BW Pite
Lieut-Col
Comdg: 8th (S) Bn. Gloucestershire Regt.

8(S) Bn Gloucester Regt

WAR DIARY
INTELLIGENCE SUMMARY.
(Erase heading not required.)

Army Form C. 2118.

21.M.
5 sheets

Place	Date	Hour	Summary of Events and Information	Remarks and references to Appendices
CANDAS	1/1/19		Training was carried out as per Programme 2.	
"	2/1/19		do	
"	3/1/19		do	
"	4/1/19		Two Lectures were given at the Kinema Hall at 11.00 hours and 17.00 hours respectively.	
			1st Lecture - "Political & Social Manufacture of Russia."	
			2nd Lecture - "Soviet heat Reconstruction of Russia."	
			A Cross-Country run took place. — Teams 25 for Bn. met at the Kinema at 10.30 hours.	
"	5/1/19		DIVINE SERVICES. 1 Officer and 100 other ranks to company parade at Bn. Headquarters at 10.20 hours for Divine Service.	
			Roman Catholics paraded at 08.55 hours for Mass.	
"	6/1/19		Training was carried out as per Programme 3.	

Army Form C. 2118.

WAR DIARY
or
INTELLIGENCE SUMMARY.
(Erase heading not required.)

Instructions regarding War Diaries and Intelligence Summaries are contained in F. S. Regs., Part II. and the Staff Manual respectively. Title pages will be prepared in manuscript.

Place	Date	Hour	Summary of Events and Information	Remarks and references to Appendices
CANDAS	7/1/19		Training programme carried out as per Programme. A Lecture was given by Lieut. Col. Montgomery DSO. at the Cinema Hall at 11.45 hours :- Subject - "Organisation of a Division"	
"	8/1/19		Training was carried out as per Programme.	
"	9/1/19		The Ba'ts were allotted to the Battalion. In addition Companies carried out 1 hour Arm Drill.	
"	10/1/19		The Battalion paraded for a Route March at 0900 hours. ROUTE. CANDAS — FIENVILLERS — MONTRELET.	
"	11/1/19		Companies were at the disposal of Company Commanders for kit inspection, and general cleaning up of army equipment and billets.	
"	12.1.19		DIVINE SERVICES. 2 Officers and 75 other ranks (or Coy. (Less A'Coy) paraded at Bn. HQrs at 0950 hours for Divine Service at the Cinema Hall. Roman Catholics paraded at 0850 hours for Mass.	

WAR DIARY
INTELLIGENCE SUMMARY.
(Erase heading not required.)

Army Form C. 2118.

Place	Date	Hour	Summary of Events and Information	Remarks and references to Appendices
CANDAS	13.1.19		Training was carried out as per Programme of training.	
"	14.1.19		do	
"	15.1.19		do	
"	16.1.19		Training was carried out as per Programme. "A" Company were allotted the 900 x Range. The 13th Company paraded at 09.00 hours for Route March. ROUTE FIENVILLERS — MONTRELET — CANDAS.	
"	17.1.19		Training was carried out as per Programme. Lt. "Peter Dreyfelder" was allotted to 13th Company.	
"	18.1.19		The battalion paraded on the Bn. Parade Ground at 10.00 hours. DRESS — Drill Order. N.C.O's and men selected as escort to the Colours paraded at 09.00 hours at Batty. H.Q. under Capt. J.H. ALLEN. The men fell in at 11.30 hours by Capt. Franks. A Lecture has given in the Cinema Subject:- The Independent State of India.	

Army Form C. 2118.

WAR DIARY
or
INTELLIGENCE SUMMARY.
(Erase heading not required.)

Place	Date	Hour	Summary of Events and Information	Remarks and references to Appendices
CANDAS	19.1.19		DIVINE SERVICES. Celebration of Holy Communion in the Cinema Hall at 0800 hours.	
"	20.1.19		2 Officers & 60 other ranks for Company Parades at Bates Farm at 0935 hours for Roman Catholic Divine Service. Roman Catholics paraded at 0850 hours for Mass. Bates were allotted to H.Q. "Band" & "C" Coys. In addition Companies carried out 1½ hours training.	
"	21.1.19.		Training was carried out as per Programme.	
"	22.1.19		"C" and "Z" Companies. The Battalion paraded at 09.45 hours for rehearsal of Colour Presentation. Bands were allotted to later.	
"	23.1.19		Training was carried out as per programme.	
"	24.1.19		Battalion paraded at 09.45 hours for rehearsal of Colour Presentation.	
"	25.1.19		The Divisional Commander presented the Kings Colour to the Battalion.	

Army Form C. 2118.

WAR DIARY
or
INTELLIGENCE SUMMARY.
(Erase heading not required.)

Place	Date	Hour	Summary of Events and Information	Remarks and references to Appendices
CAIRO	26.1.19		DIVINE SERVICES. 2 Officers and 50 other ranks of Company paraded at Batt. Headquarters at 10.15 hours for Divine Service. Roman Catholics paraded at 08.50 hours for Mass.	
"	27.1.19		Training was carried out as per programme.	
"	28.1.19		Training was carried out as per programme.	
"	29.1.19		A Company carried out education. The token disinfector was allotted to "D" Coy. "B" and "C" Companies were employed on fatigues.	
"	30.1.19		"B" Company carried out Education. "A" and "C" Coys were employed on fatigues. Brig. Gen. Eccles. D.S.O gave a lecture on CHINA at the Kinema Hall at 11.00 hours.	
"	31.1.19		"C" Company carried out Education. "D" Company paraded at 09.00 hours for Foot Drill. "A" & "B" Coys carried out the following 09.00 to 09.30 hours Cleaning of rifles. 09.30 to 10.30 hours Arms and Saluting drill. A lecture was given by the Rev. H.S. Kirkland in the Kinema Hall at 11.00 hours. Subject PALESTINE.	

W. Parkes Major

Comdg. 8'(S) Bn B. Chuwcestashire Regt.

Army Form C. 2118.

WAR DIARY
INTELLIGENCE SUMMARY.
(Erase heading not required.)

8th Gloucester Regt.

Vol 4

Place	Date	Hour	Summary of Events and Information	Remarks and references to Appendices
CROUY	1/2/19	—	The Baths situation at CROUY were allotted to Companies as follows:- "B" Coy 09.30 hours to 10.45 "A" Coy 10.45 hours to 12.00 "D" Coy 12.00 hours to 13.00 hours transport Men from 12.00 hours to 13.30 hours.	
	2/2/19		Baths were allotted to Companies as under:- "B" Coy 07.30 hours to 08.30 hours. "C" Coy and Fatigue Party of "D" Coy 08.30 hours to 09.30 hours. DIVINE SERVICE. 2 Officers and 50 Other Ranks per Company (less C Coy) paraded at Battalion HQ. Non-Conformists paraded at Battn HQ at 08.55 hours for their respective services. Roman Catholics paraded at Battn HQ at 08.55 hours for their respective service. Church of England paraded at Battalion HQ at 09.50 hours.	
	3/2/19		Programme of work for the day for companies carried out. Education. General cleaning up of Billets. 09.00 to 09.30 hours – General cleaning up of Billets. 09.30 to 10.00 hours – Lighting and Arms Drill. 10.30 to 11.30 hours – Route March.	

Army Form C. 2118.

WAR DIARY
or
INTELLIGENCE SUMMARY.
(Erase heading not required.)

Instructions regarding War Diaries and Intelligence Summaries are contained in F. S. Regs., Part II. and the Staff Manual respectively. Title pages will be prepared in manuscript.

Place	Date	Hour	Summary of Events and Information	Remarks and references to Appendices
CHAPPEL	4/4/19	—	Training carried out as follows:— "Band Blows" 09.00 hours to 09.30 Inspection 09.30 " to 10.00 Saluting Drill 10.00 " 12.00 Route March	
"	5/4/19		E Coy 09.00 am to 11.00 Cleaning up and Inspection 11.00 noon to 12.00 Route March. D Coy Carried out Education. HQrs, B Coy, Carried out Education. At 11.00 hours the Company Officers Paraded for Route March. Head HQ Coy. carried out the following:— 09.00 to 09.30 hours General cleaning up 09.30 to 10.00 " Turns out & Saluting drill 10.15 to 12.00 " Route March	
"	6/4/19		Bakers were allotted to Companies as under. E Coy 07.30 to 08.45 hours D " 08.45 to 09.30 hours A Band D Companies were employed in clearing up Battalion from huts.	

Army Form C. 2118.

WAR DIARY
or
INTELLIGENCE SUMMARY.
(Erase heading not required.)

Instructions regarding War Diaries and Intelligence Summaries are contained in F. S. Regs., Part II. and the Staff Manual respectively. Title pages will be prepared in manuscript.

Place	Date	Hour	Summary of Events and Information	Remarks and references to Appendices
CANDAS	7/9/19		"A" & "C" Company carried out Educational Training. "B", "D" and "T" Infantry carried out the following:— 09.00 to 10.00 hours. Compt cleaning up of arms and equipment. 10.00 to 12.00 hours. Route March.	
"	8/9/19		Both "D" Company carried out Education. "A", "B" and "C" Carried out the following:— 09.00 hours to 10.30 hours. General cleaning of arms and equipment. DIVINE SERVICES. All available NCOs and men of C of E Denomination paraded at Battalion Headquarters at 11.20 hours for Divine Service. Roman Catholics paraded at 08.55 Non Conformist paraded at 09.45 hours. Remainder of day was allowed as hours for Men.	
"	9/9/19		Companies carried out the following:— 09.00 hours to 09.15 hours General cleaning up. 09.15 hrs to 10.00 hours Extended Order Drill. 10.00 hours Battalion paraded in Full Marching Order. Dress DRILL ORDER.	

Army Form C. 2118.

WAR DIARY
or
INTELLIGENCE SUMMARY.
(Erase heading not required.)

Instructions regarding War Diaries and Intelligence Summaries are contained in F. S. Regs., Part II. and the Staff Manual respectively. Title pages will be prepared in manuscript.

Place	Date	Hour	Summary of Events and Information	Remarks and references to Appendices
CAMPLES	11/2/19		Companies carried out the following:– 09.00 hours to 09.15 hours. General cleaning up. 09.15 hours to 10.00 Saluting drill. At 10.00 hours the Battalion paraded for Route March.	
"	12/2/19		do.	
"	13/2/19		NCOs and men of "A" and "D" Companies undergoing education reported to the Educational Officer at 09.00 hours. NCOs and men detailed for transfer to the T/5 Glouc. Regt. sent at the disposal of Company Commander. NCOs and men not detailed as such paraded at Bn Headquarters for Route March. Bn H.Q. were allotted to the battalion from 07.30 hours to 13.30 hours.	
"	14/2/19		In addition Companies carried out 2 hours training in proximity of their billets.	

Army Form C. 2118.

WAR DIARY
or
INTELLIGENCE SUMMARY.
(Erase heading not required.)

Place	Date	Hour	Summary of Events and Information	Remarks and references to Appendices
CANDAS	15/2/19	-	Officer Commanding Companies carried out the following:-	
			09.15 - 09.30 hours General cleaning up.	
			09.30 - 11.00 " Kit inspection	
			11.00 - 12.00 " Short Route March.	
"	16/2/19		DIVINE SERVICES All available NCO's and men paraded at Bn Headquarters at 10.15 hours for Divine Service. Roman Catholics paraded for Mass. Non-Combatants paraded at Bn HQ at 09.45 hours and proceeded to YMCA Hut for Service.	
"	17/2/19		"B" Company was at the disposal of the 2nd in Command for cleaning up. "A" "C" and "D" Companies carried out the following training:-	
			09.00 - 09.30 General cleaning up.	
			09.30 - 10.30 Arms & Saluting drill.	
			11.00 - 12.00 Squad and Platoon drill.	

Army Form C. 2118.

WAR DIARY
INTELLIGENCE SUMMARY.
(Erase heading not required.)

Place	Date	Hour	Summary of Events and Information	Remarks and references to Appendices
Camp A9.	18/4/19		O/C Companies carried out the following:- 09.00 – 09.30 hours General cleaning up. 09.30 – 10.30 " Arms and Saluting drill. 11.00 – 12.00 " Squad and Platoon drill.	
"	19/4/19		O/C Companies carried out the following:- 09.00 – 09.30 hours General cleaning up. 09.30 – 10.30 " Arms and Saluting drill. A lecture was given in the Kinema Hall at 11.00 hours by M. VIRREEST. Subject:- MOROCCO and TANGIERS. Baths were allotted to Companies as follows:- "A" Coy 09.00 – 10.00 hours "B" Coy 10.00 – 11.00 hours "C" Coy 11.00 – 12.00 hours "D" Coy 12.00 – 13.00 hours	
"	20/4/19		O/C Companies carried out the following:- 09.00 – 09.30 hrs General cleaning up. 09.45 hrs to 10.30 hrs Arms & Saluting drill. 11.00 hrs to 12.00 hrs Squad and Platoon drill	

Army Form C. 2118.

WAR DIARY
or
INTELLIGENCE SUMMARY.
(Erase heading not required.)

Instructions regarding War Diaries and Intelligence Summaries are contained in F. S. Regs., Part II. and the Staff Manual respectively. Title pages will be prepared in manuscript.

Place	Date	Hour	Summary of Events and Information	Remarks and references to Appendices
CANDAS	2/2/19		A draft of 10 Officers and 163 other ranks entrained at CANDAS Station to proceed and join 2/5 E. Lorne Regt. for Army of Occupation.	
	22/2/19		Hanging over of Billets.	
	23/2/19		DIVINE SERVICE. All available NCO's and men paraded at Bn. HQrs at 10.20 hours for Divine Service. Roman Catholics paraded at B. HQrs at 08.50 hrs for Mass. Non-Conformists paraded at 09.55 hours and proceeded to YMCA Hut for Services.	
	24/2/19		Lieut. "A" Company seen at the disposal of the 2nd in Command.	
	25/2/19		"A" Company men employed in clearing up billets.	

Army Form C. 2118.

WAR DIARY
or
INTELLIGENCE SUMMARY.
(Erase heading not required.)

Instructions regarding War Diaries and Intelligence Summaries are contained in F. S. Regs., Part II. and the Staff Manual respectively. Title pages will be prepared in manuscript.

Place	Date	Hour	Summary of Events and Information	Remarks and references to Appendices
Cin9Mt	24/2/19		Lectr. "A" Company was employed in clearing up billets	
"	27/2/19		do	
"	28/2/19		"A" Company was employed in clearing up billets. A draft of 43 other Ranks was sent to XVII Corps Concentration Camp for Demobilization.	

M. Parker
Lieut Col.
Comdg. 8th Bn. Gloucestershire Regt.

Army Form C. 2118.

WAR DIARY
or
INTELLIGENCE SUMMARY
(Erase heading not required.)

8-(S) Batt. Gloucestershire Regt.

Vol 43

Place	Date	Hour	Summary of Events and Information	Remarks and references to Appendices
CANDAS	1/3/19		Letter "H" Company men employed in clearing up billets.	
	2/3/19		**DIVINE SERVICES** O/C "H" and "L" Companies detailed the following to attend Divine Service. "A" Coy 1 Officer and 30 other ranks, "Z" Coy 5 other ranks at Battalion Headquarters at 09.50 hours. Non-Conformist paraded at 09.50 hours for Service. Roman Catholics paraded at 09.00 hours for Mass.	
"	3/3/19		Letter "H" Company were employed in cleaning up of the bootas.	
"	4/3/19		Letter "H" Company were employed in sweeping & cleaning up the road near the Baths and also from CANDAS Church to CANDAS NORD STATION.	
"	5/3/19		do	

WAR DIARY
or
INTELLIGENCE SUMMARY.

(Erase heading not required.)

Army Form C. 2118.

Place	Date	Hour	Summary of Events and Information	Remarks and references to Appendices
Chayps.	6/3/19		Bttn. "A" Company carried out general cleaning up of the Battalion Area.	
"	7/3/19		Bttn. "A" Company was employed in cleaning up the Battalion Area.	
"	8/3/19		Bttn. "A" Company was employed in cleaning up the Battalion Area.	
"	9/3/19		DIVINE SERVICES. Roman Catholics paraded at the Orderly Room at 08.55 hours for Mass. Non-Conformists paraded at 09.55 hours for Service in the Y.M.C.A.	
"	10/3/19		Bttn. "A" Company was employed in changing billets.	
"	11/3/19		"A" Company was employed in cleaning up billets. The Medical Officer gave a Lecture to all Officers and men of the battalion at 11.00 hours.	

WAR DIARY
or
INTELLIGENCE SUMMARY.
(Erase heading not required.)

Army Form C. 2118.

Place	Date	Hour	Summary of Events and Information	Remarks and references to Appendices
CHIVRES	12/3/19		O/C "A" Company detailed the following working parties:- 1 NCO and 10 men to clean all Lewis Guns. Remainder of the Company reported at the Quarter Masters Stores at 07.00 hours for fatigues.	
"	13/3/19		Left "A" Company were employed in cleaning up the battalion area.	
"	14/3/19		"A" Company were employed in cleaning up the battalion area.	
"	15/3/19		The Baths were allotted as follows:- "A" Company 11.30 to 12.30 hours. "B" Company (including Transport) 12.30 to 13.30 hours. 5 Other Ranks were sent to the XVII Corps Concentration Camp for Demobilization.	
"	16/3/19		DIVINE SERVICES. Roman Catholics paraded at 08.55 hours for Mass. "A" Company were employed in cleaning up billets.	

Army Form C. 2118.

WAR DIARY
or
INTELLIGENCE SUMMARY.
(Erase heading not required.)

Instructions regarding War Diaries and Intelligence Summaries are contained in F. S. Regs., Part II. and the Staff Manual respectively. Title pages will be prepared in manuscript.

Place	Date	Hour	Summary of Events and Information	Remarks and references to Appendices
Chaulnes	17/3/19		Rstes. "A" Company were employed in cleaning up the Battalion area.	
"	18/3/19		do.	
"	19/3/19		do.	
"	20/3/19		do.	
"	21/3/19		do.	
"	22/3/19		Baths were allotted to the Battalion. All N.C.Os and men forming the Cadre paraded outside the Battalion Orderly Room at 12.30 hours.	
"	23/3/19		DIVINE SERVICE. Church of England. A Voluntary Service followed by Holy Communion on was held in the Cinema Vallak 17.30 hours. Rstes. "A" Company was employed in cleaning up the Battalion Area.	
"	24/3/19			
"	25/3/19		do.	

Army Form C. 2118.

WAR DIARY
or
INTELLIGENCE SUMMARY.
(Erase heading not required.)

Instructions regarding War Diaries and Intelligence Summaries are contained in F. S. Regs., Part II. and the Staff Manual respectively. Title pages will be prepared in manuscript.

Place	Date	Hour	Summary of Events and Information	Remarks and references to Appendices
Cinqrues	26/3/19	—	Batts. "A" Company were employed in clearing up the battalion Area.	
"	27/3/19		Batts. "A" Company were employed in clearing up the battalion Area.	
"	28/3/19		Batts. "A" Company were employed in clearing up the battalion Area.	
"	29/3/19		Batts. "A" Company were employed in clearing up the battalion Area.	
"	30/3/19		Batts. "A" Company were employed in clearing up the battalion Area.	
"	31/3/19		Batts. "A" Company were employed in clearing up the battalion Area.	

31.3.19

A. Pickering Major.

Commdg: 8th(S) Bn. Gloucestershire Regt.

www.ingramcontent.com/pod-product-compliance
Lightning Source LLC
Chambersburg PA
CBHW080913230426
43667CB00015B/2669